PRACTICE-BASED RESEARCH IN CHILDREN'S PLAY

Edited by
Wendy Russell, Stuart Lester and Hilary Smith

First published in Great Britain in 2018 by

Policy Press
University of Bristol
1-9 Old Park Hill
Bristol
BS2 8BB
UK
t: +44 (0)117 954 5940
pp-info@bristol.ac.uk
www.policypress.co.uk

North America office:
Policy Press
c/o The University of Chicago Press
1427 East 60th Street
Chicago, IL 60637, USA
t: +1 773 702 7700
f: +1 773-702-9756
sales@press.uchicago.edu
www.press.uchicago.edu

© Policy Press 2018

British Library Cataloguing in Publication Data
A catalogue record for this book is available from the British Library

Library of Congress Cataloging-in-Publication Data
A catalog record for this book has been requested

ISBN 978-1-4473-3004-2 paperback
ISBN 978-1-4473-3003-5 hardcover
ISBN 978-1-4473-3005-9 ePdf
ISBN 978-1-4473-3006-6 ePub
ISBN 978-1-4473-3007-3 Mobi

The right of Wendy Russell, Stuart Lester and Hilary Smith to be identified as editors of this work has been asserted by them in accordance with the Copyright, Designs and Patents Act 1988.

The statements and opinions contained within this publication are solely those of the author and not of the University of Bristol or Policy Press. The University of Bristol and Policy Press disclaim responsibility for any injury to persons or property resulting from any material published in this publication.

Policy Press works to counter discrimination on grounds of gender, race, disability, age and sexuality.

Cover design by Clifford Hayes
Front cover image: iStock
Printed and bound in Great Britain by Clays Ltd, St Ives plc
Policy Press uses environmentally responsible print partners

We dedicate this book to Dr Stuart Lester who passed away in May 2017. In your gentle, playful, provocative and radical way, you have encouraged so many people to think differently about children's play. You are greatly missed, but your influence and legacy live on in many ways, including through your own extensive writing and the practice and research of your students, an example of which is presented in this volume.

Contents

List of figures

Notes on contributors

Hattie Coppard is founder and Director of Snug & Outdoor, an artist-led company who design original playful environments in the public realm. For more than 30 years she has explored the relationship of environment and playful behaviour through exhibitions, public art, urban design schemes and experimental play projects. Frustration with conventional evaluation methods that equate lived experience with measureable outcomes led her to an MA in Play and Playwork in search of theoretical ideas that could provide a fundamentally different way of understanding playful behaviour. Once started along this road she was hooked and is now undertaking a PhD investigating the relationship of play and place-making and the insights an artist's process of enquiry can bring to understandings of play in the public realm.

Megan Dickerson is a curator, researcher and playworker who develops playful exhibitions at The New Children's Museum in San Diego, CA. Previously, she worked at Boston Children's Museum, the Massachusetts Museum of Contemporary Art and the Peabody Essex Museum, among others. Megan holds her BA in History and Museum Studies from the University of California, Los Angeles and is a MA candidate in Play and Playwork at the University of Gloucestershire. She blogs at www.takeplayseriously.org.

John Fitzpatrick is manager of Gwealan Tops Adventure Playground (job share) and play and playwork tutor and assessor for Hackney Play Association. He has worked within the playwork sector for over 30 years on adventure playgrounds, afterschool clubs, mobile play projects and for regional organisations. He developed 'Playwork Beyond Quality', a quality framework for playwork and afterschool clubs in Cambridgeshire which has been launched nationally. He has a Postgraduate Certificate in Play and Playwork from the University of Gloucestershire and has co-authored a research paper on 'Co-creating an Adventure Playground (CAP): Reading playwork stories, practices and artefacts' (2014, Gloucester: University of Gloucestershire) with the university and has co-authored a related article with Bridget Handscomb in the *Journal of Playwork Practice* (November 2015). He co-edited *Playwork Voices* (2007) with Bridget Handscomb and Wendy Russell and contributed a chapter entitled 'The Fen man and the cowboy'.

Bridget Handscomb is manager of Gwealan Tops Adventure Playground (job share) and quality assurance manager and tutor for Hackney Play Association's training and assessment centre. She has worked in the playwork sector for over 30 years in many different roles with children and adults. She is committed to supporting children's play and playworkers' professional practice and has been a regular presenter at national and regional events. Bridget has a first class BA Hons Degree in Play and Playwork and a Postgraduate Certificate in Education in the Lifelong Learning Sector. She has contributed to research with the University of Gloucestershire on 'Co-creating an Adventure Playground (CAP): Reading playwork stories, practices and artefacts' (2014, Gloucester: University of Gloucestershire) and has co-authored a related article with John Fitzpatrick in the *Journal of Playwork Practice* (November 2015). She co-edited *Playwork Voices* (2007) with John Fitzpatrick and Wendy Russell, wrote a piece called 'The playwork ABC' and co-authored a chapter with Michelle Virdi entitled 'Playwork learning: sharing the journey'.

Paula Harris began her career in playwork in the late 1980s working in a variety of settings including junior youth clubs, pre-school playgroups, afterschool clubs and holiday play schemes. Since then she has worked as a play development officer, a play project co-ordinator, a playwork trainer and as the Regional Executive Officer for Tri-County Play Association, covering Caerphilly, Blaenau Gwent and Merthyr Tydfil in South Wales. She is currently employed by Duffryn Community Link as the Senior Director of the Forest Family Centre in Duffryn Newport. She completed her MA in Play and Playwork at the University of Gloucestershire in 2012.

Claire Hawkes is passionate about the value of play with over 25 years' experience as a playworker, trainer and development officer, both for the voluntary sector and local authorities. Currently working for Buckinghamshire County Council as Business Manager of Children's Services, Claire's creativity and passion for play have flowed into a variety of work, from running play activities in children's centres, youth clubs and schools, getting messy with muddy play, organising playdays to play therapy. From policy to practice she places importance on freely chosen play, ensuring children's voices and rights are heard and respected by decision makers. Over the last five years Claire's interests leaned towards a therapeutic view, focusing on nature play, playful relaxation and creative play. Always known as a bag lady, Claire is usually seen with random stones, twigs, soldiers, anything shiny and other loose parts 'just in case' the need for play arises.

Denise M Hill is a Lecturer in Sport and Exercise Psychology at the University of Portsmouth. She was previously the Course Leader for the MSc Sport and Exercise Psychology course at the University of Gloucestershire. Her research specialism lies within choking in sport, although she has a broad range of academic interests that include exercise and mental health, athletic wellbeing, application of motivational theory and performance psychology.

Rebekah Jackson is Childcare Coordinator for Wrexham County Borough Council. She stumbled across playwork early in her career working with children and young people. After focusing on developing playwork practice in out of school childcare across Cheshire she completed her MA in Play and Playwork at University of Gloucestershire and continues to support the development of playwork and childcare practice alongside being a member of the Editorial Board of Journal of Playwork Practice.

Lindsey Kilgour is a former Course Leader for the MSc Physical Activity, Exercise, and Health Practice at the University of Gloucestershire. Her research expertise lies in exercise psychology, specifically preventive aspects of health with a focus on women's engagement in physical activity, children and young people, and workplace and community-based programmes. Lindsey is now a sessional lecturer at the University of Worcester, teaching on the MSc Nutritional Therapy and Diet, Nutrition and Health courses.

Linda Kinney: For the past 17 years, Linda has worked in the Education Division at the North Carolina Zoo. Linda manages the zoo's school outreach and Nature Play programmes, and leads professional development trainings for educators. She is utilising her MA in Play and Playwork to supplement her work on approaches to facilitating play as a means of support for professionals who encourage children and young people's opportunities to play. Linda is committed to advocating for playing children and can often be found playing outside.

Stuart Lester: After working for many years on adventure playgrounds and community play projects in the northwest of England, Stuart worked as senior lecturer on the postgraduate 'Professional Studies in Children's Play' programme at the University of Gloucestershire and as an independent researcher and consultant. His key research interests focussed on the nature and value of children's play, playful production of time/space through everyday encounters and the conditions under which children's (and adults') playfulness may thrive, with particular focus on children's right to play. Stuart participated in a number of research projects that explored these themes (with adventure playgrounds, schools, museum, playwork settings, public spaces and wider studies into the implementation of the Welsh government's Play Sufficiency Duty). This led to the production of a series of research reports and contributions to numerous play and playwork publications (many in collaboration with Wendy Russell). Stuart passed away in May 2017.

Chris Martin is a playworker, writer and researcher. After receiving his MA at the University of Gloucestershire he started a PhD at the University of Leicester, expanding his research on children, young people and mobile technology in outdoor play. He works at an adventure playground as well as being active nationally and internationally. He is on the board of the England, Wales and Northern Ireland branch of the International Play Association, was a member of the steering group rewriting the UK Playwork National Occupation Standards, and until 2015 was the Playwork Convenor with Unite the Union. He was the main writer of the *UK Play and Playwork Education and Training Strategy 2011–2016* and has been published in the *Journal of Playwork Practice* and *International Journal of Play*.

Nic Matthews is a Principal Lecturer and Head of Department for Tourism, Hospitality and Events Management at Cardiff Metropolitan University. She was formally a Principal Lecturer in the School of Leisure at the University of Gloucestershire. Her research interests focus on the qualitative exploration of health and wellbeing issues among young people. Her current teaching and previous programmes of research have focused on interest mediation in sport and physical activity policy networks.

Wendy Russell currently works as a Senior Lecturer in Play and Playwork at the University of Gloucestershire and as a consultant on children's play and playwork. She has worked in the playwork sector in the UK for over 40 years, first as a playworker on adventure playgrounds in London, then in a number of roles including development work, research and education and training. Her freelance work has included working on a range of training, development, evaluation and research projects for local authorities, the private sector and local and national voluntary organisations. Key publications include two edited volumes on the philosophy of play (Routledge, 2013, 2015, with Malcolm MacLean and Emily Ryall), plus (with Stuart Lester) *Children's right to play: An examination of the importance of play in the lives of children worldwide* (Bernard van Leer, 2010) and *Play for a Change: Play, policy and practice – a review of contemporary perspectives* (Play England, 2008).

Hilary Smith is the Course Leader for the MA Professional Studies in Children's Play and a Senior Lecturer in the School of Liberal and Performing Arts at the University of Gloucestershire. Her research interests are in the realm of children's play and links with physical literacy, health and wellbeing.

Stephen Smith began his career in play as a volunteer at Barnardo's in 1998. During his ten-year career at Barnardo's Stephen helped to establish the young carers service and became a senior manager of the afterschool and weekend clubs for disabled children and young adults. During this time Stephen completed a degree in Playwork and Youth Studies and became an assessor and verifier. Stephen left Barnardo's to pursue a career in training and adult education, and in 2012 he completed his MA in Play and Playwork at the University of Gloucestershire. He is now a project manager at a training provider where he manages playwork qualifications.

Becky Willans has been avoiding an office job for 14 years. Instead she has been having fun in the playwork sector. Her experience includes five years teaching playwork, therapeutic playwork and youth studies in higher education, external examining and working with children and young people, specifically disabled children and young people in a variety of play settings. Becky is a manager at KIDS Lady Allen Adventure Playground and currently spends her time wearing fancy dress clothing while hanging out with some of the coolest and most amazing children and young people in the world, ever! She completed her MA in Play and Playwork at the University of Gloucestershire in 2012.

Tom Williams was born in London in 1966 where he played on a South London adventure playground (APG) staffed by art students, before moving to mid-Wales in 1972 for a free range hippy childhood. After art college and political demonstrations he worked on APGs in Cardiff before becoming a LAPA trainee and working on APGs in London for ten years. In 2000 he moved to Bristol, where as Play Officer he developed Council Play Policies, managed five APGs and started many successful play development projects including: Scrapstores PlayPods in Primary Schools and Playing Out street closures. In 2013 he completed his MA in Play and Playwork at the University of Gloucestershire. Now a freelance play consultant, Tom chairs the Bristol Play Network and founded Woodland Tribe, which promotes a European model of adventure play, with an emphasis on children's construction, to new audiences at UK family festivals.

Acknowledgements

Our heartfelt thanks go to all those who were involved in the studies presented here, either as participants or supporters. Many of the studies are presented anonymously for ethical reasons, but participants and supporters are acknowledged here even though they cannot be named. Those who can be named are Homerton Adventure Playground and Hackney Play Association, The New Children's Museum San Diego, Gordon Sturrock and Play Gloucestershire. We would also like to say a big 'thank you' to Professor Berry Mayall who first encouraged us to publish these research studies and who has very kindly provided a foreword. Finally, we would like to thank the University of Gloucestershire for supporting the production of this book.

Foreword

Berry Mayall

This important book breaks new ground, in bringing together a number of empirical research studies that focus on a wide range of settings in which children play, and address important theoretical issues in order to understand the findings. This contribution from me is slight, limited and angled towards what I myself have found through research and through reading.

My association with this great play project began, I think, because students on the University of Gloucestershire postgraduate programmes on play had been asked to read some of my written work; and subsequently I was invited to attend a conference (in January 2013), where the staff and students presented their work. This was a great experience for me, an eye-opener and the beginnings of insight into how thinking on play has moved on through the engagement of the staff and students on the course. In an age when the character of childhood is increasingly controlled by 'education' agendas affecting not only schooldays, but experiences outside school, I thought then – and now – that it was important to make the students' work available to a wider audience. And now this book is seeing the light of day! So first I want to congratulate everyone concerned for the massive amount of work, including thought, study, emotional engagement, pioneering spirit, and openness to experience that is so evident in the chapters that follow. It is, in part, because the authors are, or have been, engaged practitioners, that they provide such creative insights into the material with which they engage.

The explorations in the following chapters point to a range of physical environments in which play takes place, including streets, clubs, adventure playgrounds and museums. However, a key enabling condition is the loosening of adult control over children's activities, so that children are freed up to develop their play. For as sociologists of childhood have pointed out childhood is a subordinate social group, in tension and in relations with adulthood (for example, Qvortrup, 2009). Children have to seek out environments relatively free from adult control. A dramatic example of a physical, but also emotionally laden environment hostile to play is provided by that acute observer of childhood, Charles Dickens in *Great Expectations*. His young protagonist, Pip, is asked to play at Miss Havisham's grand but dilapidated house, and when he gets to her room, he finds an extraordinary scene, a dressing room where time has stopped and once-white shoes and clothes are yellowing, covered with dust and cobwebs. She herself, white-haired and shrunken, is dressed as a bride, in rotting, tattered robes. This is an adult-constructed world – a nightmare adult vision – if ever there was one. So when Miss Havisham orders him to play, he has to stand up for his own perspective, and reply that this is not possible for him.

If, however, adults can bring themselves to loosen their control over both children and childhoods, then children's play, as these chapters show, does take place almost anywhere, and it includes a wide range of activities and purposes. However, I would add one point on this: I agree with Huizinga (1949, pp 2–3) when he explained, on the basis of years of study of European cultures and arts, that play is something in which human beings engage. It is separate from ordinary life; perhaps a respite, where groups and individuals engage in activities with their own rules, for no profit. Children in this view are not different from adults; they are doing what human beings do: amusing themselves, creatively, reflectively, casually, and providing commentaries on the often harsh conditions of daily life.

As the editors point out in their opening chapter, one of the problems besetting children and childhood is the assumption, developed within psychological paradigms over many years, that key to understanding children's journeys to adulthood is study of the function of everything they do; what they do is not interesting in itself, but it provides clues about human development (Greene, 1999). As a mind-set, this concept is not only adult-centred; it devalues children's experience in the here and now. And an extreme version of the power of this concept has been the putting into place of the notion that childhood matters only as precursor to adulthood; and that children's experiences now do not matter, as compared to their futures as adults.

Important challenges to this limited view of childhood, over the last 40 years have been provided by sociologists (as I have documented in a brief history: Mayall, 2013). They have proposed childhood as a social status, subordinate to adulthood, but where children, in active inter-relations with adults, make their way as best they can, making some gains, losing some skirmishes, making do with what is offered to them and modifying these offers to their own advantage. Key to understanding how childhood is lived, therefore, is the relations between the generations, both at the level of large-scale policies, and at the level of day-to-day transactions between children and adults.

My own work has included a number of research studies where I have discussed with children: health maintenance, child–adult relations, concepts of childhood and parenthood, what constitutes work and play, what they enjoy and dislike about their childhoods (see for instance Mayall, 2002). Always impressive is children's willingness and ability to engage with these topics; for they regard themselves as having views and as competent in discussion. And notable in their discussions is the importance of play: a time and an activity which is outside the immediate control and supervision of adults. Equally impressive is children's understanding of moral issues: justice and fair shares – both within and across generations. Though, in my experience, children do not readily talk in rights terms (the UK government has not conformed to Article 42 of the United Nation Convention of the Rights of the Child [1989]; for it has not told children about their rights), nevertheless their ideas on such issues relate directly to the terms of the Convention.

This childhood sociological movement has been slow to attract the attention of mainstream sociologists (though some progress has been made), but it has begun to be influential in other important approaches to human societies: notably anthropology, geography, development studies, history. Developmental psychology has begun to acknowledge approaches which define children as people. In all these we now see many studies which take seriously children as responsible members of society, children's rights within society, children's contributions to the division of labour, and, more generally child–adult relations and transactions in these areas. Chapters in this book harness some of these varied approaches to consider the data collected.

My own current research is addressing one of those gaps in thinking which arise when a child perspective is omitted from study. Historians and other social commentators have written reams on the development of the elementary education system in England at the start of the twentieth century, in the context of wider social and political movements (international competition, socialism, the women's rights movement): they have discussed events affecting the education system; which adults influenced change and, perhaps, progress; how the education system developed. Scholars have discussed competing (adult) views: was elementary schooling introduced and operationalised as a Foucauldian (or Marxist) system of controlling the masses; or was it a democratising enterprise, offering a chance for people to gain knowledge and to better themselves. But children's own experiences and evaluations of schooling, in the context of their daily lives, at home, playing in the neighbourhood, engaged in domestic work, going on errands and seizing the chance to do scraps of paid work where available; all this is virtually absent. So, although this study is difficult and reliant on a few autobiographies and interviews, I am piecing together some evidence and some ideas about children's lives at this time, including their participation in the war effort during the first world war.

That example points to the importance of taking account of a wide range of social groups, in attempts to understand social life. And that, in the end, is why this book – which enlarges our understanding of play as a component of social life – is important. It helps us to grasp more fully children's social positioning in society, the value of play in their lives; and, for us adults, the necessity of making space, time and enabling environments, where children are free to play.

References

Dickens, C. (1861) *Great Expectations*, London: Chapman and Hall, chapter 8.

Greene, S. (1999) 'Child development: Old themes, new developments', in M. Woodhead, D. Faulkner and K. Littleton (eds) *Making sense of social development*, London: Routledge, pp 250–68.

Huizinga, J. (1949) *Homo ludens: A study of the play element in culture*, London: Routledge and Kegan Paul.

Mayall, B. (2002) *Towards a sociology for childhood: Thinking from children's lives*, Buckingham: Open University Press.

Mayall, B. (2013) *A history of the sociology of childhood*, London: Institute of Education Press.

Qvortrup, J. (2009) 'Childhood as a structural form', in J. Qvortrup, W.A. Corsaro and M.-S. Honig (eds) *The Palgrave handbook of childhood studies*, London: Palgrave Macmillan.

ONE

Perspectives on play research: the practice-theory-research entanglement

Wendy Russell, Stuart Lester and Hilary Smith

"I wish I'd done this 20 years ago, but none of this stuff was written then. It's done amazing stuff for my practice and my interest in children's play." (From a conversation with contributors)

For me it was like I'd suddenly found the exact subject area I was really passionate about. I have been skating on the edges and thought that I knew what path I wanted to be on but the more I read the more I realised this was the material that I was interested in…Doing action research suited my needs of wanting to develop this further, a selfish hunger pang for knowledge and the self-reflection opportunity. It inspired me, considering I was at the end of part time studying and the balancing act of work, family life and studying, it still intrigued me and gave me the energy to research (and continue to research and develop my own self-reflection). (Email from one of the contributors)

The ideas I am drawn to are those that seem most relevant to my way of thinking and mainly this has been the non-representational, post humanist stuff, which though often convoluted and abstract seems most pertinent to current thinking about public space and playfulness. When I think of my practice in terms of urban design (and all the negotiations and politics that this involves) then I can see how this theoretical knowledge and research can be relevant and practically useful. But when I am engaged in the creative design process itself then I am not sure that knowing the theory comes into it. On the other hand,

> play (and art) is a form of research in its own right and perhaps this is more a question of language and what we mean by knowledge – text versus affect? And then again text affects…at this point words start to wobble…loop the loop…giggle… (Email from one of the contributors)

Every book has a number of stories behind it, and this introductory chapter aims to tell some of the stories behind this one. They are stories of shared explorations not only of children's play and adults' relationships with it, but also of knowledge itself, and the entanglements of theory, research and practice. A starting point is to recognise that the process of knowledge production is inherently situated, political and ethical. Theory is not neutral, nor does it precede or 'underpin' practice or research, all are mutually implicated in each other. Whatever questions chosen to explore, whatever epistemology and methodology used, whatever methods and approaches to data analysis, these will inevitably include some things and exclude others. Selected research methods help to 'reproduce a complex ecology of representations, realities and advocacies, arrangements and circuits' (Law et al, 2011, p 13) that drags order from the proliferation of life in an exclusive manner (MacLure, 2013). They perform a 'cut' (Barad, 2007), and no matter how comprehensive these accounts, not everything can happen at the same time: 'if things are made present…then at the same time things are also being made absent (the world "itself")' (Law, 2007, p 600). Representations of the real can never be total or complete and dangers arise if this incompleteness and associated exclusions are denied. Given this, those whose work is all about knowledge production have an ethical responsibility to imagine how things might be otherwise, to deliberately seek a different cut in order to bring to light what our habitual perspectives exclude. This is not simply as an act of wilful deconstruction but one of questioning why certain discourses and their material effects come to matter and for whose benefit and loss. Such a political and ethical endeavour also recognises that knowledge will always be situated, in the sense that it is always 'from' somewhere and carries with it the histories and exclusions of that place; this is what Mignolo (2009) terms the 'locus of enunciation'. For this book, then, the geographical locus is Anglo-American; it does not seek to make universal claims but rather explores children's play and adults' place in supporting it within specific Anglo-American loci, language, cultures and histories. In addition, the worldview loci of the book's contributors are multi-layered and diverse, although all sharing a wealth of experience in working in support of children's play.

The claims made to date apply to any form of knowledge production, but there is perhaps a particular case to be made in terms of research into children's play. As the great play scholar Brian Sutton-Smith (1999, p 240) states, 'what practically all theorists of this [the twentieth] century have had in common has been the desire to show that play is useful in some way or other'. For children, this usefulness relates mostly to their learning and development, what he calls the progress rhetoric, but also to play's potential for addressing other adult concerns for children, including obesity and other health-related issues, delinquency and even poverty (Lester and Russell, 2013). From this perspective the value of play may say more about adults' anxieties and hopes for the future than children's own experiences of playing. The evolutionary argument that play must have some value simply because it has persisted among juveniles – as well as adults – across a range of species is compelling, but perhaps alternative ways of approaching the question are necessary in order to think away from the habitual focus on progress and towards other forms of value. It is this, coupled with adults' power to prescribe and proscribe children's use of space and time (although of course children find ways of resisting and subverting such constraints), that brings issues of politics and ethics into the research arena.

Practice-based Research in Children's Play is a collection of research projects carried out by experienced practitioners in the play and playwork sector in the UK and USA, who were also students, graduates and staff on the University of Gloucestershire's postgraduate 'Play and Playwork' and 'Professional Studies in Children's Play' programmes. These postgraduate programmes are part time and distance learning, and are aimed at an international studentship of practitioners working at a senior or strategic level in their field, including playwork (including play rangers), play equipment and playground design, architecture and landscape architecture, schools, children's zoos, children's museums, play development work, and management, education and training. The coming together of such a diverse group of passionate, mature and experienced professionals offers a unique space for thinking differently about children's play and adults' relationship with it, and for practice-based research in children's play. The programmes explicitly aim to develop critical approaches to disciplinary studies of children's play. While they acknowledge the contribution of traditional psychology approaches (developmental, depth and evolutionary) they also introduce lesser known disciplines such as anthropology, geography, sociology, philosophy and postmodern perspectives, looking towards a trans-disciplinary approach that not only works across and in-between disciplines but creates something new. They deliberately look for different questions to ask, different ways to see, feel and do the production of knowledge about children and playing, and to pay attention to the conditions of the questions asked, and to the particularity of 'a time, an occasion, the circumstances, the landscapes and personae, the conditions and unknowns of the question' (Deleuze, 1991, p 471) rather than seeking universal claims that elide difference. This is a process without end, and not always a comfortable one, often requiring the undoing of what we thought we could not think without (Lather, 2015). It is a process that extends to approaches to research and one that includes staff as well as students: staff members on the programmes have a long standing in the play and playwork fields and are actively involved in their own research.

Many of the contributors to this book might be seen as novice researchers in terms of their engagement in formal academic research. At the start of their studies, they might also have been regarded as newcomers to the academic theories – what some have termed 'propositional knowledge' – with which they engaged. Yet they brought with them extensive practice knowledge: a pragmatic and embodied combination of skills and craft (what Aristotle termed *techne*), codified and tacit knowledge (Polanyi, 1966, p 4: 'we can know far more than we can tell'), situated knowledge developed through communities of practice (Lave and Wenger, 1991) and a relational knowledge of context (where 'context' is understood not as something fixed and stable that practitioners operate *within*, but as constantly co-produced through praxis). Such knowledges work with the messiness, uncertainty, contingency and co-emergence of lived experience, perhaps setting them apart from the implicit claims of propositional knowledge as being objective, universal, neat and certain (Keevers, 2009). Yet, as MacLure (2010, p 277) argues, 'the value of theory lies in its power to get in the way. Theory is needed to block the reproduction of banality and thereby, hopefully, open new possibilities for thinking and doing.' Acknowledging that theory may have become too set apart from such practice knowledge, and drawing on the work of Brian Massumi (2002), MacLure proposes using 'exemplary practices, in which theory proliferates from examples' (MacLure, 2010, p 277). In this context 'exemplary' refers not to an ideal model to which concepts can be applied, but to working at the level of specificities and singularities to note connections and generate new concepts. As Massumi (2002, p 18) notes, 'exemplification activates detail. The success of the example hinges on the details. Every little one matters.' The studies in this collection are examples. Although many use traditional research methods, they make no claims to universality, generalisability, replicability or other such tenets of traditional forms of knowledge production.

Bringing such practice knowledges to an engagement with propositional knowledge highlights the impossibility of separating theory from research from practice, thereby offering a particular perspective on practice-based research. Each of the studies presented here brings something of the researcher, their practice knowledge, the theory and the processes of engagement with the research process, including contexts, participants, supervisors and fellow students.

During the process of writing this introductory chapter, the editors invited contributors to engage in conversations about how they felt as experienced practitioners when they first engaged in formal academic research, recognising of course that practice is always about (re)searching. These conversations, some by email and some by Skype, showed a range of experiences and expectations of what research is, could be and might deliver, as well as the interconnectedness of research, theory and practice. As practitioners, many contributors expressed frustration with the lack of value attributed to children's play unless it was linked to instrumental outcomes, and a perceived lack of acknowledgement of the value of those who work to support children's play. Much of this is to do with dominant and common sense understandings of the nature and value of childhood itself as well as children's play, an issue addressed in more detail in the concluding chapter. Some felt that the status afforded to academic research could help researchers gain access both to contexts or children's experiences not often addressed in academic, professional or mainstream literature (for example, disabled children hidden from view in the institutions of childhood) and also to academic publishing, thereby going some way towards addressing this lack of appreciation.

Some of the contributors researched their own workplaces or work contexts, and were occasionally surprised by what the research process uncovered for their own process of making sense of practice. For example, one said that talking to colleagues about how they played as children revealed to her their appreciation of play's intrinsic value, even though its value in the workplace was largely instrumental. This realisation allowed her to reframe her management practice.

Although many used traditional research methods, others felt that they wanted to use the opportunity to explore new ground, to be experimental in their approaches to research, to *play* with it perhaps. They had deliberately chosen forms of research (for example, performative or non-representational approaches) that offered another way of exploring children's play and adults' roles in supporting it, without any expectation in terms of what that might mean for their practice or role as advocates for children's play. In responding to the question of how what we choose to research might relate to ethical practice, one respondent suggested that was a very instrumental way to think about the process of research. The conversation went on to explore how such a relationship can be seen as a deep mutual implication rather than a singular, linear cause and effect in terms of praxis. The intrinsic value of research, evident in moments that students varyingly described as surprising, exciting, 'aha', disturbing, fascinating, confusing, mind boggling and more (including the wobbling and giggling in one of the opening quotations), is not something separate from its effects, although those effects may not be as predictable or identifiable as students may think (or hope) beforehand.

This raises questions regarding the claims made of research and its relation to something we might call 'truth' or 'reality'. One contributor said 'I thought research was...ethnographic/anthropological fieldwork, or something scientists did in labs with rats and children deprived of sleep and prodded with cattle prods and things.' Much of the twentieth-century play scholarship to which Sutton-Smith (1999) refers sits within a broadly positivist frame that assumes a real world existing independently of the researcher, that can be known, and by implication, predicted and controlled. This basic premise continues with the constructivist post-positivists who, although acknowledging the inevitability of researcher fallibility and the complexities of the real world, still believe pre-existing and objective truths can be known through triangulation techniques to mitigate those fallibilities. Such a perspective can be applied to both quantitative and qualitative research in the natural and social sciences. It increasingly underpins the current evidence-based policy paradigm and the UK government's suite of 'What Works' evidence centres for social policy (Cabinet Office, 2013) that take as their gold standard the work of the National Institute for Health and Clinical Excellence (NICE), and particularly the keystones of 'big data' and random controlled trials.

This view of research and knowledge has become so accepted as to be seen as common sense. It is challenged through Denzin and Lincoln's (2005, pp 3–4) definition of qualitative research:

> Qualitative research is a situated activity that locates the observer in the world. It consists of a set of interpretive, material practices that make the world visible. These practices transform the world...into a

6

series of representations, including field notes, interviews, conversations, photographs, recordings, and memos to the self...[Q]ualitative researchers deploy a wide range of interconnected interpretive practices, hoping always to get a better understanding of the subject matter at hand.

Yet the interpretive nature of qualitative research, while asserting the impossibility of objectivity and therefore recognising the power and authority of the researcher to interpret their data from their own worldview, still leaves this power problem largely unaddressed other than through the diversity of scholars themselves and the emergence of standpoint epistemologies and other critiques that challenged existing orthodoxies, including feminism, post-colonialism and queer theory and their more recent developments.

> Ethnography is a not an innocent practice. Our research practices are performative, pedagogical and political. Through our writing and our talk, we enact the worlds we study. These performances are messy and pedagogical. They instruct our readers about this world and how we see it. The pedagogical is always moral and political; by enacting a way of seeing and being, it challenges, contests, or endorses the official, hegemonic ways of seeing and representing the other. (Denzin, 2006, p 422)

Denzin and Lincoln (2005, p 3) recognise this in their identification of eight 'moments' of qualitative research over the last century that 'overlap and simultaneously operate in the present', and that see a meandering journey from positivism, through a number of critiques, towards a crisis of representation and beyond. These later moments and movements attempt to confront issues of power, politics and representation through dissolving long-held assumptions, category boundaries and relationships not only among humans but with all matter. Theories of knowledge (epistemology) become entangled with theories of being (ontology) and ethics (Barad, 2007). The challenge to the dominance of the twentieth century's focus on the isolated psychological subject towards ideas of space (as explored in some of the chapters here, notably those in Part Two but also elsewhere), and countering the privilege afforded to language through a turn towards other non- or more-than-representative methodologies are two examples. A closer examination of what has been termed 'post-qualitative research' (Lather and St Pierre, 2013) is given in the final concluding chapter as a part of reflections on the state of research into children's play and adults' role in supporting it.

These issues are central to critical studies of research methods in general, and it can be argued that they are particularly pertinent to studies of children's play for a number of reasons. One might be children's relative lack of power in what Rose (1999) calls 'major' politics (the formal politics of governments, corporate and financial giants and spatial planners) and also at more local levels in terms of adult organisation of time and space throughout the day. A shift towards 'minor' politics of small everyday actions might frame play as resistance, a political taking of time and space for momentarily being something other than the developing child of adult imaginings. Another might be the nature of play itself as both apart from and also a part of what might be called 'reality', an actualisation of an alternative – or virtual – reality where children can suspend the normal rules of how the world works to create worlds of their own. Yet another might be a shift away from seeing play as a tool for learning and development towards looking at the value of the pleasure and vitality that an affective and embodied engagement in created worlds brings for the moment of playing. These are but a few examples of how we might think differently about children's play and adults' role in supporting it.

In bringing these discussions, and the studies themselves, to a broader audience through this book, the hope is that more can be encouraged to think differently also. The rest of this chapter introduces the studies themselves. A range of qualitative research methodologies have been employed, including participatory and action research, ethnography, auto-ethnography and case studies; similarly, the research methods used also vary across observation, interviews, questionnaires, focus groups, spatial and cartographic methods, performative and non-representational methods, audio-visual and other sensory approaches including photo elicitation. Many studies use traditional qualitative approaches; some have taken tentative steps towards exploring alternatives. In terms of ethics, all researchers adhered to the university's protocols for voluntary informed consent, confidentiality and guilty knowledge. Some projects explored issues of ethics in more depth beyond procedural matters towards how ethical issues can be addressed through ongoing relational processes and caring about fellow participants.

Introducing the chapters

Editors always face a challenge in deciding how to arrange the chapters from contributors, as any decision inevitably imposes one of many possible structures for the book, or in the context of the discussion to date, performs a cut in which singular disorderly accounts are ordered. Here, we have grouped the chapters across three fairly loose themes of time, space and wellbeing (including playfulness). What they all have in common is their exploration of adults' relationships with children at play, whether that is in the institutions of childhood, in public space, or in terms of what children's adult-free experiences of playing can tell us about how professionals might help create conditions that support playing. The brief introductions offered here aim to help readers decide which ones are of interest to them, either in terms of the topic of enquiry or the research methodology.

The three chapters in Part One ('Now and then') present historical perspectives aimed at informing contemporary practice. Paula Harris' study considers how nostalgia may play a part in adults' own memories of playing out in a south Wales valleys town, and how this, together with stories in the media, may colour their perception of children playing out today in the same town. Harris used semi-structured interviews with adults to elicit their own memories of playing, their feelings about children's play today, and the influences on those feelings, including the media and their own experiences. She then adapted a combination of approaches to measuring nostalgia in order to explore levels of nostalgia in the adults' accounts. She also talked to children about their own experiences of playing. In her conclusion she suggests that an understanding of the role of nostalgia, together with media influences, may be useful for adults trying to advocate for children's right to play.

Becky Willans also used oral histories and semi-structured interviews in her exploration of experiences of playing out during the second world war. Alongside the horrors of war and the bombings in East London, her participants told of how they had freedom to roam and were able to explore their neighbourhoods and discover all sorts of (often dangerous) things to be played with. Analysing the delightful stories from her participants, she draws on the literature on affordances (Kyttä, 2004), loose parts (Nicholson, 1971) and risk to offer food for thought in terms of what these experiences might tell contemporary playworkers about the conditions that can support children's play.

It was in the wake of the second world war that the adventure playground movement was established in the UK, following Lady Marjorie Allen's serendipitous visit to the junk playground in Emdrup, Copenhagen. Springing up on bomb sites in working class urban areas, these places offered children opportunities to build dens, to play with whatever could be scrounged, to light fires and generally engage in forms of outdoor play under the permissive supervision of a play leader. Contemporary UK playwork theorising has its roots in the adventure playground movement (for example, Brown, 2003; Sturrock and Else, 2005; Hughes, 2012). These playgrounds have changed much over the years, with a chequered history of support from the authorities. In the final chapter in this section, Tom Williams uses a range of autoethnographic, performative and narrative methods to explore his own 40-year relationship with adventure playgrounds from his childhood to his role as manager of adventure playgrounds in a major English city and beyond. He revisits a number of playgrounds and also enlists the help of participants to access their and his own memories, applying unorthodox methodologies to unorthodox spaces in order to explore what makes them so special.

The six chapters that make up Part Two ('Here and there') look at contemporary settings for children's play and explore how these spaces work. A particular hallmark of the postgraduate programmes in children's play at the University of Gloucestershire is the inclusion of geography and Continental philosophy, perspectives not drawn on traditionally by those working in the play or broader children's sector. These perspectives move beyond the dominant focus on the isolated psychological subject, usually the developing child, to consider how spaces are produced through the entanglements and interrelationships of material and symbolic objects; sensing, moving, feeling bodies; desires, affects, expectations and histories and so on. Moving the researcher's gaze from individual (often disembodied) selves towards the always-in-the-making co-production of space is not always easy and is an example of unthinking what we have come to take as common sense understandings. Several students opted to explore these perspectives further in their research, producing new insights.

The section opens with a creative approach to researching public space as a collective achievement from Hattie Coppard. She enlists a dancer, a writer and a painter as researchers tasked with observing a busy urban public square where portable play equipment is made available and used by children alongside other inhabitants of the square that include shoppers, businesses and street drinkers. Moving away from seeking accurate and objective representations of 'reality', the researchers were asked to engage with their particular embodied modes of being and to report those in whatever format they chose. These data were supplemented with discussions, interviews and other audio-visual materials. Three themes emerged from the data that together illustrate the intricacies and 'throwntogetherness' (Massey,

2005) of making space work: movement and presence; objects and imagination; co-existence and co-formation.

The connections between play, art and space are also themes in Megan Dickerson's study into alternative research methodologies that can be employed in helping practitioners make sense of play in a new and experimental kind of Children's Museum in the USA. The museum straddles the educational world of children's museums, where play is valued for its learning outcomes, and the contemporary art world, where more attention can be paid to performative and creative processes. The study draws on performance studies, the concept of art as event, art practice as research and post-qualitative methodologies to develop a proposed hybrid ludo-artographic research methodology that she then applies across a number of art pieces in an open, creative and playful manner.

The tension between adults' perception of play as a tool for learning and its intrinsic value is also investigated in Linda Kinney's study in a children's zoo in the USA, but here the focus is 'nature play'. Drawing on data from a stakeholder analysis, questionnaires and interviews, including mind maps, Kinney analyses stakeholders' perceptions of the value of the play setting within the zoo and the implications of this for the management of the play setting. For her analytical framework she uses Beunderman's (2010) adaptation of Holden's (2006) value triangle that acknowledges the relationship between instrumental value (where the outcomes of play are valued in terms of learning and development, particularly environmental stewardship), institutional value (where the play area has an added value for the zoo as an institution) and intrinsic value (where play is valued for its own sake).

The tension between adult intentions for children's play and children's playful dispositions continues in Rebekah Jackson's study of playworkers in a UK afterschool club, where she used interviews and observations to explore how the production of the space is imbued with power relations. The spatial practices, habits and routines of the playworkers promote certain play forms over others through the layout of the space and the naming of zones, resources and activities. This creates a theory-practice tension given the espoused understanding of play as freely chosen, personally directed and intrinsically motivated. Nevertheless, children can find ways of playing that transgress adult designs and intentions, creating fields of free action alongside and overlapping the adult-intended fields of promoted and constrained action (Kyttä, 2004). She concludes that encouraging reflective practice that pays attention to how the spaces are produced may allow for a more open space.

John Fitzpatrick and Bridget Handscomb's chapter returns to adventure playgrounds and to a collaborative research project between staff and alumni of the University that used participatory action research (PAR) as an approach to reflective practice and continuing professional development for a newly established staff team. The focus is on the flows, rhythms, habits and routines of the space, and the meanings and emotions invested in them. These were documented using a range of methods, including mappings, sketches, photographs, audio and video recordings, blogs, reflective accounts and stories, together with facilitated sessions where this documentation was shared and relevant theories of the production of space introduced. The documentation and discussions helped develop an appreciation of the play space not as something pre-existing but as always in the process of being brought into being through largely unpredictable and emergent encounters of material and symbolic objects, bodies, affect and so on. Alongside this came an awareness of the complexities of these entangled encounters and the difficulties of assuming simple linear cause and effect in terms of design intentions and practices. An open-ended 'what if?' experimental approach was encouraged where the playworkers tried doing things differently just to see what might happen. The chapter also discusses how the approach has been developed further by the authors in play and playwork education and training and playwork professional practice.

An adventure playground is also the setting for Chris Martin's research into how children use mobile phones in their outdoor play. An ethnographic approach was used here, with observation, informal interviews and reflective logs to document how children used mobile phones. Moving away from dualistic arguments about 'nature' and 'technology', or the benefits and potential harms of mobile phones for children, the research shows how phones have become absorbed into the 'assemblage' that is children's play: an *ad hoc* grouping of actants, both human and non-human, that come together to produce that moment of playing.

Part Three of the book considers playfulness and wellbeing. Stephen Smith's study of playwork with children with profound and multiple learning disabilities (PMLD) raises some challenges to the understanding of play as freely chosen and personally directed, as articulated in the Playwork Principles (PPSG, 2005) given communication difficulties and the high levels of support needed for these children. In interviews the playworkers felt that such a definition of play was not applicable to, and therefore in a sense excluded, their work. Nevertheless, observations showed that the playworkers' close attention to metacommunication supported the development of playful relationships, evident both in care routines and more designated 'play' activities. In this way, playworkers were able to meet the overall aim of playwork as being 'to support all children and young people in the creation of a space in which they can play' (PPSG, 2005).

Claire Hawkes' study considers how an understanding of Sturrock and Else's (2005) model of therapeutic playwork could help playworkers in afterschool clubs to respond to issues which they faced in the clubs. Here the focus moves towards depth psychology and an appreciation of inner psychic reality in the play ecology. The model suggests that supporting children to express latent ('unplayed out') material may be curative or preventative in the development of neurosis. Through this lens, 'challenging behaviour' may be seen as a form of 'dysplay', and the playworker works to support children in expressing latent material. Applying concepts from psychotherapy to the relationship between playworker and child, playworkers can develop an awareness of their own unplayed-out material and the impact this may have on the play space. The project was part action research and part ethnography; playworkers attended an introductory course in therapeutic playwork and then reflected on its effect on their feelings about their work and on their practice.

In the final study, staff from the University of Gloucestershire (Nic Matthews, Hilary Smith, Denise Hill and Lindsey Kilgour) worked with local play rangers and children as co-researchers to explore how attending the play ranger sessions might contribute to the children's wellbeing. Creative and participatory methods were used, in particular drawings and photo elicitations, to stimulate playful conversations among the children about their feelings about play, the play rangers and wellbeing. Alongside this, training events, on-site work, focus groups and interviews with staff explored the place of wellbeing in playwork practice and how the play rangers could gather evidence to support their advocacy for play in the policy arena.

The final chapter reflects on approaches to research into children's play and playwork. It considers the socio-political context for children's play, particularly in terms of value, evidence-based policy and children's rights, ending with some recommendations regarding future directions in research into this topic.

References

Barad, K. (2007) *Meeting the universe halfway: Quantum physics and the entanglement of matter and meaning*, Durham, NC: Duke University Press.

Beunderman, J. (2010) *People make play: The impact of staffed play provision on children, families and communities*, London: National Children's Bureau.

Brown, F. (2003) 'Compound flexibility: The role of playwork in child development', in Brown, F. (ed) *Playwork theory and practice*, Buckingham: Open University Press, pp 51–65.

Cabinet Office (2013) *What works: Evidence centres for social policy*, London: Cabinet Office.

Deleuze, G. (1991) 'The conditions of the question: What is philosophy?', trans. Daniel W. Smith and Arnold I. Davidson, *Critical Inquiry*, 17(3): 471–8.

Denzin, N.K. (2006) 'Analytic autoethnography, or déjà vu all over again', *Journal of Contemporary Ethnography*, 35(4): 419–28.

Denzin, N.K. and Lincoln, Y.S. (2005) 'The discipline and practice of qualitative research', in N.K. Denzin and Y.S. Lincoln (eds) *The Sage handbook of qualitative research* (3rd edn), London: Sage, pp 1–32.

Holden, J. (2006) *Cultural value and the crisis of legitimacy*, London: Demos.

Hughes, B. (2012) *Evolutionary playwork and reflective analytic practice* (2nd edn), London: Routledge.

Keevers, L. (2009) *Practising social justice: Community organisations, what matters and what counts*, PhD thesis, University of Sydney.

Kyttä, M. (2004) 'The extent of children's independent mobility and the number of actualised affordances as criteria for child-friendly environments', *Journal of Environmental Psychology*, 24(2): 179–98.

Lather, P. (2015) 'The work of thought and the politics of research: (Post) qualitative research', in N.K. Denzin and M.D. Giardina (eds) *Qualitative inquiry and the politics of research*, Walnut Creek, CA: Left Coast Press, pp 97–117.

Lather, P. and St Pierre, E.A. (2013) 'Introduction: post-qualitative research', *International Journal of Qualitative Studies in Education*, 26(6): 629–33.

Lave, J. and Wenger, E. (1991) *Situated learning: Legitimate peripheral practice*, Cambridge: Cambridge University Press.

Law, J. (2007) 'Making a mess with method', in W. Outhwaite and S.P. Turner (eds) *The Sage handbook of social science methodology*, London: Sage, pp 595–606.

Law, J., Ruppert, E., and Savage, M. (2011) 'The double social life of methods', *CRESC working paper, no. 95*, Milton Keynes: Open University.

Lester, S. and Russell, W. (2013) 'Utopian visions of childhood and play in English social policy', in A. Parker and D. Vinson (eds) *Youth sport, physical activity and play: Policy, intervention and participation*, London: Routledge, pp 40–52.

MacLure, M. (2010) 'The offence of theory', *Journal of Education Policy*, 25(2): 277–86.

MacLure, M. (2013) 'Researching without representation? Language and materiality in post-qualitative methodology', *International Journal of Qualitative Studies in Education*, 26(6): 658–67.

Massey, D. (2005) *For space*, London: Sage.

Massumi, B. (2002) *Parables for the virtual: Movement, affect, sensation*, Durham, NC: Duke University Press.

Mignolo, W.D. (2009) 'Epistemic disobedience, independent thought and de-colonial freedom, *Theory, Culture and Society*, 26(7–8): 1–23.

Nicholson, S. (1971) 'How NOT to cheat children: The theory of loose parts', *Landscape Architecture*, 62(1): 30–4.

PPSG (Playwork Principles Scrutiny Group) (2005) *The Playwork Principles*, Cardiff: Play Wales.

Polanyi, M. (1966) *The tacit dimension*, New York: Doubleday.

Rose, N. (1999) *Powers of freedom: Reframing political thought*, Cambridge: Cambridge University Press.

Sturrock, G. and Else, P. (2005) *The therapeutic playwork readers I and II*, Sheffield: Ludemos.

Sutton-Smith, B. (1999) 'Evolving a consilience of play definitions: Playfully', in S. Reifel (ed) *Play and culture studies (Vol 2): Play contexts revisited*, Stamford, CT: Ablex, pp 239–56.

Part One

Then and now: historical perspectives

TWO

Nostalgia and play

Paula Harris

Introduction

This chapter describes a small-scale study that explored older generations' memories and feelings of nostalgia about their own childhood play experiences and compared these with their ideas about children's play today. Alongside this, children's own accounts of playing in the same town in the Welsh Valleys were collected and set against adult memories and beliefs about contemporary conditions for playing. A technique regularly employed by playwork professionals in training and advocating for the child's right to play is to ask adults to remember how they played as children and the joy they gained from this experience, invoking emotionally charged memories. Playworkers are also encouraged to use their own memories as a means of reflecting on their practice to improve the quality of provision, alongside intuition, evidence from the literature and experience of working with children (Hughes, 2001). This chapter argues that a deeper appreciation of how memory is intricately entwined with affect, emotion and place allows for a more nuanced approach to using memory as an effective advocacy tool. In the study described here, this was explored through semi-structured interviews with children and adults who had grown up in the same town, alongside the use of nostalgia measures of the adults' accounts. As Labaree (2016) notes, self-reporting can have limitations as a research method given the potential for selective memory, telescoping (right memory wrong timescale), attribution (attributing negative outcomes to external forces or to other people) and exaggeration. However, this study was less concerned with the accuracy of memory and more with what memory *does* in terms of giving meaning to children's play experiences today. This required an engagement with the affective registers of memory, and this was explored through the literature on and research approaches to nostalgia.

> Memory makes us what we are, and along with emotion/
> affect it forms the interrelating processes of our ongoing
> lives...We are conglomerations of past everyday experiences,
> including their spatial textures and affective registers.
> Memory should not be seen (simply) as a burden of the past,
> rather it is fundamental to 'becoming', and a key wellspring
> of agency, practice/habit, creativity and imagination. (Jones
> and Garde-Hanson, 2012, p 8)

Memory studies cover a wide field of disciplines. As Jones and Garde-Hansen (2012) note, memory is intimately connected to place, identity and emotion/affect. Rather than being an accurate and static image of the past, memories are continually reworked in the present, connecting to current experiences, contexts and ways of being (Jones, 2011).

Nostalgia is broadly understood as a complex emotion (Sedikides et al, 2004) and can be defined as 'a sentimental longing or wistful affection for the past, typically for a period or place with happy personal associations' (New Oxford English Dictionary). Johnson–Laird and Oatley (1989) indicate the complexity and dualistic nature of nostalgia, saying it is predominantly a 'happiness' emotion, but with a bittersweet undercurrent of a past lost, never to be regained. The discontinuity hypotheses of nostalgia suggests that 'nostalgia is an emotional reaction to discontinuity in people's lives...people who experience disruption in their lives will rate the past more favorably than those who experience continuity' (Sedikides et al, 2004, p 208). Moran (2002) argues that many nostalgic narratives idealise the childhood of our collective pasts rather than focusing on individual lived experience, describing the concept of childhood as, 'desired by adults for its innocence and the sentimentalized utopia of the middle class nursery' (Moran, 2002, p 157). Similarly, Karsten (2005, p 276) notes that '[t]here is an overall tendency...to assume that things were better in the past'. Nostalgic memories of childhood portray it as a space in time free from adult control, but feeling loved and protected by family and friends, in contrast to the restrictions placed on contemporary childhood from political, educational and legal institutions. Such a contrast may serve to feed adults' anxieties about the threats to children from outside influences (Moran, 2002; Wildschut et al, 2006). This is echoed in a survey commissioned by Play England for Playday 2007 (ICM Research, 2007), which found that when participants were asked to compare the present day to their past experiences, the past provided a picture of idyllic landscapes, safety and imagination, whereas play for the child of the present was characterised by lack of imagination, sterile environments, computers, fear and violence.

One effect of this fear and perception of violence is that parents are increasingly unwilling to let children explore the outside world unsupervised (Shaw et al, 2012; Shaw et al, 2015). The spread of mass media means that instances of violence against children by strangers are reported in great detail; parents believe such events to be more common than they are and feel anxious about their children's safety in this respect (Layard and Dunn, 2009). The Play England survey (ICM Research, 2007) shows how children's place in the general environment is coloured by personal perspective: parents identified threats to children playing out, whereas non-parents saw children and young people as a nuisance. These competing ideas of children, what Hendrick (1997) has described as the victim/threat dualism, may have contributed to adults' fears about children playing out. The idea of the child in need of protection versus the child in need of correction is a social paradigm still evident in reports linking social exclusion to criminality (Layard and Dunn, 2009).

Although nostalgia has been viewed predominantly as a positive emotion that builds a sense of self and social belonging, it has also been argued that nostalgic experience can result in a desire and yearning for a utopian past that may or may not have occurred in the life of the individual. As such, nostalgia in terms of childhood and early adolescence experience may function differently depending on the life circumstances and experiences of the individual receiving information about present childhood, how that information is given or received and on their own interactions and/or observations of children in public spaces. Nostalgia may reaffirm the adult's belief that the child of the present does not have the same opportunities as they had and so is a victim of social, cultural and political change or alternatively that children themselves are somehow responsible for any perceived change for the worse and are therefore a threat to the possibly idealistic view which the adult holds of their own childhood.

Depending on whether and how nostalgia plays a role in generating positive opinions of children's play behaviour and use of space, the practice of drawing on memory as a tool for play advocates and playworkers may either continue to be a useful tool or a case of misplaced nostalgia (Neisser, 1991). It may be pertinent therefore to query whether nostalgia triggered by anxiety in relation to perceived present-day threat to/from children may actually serve to expand the generational gap in regards to how adults view the play behaviour of children and their use of public space. In addition, nostalgia might affect adults' ability to think positively about present and future childhoods. However, by enhancing the adults' self-esteem, sense of social stability and providing a reference and meaning to their lives, nostalgia may function to draw attention to shared experiences and emphasise comparisons and continuity between generations, thus providing a platform from which to advocate for the child's right to play.

Approaching the research

The study took an inductive approach, working from the 'bottom up' to find patterns in the data collected from which new understanding may develop (Creswell, 2007). It took an epistemological position of social constructionism, which sees the 'reality' (of children's play) as mediated 'historically, culturally and linguistically' and as such is perceived differently by different individuals, allowing for more than one way of knowing (Willig, 2001, p 7). Furthermore, as reality is constructed, then the meaning given to the phenomena (children's play and adults play nostalgia) will be different for different individuals (Crotty, 1998). The research therefore explored the meaning given to children's play and use of space, from the perspective of the adult reporting nostalgic recollections of playing out as a child and from the perspective of children currently living the experience. The intention of the study was to recruit and interview adults between the ages of 18 and 65 who came from families where two or more generations had grown up in the same locality and also with children aged eight to 14 from the same town. This meant that there could be some parallels in terms of shared spaces and opportunities for playing, as well as recognition of the importance of children's relationship with space and the spatial aspects of memory (Jones, 2011). Nine adults were recruited through personal contacts of the researcher, though no participants were close personal friends or family. With the exception of one participant, adults interviewed were not currently involved in children's play projects and had no prior knowledge of current playwork thinking.

All the children who participated in the research lived in the town and the surrounding settlements. They either attended open access[1] outdoor play sessions at one of the local parks or used the park to 'hang out' with friends on a regular basis, so were known to the playworkers at the site. Ten children agreed to participate in the study and signed consent was obtained from them and their parents. Child participants were in the age range eight to 14 years old (the predominant age range of children using both the park and the open access play project) with largest numbers of children being in the eight- to nine-year-old and the 12- to 14-year-old age ranges.

The research comprised semi-structured interviews and nostalgia measures. Semi-structured or focused interviews are probably the most commonly used interview method for obtaining qualitative research data (Dawson, 2007). Using open questions enabled the interviewer to gain an individual perspective from the participant who is allowed the time and scope to express their opinions and feelings on the subject decided by the interviewer. Open-ended questions regarding children's current play experiences were prepared in advance and split into two sections. The first set of questions focused on what children liked playing, where and with whom, to what extent adults organised play opportunities, and attendance at organised activities. The second set of questions looked at the community in which the child lives, where they can and cannot play and relationships with neighbours. Similar questions were used for the adult participants, with the addition of questions to elicit adults' feelings and thoughts about contemporary children's play, changes between the past and present, concerns about children playing out today, and how their concerns and opinions were formed.

Adult participants were interviewed within their own homes in accordance with the policies and procedures for lone working of the organisation in which the researcher was employed and after providing signed consent. These interviews were recorded on a dictaphone in order that the researcher had a complete record.

Children were interviewed at a local play setting. However, due to the noise level and disturbance, it became apparent early on that the use of a dictaphone would prove difficult. Instead, handwritten notes were taken by the researcher and read back to the children after the interview. In this way they could add detail to what they had reported or amend any errors made.

During the research, three paired interviews were conducted, one with young people, one with a married couple and one with an adult father and son. In all of these cases participants stated a preference for being interviewed together. This approach can be useful where participants feel a little shy about being interviewed alone or are concerned that they may not be able to answer a question. Booth and Booth (1994) maintain that paired interviews enable people with a shared background to build on each other's responses enabling a greater depth of information through the disclosure of things which may otherwise have not come to light and challenging statements made by the other in a way an interviewer would not have. Like focus groups and group interviews, the loss of individual perspectives while trying to 'fit in' or appear in a positive light may prove to be a limitation, although when the participants are closely related or long-term friends the need to fit in is less likely to be an issue. However, it should be noted that where paired interviews took place with children/young people, peer pressure may have an impact on the responses obtained.

In addition to interviewing the adults, and in order to explore whether or not play nostalgia had a role in adults' perceptions of children's play behaviour and use of public space, a short questionnaire was completed by adult participants following the semi-structured interviews. This questionnaire was designed using a combination of approaches to measuring nostalgia, namely Batcho (1995) and Wildschut et al (2010), and also used the Positive and Negative Affect Schedule (PANAS) developed by Watson et al (1988).

Although the study used quantitative approaches to measuring nostalgia, it makes no claims to generalisation, as numbers involved were small. Rather, it explored the particular location of shared experiences between adults and children as an alternative to broad generalisations that can occlude the relationship between memory and place (Jones, 2011).

Adult perceptions of children's play behaviour and use of space

In order to interpret adult perceptions of children's play behaviour and use of space, the interview transcripts were analysed to identify emergent themes. Themes were ranked by the number of times they appeared in the interview transcripts. The predominant themes emerging from the interviews when discussing adult perception of contemporary children's play were that children do not play in the same way as adult participants had (a view expressed by all participants), that children's play is focused around occupation with technology, engaging in anti-social behaviour and 'hanging around doing nothing'. There were fewer comments made by adult participants regarding children engaging in wheeled play, sport, adult organised activities, street games and engaging with the opposite sex (themes that emerged from the interviews with children), though these were noted by a minority.

Analysis to identify where adults had observed children playing and whether their response to the space chosen to play in was viewed in a positive or negative light found a divide in adult opinion regarding children's use of the street and the park. However, the majority of adult participants felt use of green spaces and the skate park to play in was positive, whereas playing around the shops and in the car parks was viewed in a negative light.

When exploring beliefs that children's play had changed from their childhoods, adult responses fell broadly into the victim/threat duality described by Hendrick (1997). Children were described as either victims of change (societal or environmental) or at threat from other individuals, or they were perceived as a threat to others.

> "I wouldn't say I wouldn't want my children going where I went but, now there isn't a place to go and it isn't as nice to play either, definitely not, but you're more afraid of people these days." (Participant 2)

> "I don't think I would go out at night on my own, I think some of them can be very intimidating and I think some of these youngsters are very, very rude, there's no…how can I explain…they've got no civility." (Participant 8)

The main concern noted by participants about children playing outdoors was fear of other people and children, specifically abduction, molestation and bullying, reflecting national research focusing on the concept of 'stranger danger' (Pain, 2006). Furedi (2001) refers to research undertaken in Scotland in 1998, where 76 per cent of parents interviewed thought that there had been an increase in child murder by a stranger, although in fact the incidence of such events is very low and has shown no change over two decades. This confirms that there is a marked discrepancy between the threat of something bad happening and the actual situation occurring.

> "I know our E, who's nine now, plays in the avenue and I think our L may have let her to the shop but that's it. I'd be very wary now, particularly if I had a girl…You hear so much going on don't you about men picking up young girls and different things, I would be quite concerned about that." (Participant 8)

The next most mentioned concern was that children do not or will not go out due to the use of technology in their play.

> "Everything is so motivated around computers, televisions and all that type of technology that they just miss out on all the nice things, or what we did anyway." (Participant 1)

Additionally, participants were concerned by the rise in traffic around the streets where children have traditionally played and children missing out on the fun which participants had as children. Concerns about drugs, peer pressure, obesity, lack of imagination and damage to property were also highlighted during the interviews.

Adult participants who reported negative perceptions of children noted specifically that they believed children's behaviour, attitudes and manners had changed for the worse. The threat of mugging and being beaten up particularly in areas where gangs congregate was reported as a first-hand experience by two of the participants.

Questions about how these concerns are formed were added in order to establish how external sources of information might contribute to the adults' interpretation of children's play and use of space. Their information regarding children's play and use of space came from three main sources: the media, observation and direct or indirect experience.

Although there were key differences in past and present play experiences as reported by participants, these were not to as great an extent as may have been suggested within intergenerational and historical research. The main areas of difference were as expected, occupation with technology (Byron, 2008), children using the home as a play space (Karsten, 2005) and how far children can travel from home independently to play (Lester and Maudsley, 2007), although this was only really evident when participants had reached secondary school.

Comparing adult and child responses

Both children and adults were asked about their own play experiences as a means of comparing adult accounts of play experiences to those reported by children today.

Many of the places adults and children chose to play remained the same, however, more adults than children reported playing in undeveloped or natural space, for example fields and woodland. Although some children did report playing in the house with computer games, this was seen as a complement to, not instead of, playing out. What had changed were adult attitudes. Far more reported being concerned for children than they felt the adults of their childhood had been.

Both adult and child participants reported outdoor play which included wheeled play, hide and seek, building dens, skipping, mud pies and rivalry between different neighbourhoods and to a lesser extent, playing team sports, hanging out with friends, playing 'Knock, Knock, Ginger', and enjoying arts and crafts and walks. Both sets of participants, but more so the children, reported climbing trees, sliding down banks, playing imaginary games and playing on park equipment. Significant areas where play behaviour differed between adult and child participants were chasing games and computer games (considerably more children than adults said they played these games) and drinking alcohol (only adults commented on this in their memories of playing as children).

Comparing data between adult and child participants in relation to clubs and organised activities, similarities were found in attendance at sports clubs, play or youth projects, afterschool clubs, dancing and uniformed groups. More adults than children spoke about participating in church/chapel-based activities.

Both adult and child participants reported playing with friends from the street, friends of different ages, school friends, and a wider circle of friends from different areas. Children said they were more likely to play with siblings whereas adults reported they were more likely to have played in gangs. Neither adults' nor children's play was reported as being organised by adults. Although they reminisced about attending clubs and supervised activities, the adult participants did not seem to have considered this as play and although the majority of children interviewed were regular attendees at open access play sessions, they did not seem to have considered their play there as organised by the playworkers. There were also reports of playing with older family members and parents in both participant groups.

To be in by dark was reported as the most common time restriction placed on both children and adults; however, child participants were more likely to have a set time to be home, between 8 pm and 8.30 pm. The greatest difference reported was in relation to ranging behaviour. Whereas both adults and children reported staying close to home until the age of 10 or 11, once they were in secondary school, adult participants reported roaming within a three- or four-mile radius whereas over half of the older children in the study reported to staying within the locality in which the research took place.

Similarities in adult and child participants' choice of space to play were reported as follows: street, back lane, playing fields, garden and parks. Natural spaces such as woods were also reported in both groups but more so in the adult group. Main differences between the groups were the number of children reporting playing in the house. The reasons for playing in these spaces were the same for both groups: they are either close to home, out of the way of adults or family members are there. With regard to playing at home, the majority of children interviewed stated that this was due to none of their friends being out or bad weather. Adult participants also reported the presence of lots of other children being a factor in deciding where to play.

Both adults and children alike agreed that their communities were friendly, though adults noted that whereas they once knew everyone in their street this is no longer the case. Neighbours and recollections of grumpy neighbours featured in both adults' and children's interviews, as did the neighbours who were particularly nice. Whereas adults described their communities as close, children were more likely to say they were okay or that they did not really talk to their neighbours.

Nostalgia measures

While analysing research data for the study, it became apparent that establishing whether participants were feeling nostalgic could not be addressed through semi-structured interviews alone. Therefore, an additional measure of nostalgia and positive affect items was added to the research after interviews had been completed.

A number of measures of nostalgia have been developed concentrating on its effects, namely: self-continuity, instilling stability at times of change (Davis, 1979); social connectedness and affirming social bonds (Batcho et al, 2008); positive and negative affect, triggered by feelings of loneliness and sadness but acting as a repository for positive affect, strengthening bonds and re-affirming relationships (Wildschut et al, 2006); and historical nostalgia, yearning for the distant past which is evaluated in more positive terms than the present (Stern, 1992).

In order to gauge the degree to which individuals generally experienced nostalgic states, a question from Wildschut et al's (2010) study was used: 'Generally speaking, how often do you bring to mind nostalgic experiences?', with responses ranging on a seven-point scale from very rarely to very frequently. This also provided a means of comparison with the responses given by participants in the Batcho Nostalgia Inventory (BNI). Batcho (1995) created the BNI as a measure of discontinuity hypothesis based on 18 aspects of the past which individuals miss, for example, 'not having to worry', and 'my friends'. Ten items from Batcho's Nostalgia Inventory (1995) were selected and presented as a Likert scale, in order to ascertain general feelings of discontinuity/self-continuity.

The Positive and Negative Affect Schedule (PANAS) developed by Watson et al (1988) is a measure of emotional state to assess the positive or negative affect, in this case nostalgia. Nostalgia is seen as promoting positive affect (Sedikides et al, 2004) and as such, participants experiencing nostalgic episodes should score highly on the positive affect scale and lower on the negative affect scale. Within this study, participants were asked to complete the PANAS and report their feelings after discussing their own childhood (Measure 1) and again after discussing their perceptions of children playing today (Measure 2). The scales were analysed individually and then compared to show any difference in the participants' positive affect between the two measures.

Analysis of nostalgia and affect measures

In comparing participants' results on the BNI with their response to Wildschut et al's (2010) nostalgia items, those participants who claimed to feel nostalgia 'occasionally' or 'often' scored more highly on the BNI, implying higher levels of personal nostalgia and a greater likelihood to 'miss' negative things associated with their past.

On analysing the two PANAS measures (Measure 1 being the emotion level after discussing past play experiences and Measure 2 the emotion level after discussing perceptions of current play behaviour and use of space) it was found that in both measures participants recorded a higher positive affect score than negative affect. However, in Measure 2, with the exception of one participant, the positive affect score was lower than in Measure 1 and the negative affect score was higher than in Measure 1, resulting in a lower differential between positive and negative affect. This suggests that participants felt less positive when discussing children's play in the present day than when discussing their own childhood play experiences. However, this cannot be directly attributed to nostalgia, as the results may be due to participants' external sources of information regarding current childhood play experiences, or indeed an interrelated combination of all sources of information.

Analysis of adult interview transcripts with reference to nostalgia

Adults' interview transcripts were examined in order that the author could determine whether the accounts given show signs of nostalgia as identified in research. Indicators of nostalgic experience identified by Holak and Havlena (1992, 1998) and Wildschut et al (2006) were considered as nostalgic recollection in instances where the participant went into some depth to explain or describe specific incidents from their past.

In analysing the interview transcripts, it was evident that historical nostalgia played a considerable part in the reminiscences of a number of the adult participants. Of the nine participants interviewed, seven recounted nostalgic memories to the author, these nostalgic episodes were based primarily around friends, special occasions and specific play experiences.

Instances of historical nostalgia (Stern, 1992) were identified through common nostalgic generalisations, for example, adults' tendency to report consistently warm summers and snow every winter, and by past/present comparisons. Past/present comparisons were identified in the transcripts of five participants predominantly around places that have changed. Common nostalgic generalisations were identified in the transcripts of four participants focusing on weather and community relationships.

When looking at the number of instances of nostalgic accounts within interview transcripts compared to the nostalgia measure results, it would be expected that there would be a positive correlation between the two sources of data. This proved to be the case in all but one instance. Furthermore, the results suggest that there is a correlation between the nostalgia measures and positive affect. A similar relationship was identified when analysing interview transcripts and comparing those to the PANAS, those participants who recalled many nostalgic memories during interview scored higher on the Positive Affect scale. This suggested that when individuals recollect their past experiences, they feel more positive.

Correlation between nostalgia measures and nostalgia in adult interview transcripts

There was an interesting relationship between adult comparison of their play experiences with that of children today, and their scores in nostalgia measures. Adults who scored highly in the nostalgia measures provided more comparisons between their own experience and children today, viewing their own experiences as more positive. Furthermore, the spaces where children play which were viewed positively by adults were the spaces they used for their own play as children. This phenomenon could be ascribed to the nostalgia function of self-continuity (Davis, 1979), where nostalgia functions as a means of providing stability and continuity. A connection between levels of nostalgia and perception of children's play and use of space, suggests that adult participants used their own nostalgic experiences as a measure by which to interpret children's play and use of space in a positive or negative way.

There were some disparities in what adults thought about children's play and use of space and children's reports. However, what is interesting is that when looking at the way that adults viewed play and use of space, instances which mirrored their own practices as children were looked upon more favourably than those which did not, and where adults felt they themselves had engaged in behaviour which could be interpreted as anti-social, they shrugged it off as fun or at least harmless normal childhood behaviour. This may be a way of understanding why adults who recall their misdemeanours as children are able to justify them, while if they are observed in the context of current play behaviour, they are seen as disruptive or unacceptable, suggesting what McAdams et al (2001) describe as contamination.

When comparing the nostalgia measures with the transcripts, it did become apparent that participants who scored lower on the nostalgia measures were less likely to present comparisons in their interviews. However, the majority of adult participants who scored highly on the nostalgia measures presented more nostalgic experiences and comparisons between their play behaviours and use of space with those of children today. These comparisons were negative towards current experiences in all cases.

> "Children have changed, there's a lot of bullying, and um they do things don't they, they carry weapons, I never seen anything of that and I never seen any bullying when I was younger. But I do think children have changed." (Participant 2)

Closing thoughts: implications of the research for the playwork profession

Ramey (2010) suggests that recollection of childhood memories provides a useful tool in advocating for unstructured 'natural' play opportunities today. This technique is commonly used by playwork professionals in making a case for children's freely chosen play and by playwork trainers in advocating the need for development of play opportunities and play space.

The research found that nostalgic recollection resulted in positive affect in adult participants; recalling their own childhoods made them happy. However, when discussing present-day play experiences of children, positive affect lowered and negative affect rose. This suggests that when playwork professionals use nostalgia as an advocacy tool, they are raising positive affect, only to lower it when comparisons are made with the present-day situation. This can be helpful when advocating for development of play spaces or for more tolerance of children playing in the public realm. Although comparisons were negative, more leaned towards the child as a victim of societal and environmental change and adult participants sympathised that children did not have the same opportunities available to them. This raises the question as to whether playwork professionals should be emphasising the child as an object of sympathy who requires an intervention to compensate for what adults interpret as lack of opportunity and space to play when compared to their own childhoods.

Hughes (2001) suggests using the IMEE (intuition, memory, experience and evidence) process of reflection in supporting playwork practice. Though widely used, it could become easy for playworkers' reflections to slip into emotional nostalgia leading to a rose-tinted glasses view of their past play experiences and an attempt to recreate them, which may support their needs but be less likely to support the needs of the child.

The research presented in this chapter highlights many similarities between past play experiences and current childhood play experiences. It may be pertinent, however, to query the efficacy of using play memories as an advocacy tool, because, although nostalgia may enhance the adults' self-esteem, sense of social stability and by providing a reference and meaning to their lives, it also has the potential to regard the experiences of contemporary children in a negative light because it does not match the ideal of their own childhoods.

Notes

[1] 'Open access' is a term used in the UK to refer to staffed play provision where children are free to come and go, in contrast to childcare where children stay at the setting until collected by a caregiver.

References

Batcho, K.I. (1995) 'Nostalgia: A psychological perspective', *Perceptual and Motor Skills*, 80(1): 131–43.

Batcho, K.I., DaRin, M.L., Nave, A.M. and Yaworsky, R.R. (2008) 'Nostalgia and identity in song lyrics', *Psychology of Aesthetics, Creativity, and the Arts*, 2(4): 236–44.

Booth, T. and Booth, W. (1994) *Parenting under pressure: Mothers and fathers with learning difficulties*, Buckingham: Open University Press.

Byron, T. (2008) *Byron Review: Safer children in a digital world* (executive summary), Nottingham: Department for Children, Schools and Families and the Department for Culture, Media and Sport.

Creswell, J. (2007) *Qualitative inquiry and research design: Choosing among five approaches* (2nd edn), Thousand Oaks, CA: Sage.

Crotty, M. (1998) *The foundations of social research: Meaning and perspectives in the research process*, London: Sage.

Davis, F. (1979) *Yearning for yesterday: A sociology of nostalgia*, New York: Free Press.

Dawson, C. (2007) *A practical guide to research methods: A user-friendly manual for mastering research techniques and projects* (3rd edn), Oxford: How To Books.

Furedi, F. (2001) *Paranoid parenting*, London: Allen Lane.

Hendrick, H. (1997) 'Constructions and reconstructions of British childhood: An interpretative survey, 1800 to the present', in A. James and A. Prout (eds) *Constructing and reconstructing childhood: Contemporary issues in the sociological study of childhood*, London: RoutledgeFarmer, pp 34–62.

Holak, S.L. and Havlena, W.J. (1992) 'Nostalgia: An exploratory study of themes and emotions in the nostalgic experience', *Advances in Consumer Research*, 19: 380–7.

Holak, S.L. and Havlena, W.J. (1998) 'Feelings, fantasies, and memories: An examination of the emotional components of nostalgia', *Journal of Business Research*, 42(3): 217–26.

Hughes, B. (2001) *Evolutionary playwork and reflective analytic practice*, London: Routledge.

ICM Research (2007) *Attitudes towards street play*, London: ICM, www.playday.org.uk/media/2681/attitudes_towards_street_play.pdf.

Johnson-Laird, P.N. and Oatley, K. (1989) 'The language of emotions: An analysis of semantic field', *Cognition and Emotion*, 3: 81–123.

Jones, O. (2011) 'Geography, memory and non-representational geographies', *Geography Compass*, 5(12): 875–85.

Jones, O. and Garde-Hansen, J. (2012) 'Introduction', in O. Jones and J. Garde-Hansen (eds) *Geography and memory: Explorations in identity, place and becoming*, London: Palgrave-Macmillan, pp 1–23.

Karsten, L. (2005) 'It all used to be better? Different generations on continuity and change in urban children's daily use of space', *Children's Geographies*, 3(3): 275–90.

Labaree, R.V. (2016) *Organizing your social sciences research paper*, Los Angeles, CA: University of Southern California, http://libguides.usc.edu/writingguide.

Layard, R. and Dunn, J. (2009) *Good childhood: Searching for values in a competitive age*, London: Penguin Books.

Lester, S. and Maudsley, M. (2007) *Play, naturally: A review of children's natural play*, London: National Children's Bureau.

McAdams, D.P., Reynolds, J., Lewis, M., Patten, A.H. and Bowman, P.J. (2001) 'When bad things turn good and good things turn bad: Sequences of redemption and contamination in life narrative and their relation to psychosocial adaptation in midlife adults and in students', *Personality and Social Psychology Bulletin*, 27(4): 474–85.

Moran, J. (2002) 'Childhood and nostalgia in contemporary culture', *European Journal of Cultural Studies*, 5(2): 155–73.

Neisser, U. (1991) 'A case of misplaced nostalgia', *American Psychologist*, 46(1): 34–6.

Pain, R. (2006) 'Paranoid parenting? Rematerializing risk and fear for children', *Social and Cultural Geography*, 7(2): 221–43.

Ramey, L. (2010) 'Rekindling memories of yesterday's children: Making the case for nature-based unstructured play for today's children', *Journal of Sustainability Education*, 1(1): 228–54.

Sedikides, C., Wildschut, T. and Baden, D. (2004) 'Nostalgia: Conceptual issues and existential functions', in J. Greenberg, S.L. Koole and T. Pyszczynski (eds) *Handbook of experimental existential psychology*, New York: Guildford Press, pp 200–14.

Shaw, B., Watson, B., Frauendienst, B., Redecker, A., Jones, T. with Hillman, M. (2012) *Children's independent mobility: A comparative study in England and Germany, 1971–2010*, London: Policy Studies Institute.

Shaw, B., Bicket, M., Elliott, B., Fagan-Watson, B., Mocca, E. with Hillman, M. (2015) *Children's independent mobility: An international comparison and recommendations for action*, London: Policy Studies Institute.

Stern, B.B. (1992) 'Historical and personal nostalgia in advertising text: The fin de siècle effect', *Journal of Advertising*, 21(4): 11–22.

Watson, D., Clark, L.A. and Tellegen, A. (1988) 'Development and validation of brief measures of positive and negative affect: The PANAS scales', *Journal of Personality and Social Psychology*, 54(6): 1063–70.

Wildschut, T., Sedikides, C., Arndt, J. and Routledge, C. (2006) 'Nostalgia: Content, triggers, functions', *Journal of Personality and Social Psychology*, 91(5): 975–93.

Wildschut, T., Sedikides, C., Routledge, C., Arndt, J. and Cordaro, F. (2010) 'Nostalgia as a repository of social connectedness: The role of attachment-related avoidance', *Journal of Personality and Social Psychology*, 98(4): 573–86.

Willig, C. (2001) *Introducing qualitative research in psychology: Adventures in theory and method*, Buckingham: Open University Press.

THREE

Debris and delight: children's play during the second world war

Becky Willans

Introduction

The second world war (WWII) is perhaps the best known time in modern history when children in the UK were subject to large-scale destruction and devastation, while still having periods of free time away from adults to largely do as they pleased (Westall, 1995; Magee, 2008). Yet little is known about children's opportunities and experiences of play during WWII; literature and documentation on children's experiences of this period is limited. Books, diaries, memoirs, news articles and photography mainly relate to evacuation or childhood in general rather than focusing on the leisure time of children, the opportunities for play during this time (for example, Tymoczko and Blackmun, 2000; Werner, 2001; Andrews-Brown, 2004; Ashman, 2006; Rex, 2008; Veale, 2008). These records of wartime childhood are frequently negative, highlighting experiences of rationing, air raids and evacuation rather than the more positive aspects of childhood, particularly personally directed play experiences.

The small-scale study described in this chapter interweaves the rich oral histories of five people who were children in the East End of London during the war with the literature on children's wartime experiences and also that on play and resilience (Lester and Russell, 2008), Kyttä's (2004) work on affordances and Nicholson's (1971) theory of loose parts, to document and theorise children's opportunities for playing during WWII and how this might inform contemporary playwork practice. The chapter opens with a discussion on childhood during WWII and then moves on to a description of the research process. Four key themes emerged from the data analysis: opportunities for playing; affordances; loose parts, toys and games; resilience and risk. Each theme is introduced through the literature and illustrated from the participants' stories.

As Thompson (2000, p 1) states: 'All history depends ultimately upon its social purpose.' The purpose of the history told here grew out of the coming together of a number of interests: the researcher's involvement in playwork; her observations of and curiosity about children's creation/use of spaces for playing; and an interest in exploring how the play experiences of children during WWII may offer insights for making sense of the Playwork Principles (PPSG, 2005) in practice, particularly in terms of supporting children in the creation of a space where they can play on their terms with fewer adult–imposed expectations and demands.

Second world war childhoods

When war first broke out in 1939, it had little impact on people's lives initially. The events of Saturday 7 September 1940, or 'Black Saturday' were unanticipated by many (Gardiner, 2010). There was a general feeling of shock when the Luftwaffe struck. Bombs rained down on the residential and industrial areas of East End London, in what was to be the first of 57 consecutive nights of bombing. Gardiner (2010) states that the main target of the bombing campaign were the docks in the area of Silvertown, where the river Thames bends back on itself to create a 'U' shape. The bombing campaign was not specifically restricted to the docks. The attacks commenced along both sides of the river, in the East End from Dagenham to Tower Hill, and to the south of the river from Woolwich to Bermondsey, areas where there were high levels of integration between industry and housing (Gardiner, 2010) (see Figure 3.1).

The East End was a dangerous place to live at this time. The bombing was so severe it resulted in the destruction of a high proportion of both residential and commercial areas. However, despite the widespread desolation and ruin, life for the East Ender continued. Although the evacuations of children and some women or families were encouraged, O'Neill (2003) suggests that this was not really an option for those residing in the East End as they were not people of privileged backgrounds; even if the opportunity of evacuation did arise, East End families chose to stay together. The pain of separation was more powerful than the fear of the dangers war would bring. And so, life and the sense of community remained, families continued to socialise out the front, knitting, reading the paper and chatting to the neighbours, while the children played in the street.

Most people had little in terms of material wealth, having 'just the sheer milk of human kindness towards one another, which obviously

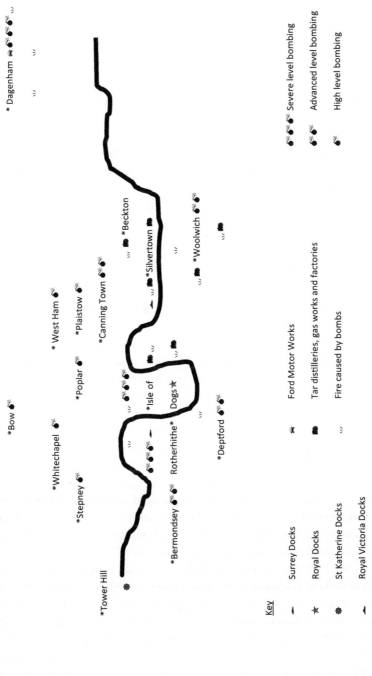

Figure 3.1: River Thames, East End, London: sites of bombing, bomb fire and destruction

Key

⚓	Surrey Docks	Ford Motor Works
★	Royal Docks	Tar distilleries, gas works and factories
⚙	St Katherine Docks	Fire caused by bombs
⚓	Royal Victoria Docks	

Severe level bombing
Advanced level bombing
High level bombing

Source: Becky Willans

37

when faced with adversity brought it through more and more in people's attitudes towards one another' (Taylor, 1981). This suggests a resilient community of both adults and children who found ways of coping despite living in a war zone.

Garbarino et al (1991) suggest the sheer fact that children survive a war is a testimony to their resilience. They highlight a number of factors that support resilience in times of adversity, including: actively trying to cope with stress, cognitive competence, supportive environments, stable relationships and the support of their community. In their review of contemporary literature on children's play, Lester and Russell (2008) show how playing can contribute to these factors, particularly noting its potential across the following themes: pleasure and enjoyment; emotion regulation; stress response systems, uncertainty and risk; creativity and openness to change and novelty; attachment to peers and to place. These ideas are further developed throughout the chapter as the opportunities for play are illustrated both in the stories of the participants and the literature.

How the research happened

The epistemological position of social constructivism was used for the research, acknowledging that people construct their realities through the processes of engagement in the world. In this sense, meanings are fluid, situated and contextual both in time and place. A theory of meaning was sought rather than beginning with a theory or imposed meaning (Crotty, 1998; Creswell, 2007). This was combined with the methodological approach of oral histories in order to gather the memories and experiences of those who were children during WWII. Human memory is partial and subjective, therefore it is often difficult to challenge or develop the views and opinions gathered through the use of research methods such as a questionnaire, where little or no face-to-face contact occurs. Oral histories and semi-structured or unstructured oral methods allow the researcher to question and delve more deeply, allowing for two-way questioning, cross questioning and expansion of points for further clarification and interest (Thompson, 2000).

Oral histories, in essence, follow the data collection principles of unstructured or semi-structured interviews (Blaikie, 2009). This type of interviewing allows for descriptive story-like narratives to occur and flow naturally without the interruption or rigidity of formal or structured questioning (Creswell, 2007). The progression of the discussion allows the researcher to draw attention to interesting points talked about on the way. Bearing this in mind, the following topic areas were used to focus the interview, and move from simple and straightforward contextual questions into more open ones that can allow for a free flow of conversation:

- Background: age, family members, parents' jobs during war
- Where did you live?
- Were you evacuated?
- Was your home damaged?
- Did you have your own shelter?
- What did you do in the shelters?
- Who did you play with?
- What did you play?
- Where did you go to play?

It was also worth considering that due to the length of the interviews and the age of the participants, the most appropriate form of interviewing was face-to-face. In order to provide a complete record of each interview, a voice recorder was used (Creswell, 2007).

The participants needed to have lived in the East End in the following postal areas, E1, E2, E3, E8, E9, E14, E18, IG1, IG3 and IG8. The reasoning behind this choice is that these areas, due to their close proximity to the docks and factories, were subject to frequent and heavy bombing and devastation throughout WWII (Gardiner, 2010). It is likely that this would have had a significant impact, both positive and negative, on children's opportunities for playing. Participants needed to satisfy specific conditions in order to provide some focus and common factors to the research. They had to have been born between the years of 1924 and 1939. This was to help ensure that their experiences of, and opportunities for playing occurred during or shortly after WWII. Participants had to have grown up on the home front and if they were evacuated this could be for no longer than one year. Five participants were recruited who met these criteria and still offered some diversity of experience: Bob, Paul, Bonnie, Ann and Susan.

The research design was approved by the University of Gloucestershire's Faculty Research Ethics Committee. All participants received an information sheet about the study, discussing research ethics, highlighting any risks and requesting permission to use their spoken word for the research. Pseudonyms were used throughout to protect the participants' identity.

Data analysis followed Creswell's (2007) Data Analysis Spiral, where the researcher 'engages in the process of moving in analytic circles rather than using a fixed linear approach' (Creswell, 2007, p 150). The data were interpreted, compared and categorised in relevant topic areas using memoing (notes of insights gathered during the coding process) and reflection, allowing a representation of the research account to be produced. Each transcript was read through and recordings listened to, making notes in the margins. This allowed the formation of initial codes or themes which overlapped in the individual accounts of participants. After this initial coding process, themes, stories and categories which occurred as commonalities across all participant accounts were noted. Creswell (2007, p 151) describes the interpretation, comparison and categorisation loop of the data analysis spiral as 'the heart of qualitative data analysis'.

There were seven categories first used when analysing the data. These were: home (accommodation and family life); evacuation; bombing (housing and shelters); health; school; leisure (cinema and dancing); play. Any data which did not fit in to these categories were discarded. As the seven categories were further explored, four cross-cutting themes emerged. These themes were somewhat of a surprise as they did not specifically correlate with the original categories or pre-conceived beliefs that children would have been fearful of the dangers of war. The seven categories had been designed in order to record how the participants' play experiences could inform contemporary playwork. However, in the event, their accounts were enthralling and highlighted the many fond memories they had from their childhoods. As they talked about their childhoods and play experiences, the topic areas soon faded into the background, allowing for a free flowing conversation to occur and provided richer accounts of play experiences during WWII. The four cross-cutting themes were: opportunities for playing; affordances; loose parts, toys and games; and resilience and risk.

Opportunities for playing

The literature on childhood during WWII documents the extensiveness of bombing and consequent widespread damage and destruction. Although it created dangerous and hazardous areas, they became rich exploration sites for children. For example, Sark (2003) recounts 'we were told not to play on bomb sites, a very sensible restriction which we all ignored'. In some ways, although structurally dangerous, bombed out and dilapidated buildings provided playgrounds rich in potential. These spaces were perceived by adults as undesirable, yet they provided children with opportunities to take risks and develop the skills needed for resilience. Along with the exploration of bomb sites, RAF barracks offered exciting, yet dangerous opportunities for playing. Frequently, children 'borrowed' unexploded cannon and cartridge shells to use as ornaments or to create their own explosives (Werner, 2001; Ashman, 2006; Rex, 2008). One diary entry in Ashman (2006) describes how one day a boy and a friend packed the powder from an incendiary bomb into the holes of the pavement and set it alight from distance. The expected outcome was a little damage; however, the overall result caused a crater in the road.

For the research participants in this study, opportunities for playing presented themselves frequently throughout the war. Bonnie clarifies, "we used to play a lot, we were out in the street ever such a lot". Paul, Bonnie and Bob discussed the changes to time during the war. Double British summertime occurred, "so in fact it wouldn't get dark until about 11 pm in those days [summer]. So we used to be out playing really". However, during the winter months, darkness came by roughly 3 pm, making this period a very dark and depressing time for children.

During WWII it would have been unusual for parents to take their children to school in personal transport. Some children, like Ann would have used public transport to travel to school, but most children, such as Bob, Paul and Bonnie, walked to school with their siblings and friends. Paul describes his journey: "Sometimes we used to leave school at 4 pm and I never got in til 6 pm...You would take the longest route home and play [marbles] all along the gutter." Parents were often absent, serving in the forces, at work or preoccupied with the war effort. This resulted in a greater sense of freedom for children than is perhaps possible in the modern day. Paul commented that there was no-one around to tell you what to do.

Affordances

The availability of an environment which provided stimulation for creativity and imagination would have affected the opportunities for playing for children during WWII. The possibilities available to the child in an environment are known as affordances. Kyttä (2004) highlights that affordance can occur in two ways: potential affordance, where there are infinite possibilities available to the child, and actualised affordances where the child acts on the possibilities available within their play experience. The potential for actualising affordances can be split into three 'fields of action'. The field of promoted action (FPA) is a socially approved way of using an environment at a specific place or time. The field of constrained action (FCA) is restricted either by the physical design or social prohibition. The field of free action (FFA) is the affordance which provides the most stimulation and opportunities for playing and exploration, these can be either socially promoted or socially constrained, meaning that the affordance can be actualised in either socially acceptable or socially unacceptable ways, with or without adult permission.

The places in which all the participants recounted playing were rich in actualised affordances (Kyttä, 2004) being either FPAs, for example, Victoria Park and the street, and/or FFAs, such as, marshland, fields, bomb sites and disused factories. Susan, Ann and Bob used to play in Victoria Park. Their experiences included swimming, paddling, football, cricket, games around the water fountain and play on the park equipment.

Bob talked at length about his experiences playing and exploring with his friends on Hackney Marshes. This area was largely free from adults and as the marshes were being used as a refuse site, there was a wealth of material and objects available. Bob recalls watching and befriending troops who were digging trenches in the area and watching mainly intact bombs being transported and disposed of. The marshes were next to the river Lea, which gave rise to opportunities for fishing and paddling with friends.

Of all the participants, Paul had the greatest range of areas used for play. He discussed these areas in depth and the experiences of playing there. He recalled a field used for play by him and his brothers: "10 foot high, just a complete maze of undergrowth and we used to have dens in there." These were places where adults were not present and children governed the area.

Paul and Bob talked about playing in old abandoned or bombed-out factories during the war, the exploration occurring either by chance or boredom and wanting something exciting to do. This was similar to Bonnie's experiences of playing in abandoned churches. She stated, "I mean you're not really supposed to go into them but we all did." She also spoke about her explorations of bombed-out churches: "Well I mean there were things that you could find, it was just interesting." Kyttä (2004) suggests that these kinds of areas provide the most stimulation and opportunities for playing and exploration. This is perhaps why the participants were so drawn to them as children. Bombed out and derelict buildings afforded opportunities for playing as they represented a FFA (Kyttä, 2004) for children and were rich in the availability of loose parts (Nicholson, 1971), and it is to this concept that the chapter now turns.

Loose parts, toys and games

When discussing children's playful engagement with space, Nicholson (1971, p 6) states 'In any environment, both the degree of inventiveness and creativity, and the possibility of discovery, are directly proportional to the number and kind of variables [loose parts] in it.' Variables or loose parts can take many forms including stones and rubble; sand, dirt, wood and twigs; fabric, rope and dilapidated household furniture. As the East End was heavily bombed, these kinds of materials and objects could be found in abundance. They provided children with plenty of choice about what and how they could play with the items they found. Due to their adaptability and manipulability the same object could be used to facilitate a variety of different play forms and themes. The availability of loose parts facilitated and afforded inventiveness for play. Children were able to design and create a space which fulfilled their desire for playing, creativity and experimentation.

While commercial toys were scarce in the East End during WWII, materials to build and create were readily available, many children made their own toys (Werner, 2001; Ashman, 2006; Rex, 2008; Veale, 2008). These included teddy bears, peg dolls and rag dolls made from scraps of material, bones, wood and clay (Rex, 2008). Other toys and pastimes included marbles, a whip and top, hoops made from bicycle wheels, football, twosy-threesy, cricket, marbles, skipping and hopscotch. Lamp posts were popular places for children to play chasing and tag games, group skipping games and for rope swings (Lovet Watson, 2008; Little Bobby, 2003; Rex, 2008; Veale, 2008). Pop guns were also a popular toy to design and make. They were constructed using an elder tree branch and an acorn (Rex, 2008). The pop guns were then used by children during dramatic re-enactments of battles with friends or with small-world scale replica toys.

What is demonstrated from the memories and recollections of all participants is that they were imaginative and creative with what was available to them during a time of particular hardship. This is perhaps because of the wealth of variables, resources and materials available. All participants of the study discussed at length the toys, games and play experiences they remembered from their childhoods during WWII. These ranged from activities such as shrapnel collecting to bike riding and roller skating or making their own toys or imaginary games. It was evident, through all five interviews, that mass produced toys such as cars, trains and dolls were hard to come by. If one was lucky enough to have a manufactured toy, this would be shared with other siblings and children who lived in the same street. Susan clarifies, "we all used to share our toys, cos some kiddies had toys, some kiddies didn't. People couldn't afford to buy them." For the most part, girls enjoyed playing skipping, hoops and whip, hopscotch and spinning tops while boys favoured football and fishing. Marbles was also a popular pastime of the participants.

Out of all the participants, Ann appeared to have better access to toys, particularly a camera. However, the most common theme with all participants was access to bicycles or roller-skates. This was surprising as little was found in the literature review about these items. Paul and Susan both had access to a pair of roller skates. Paul described his roller skating experiences in depth, explaining how his brother used to get wheel bearings from the garage where he worked, "we used to put them on our skates and they were like super charged". Ann, Paul and Bob all had access to bikes, with Ann being fortunate enough to own one. "He [dad] made me a bike, a green bike…as I got bigger, and he would work, he brought me a two wheeler."

Many of the participants spoke of making their own toys. Bonnie recalled tying string to cans and running along the street with them, "we just used to do it to be annoying". Bob reminisced, "wood working class I was in, I had a submarine for years that I had made". Paul could remember his brother being quite creative and making pop guns out of wood and springs and aeroplanes and houses out of cardboard. However, he could remember being disappointed when his brother, while playing, set fire to them. Perhaps as a response to the destruction that was being witnessed and experienced at that time, Bonnie suggested "he probably thought he was bombing it".

Sutton-Smith (1997; 2003) suggests that in their play children appropriate aspects of their everyday lives in order to render daily life either less boring or less scary. Such reconstructions of events going on around the children were a common aspect of playing during WWII, as both the literature and the participants' stories show. As well as found objects and loose parts, toy soldiers and small-world toys were used, particularly by boys, to re-enact situations arising in the war. Graham-White (2000) talks about the influences war had on his play experiences. He would recreate the previous day's news using toy soldiers. Andrews-Brown (2004) also reminisces about similar play experiences: "We often used to create what we called Lands. These were often built at the base of tree trunks where we laid out miniature fields planted with genuine crops." With the introduction of tanks, cannons and planes to the play, frequently one land declared war on the other, with bombing using acorns, followed by the heavy trampling of the fields by foot.

Such forms of play later came to be understood by some play and childhood scholars as indicative of violence or aggression and they were discouraged in the institutions of childhood (for a critique of this perspective, see, for example, Sutton-Smith, 1997; Holland, 2003; Smith, 2005). Yet it may be that rather than representing violence in some literal sense, such play forms had a role in the development of resilience, the final theme presented here.

Resilience and risk

During WWII children were aware, from listening to the conversations of adults and the radio, of the changes, fear and worry as a direct result of the war. However, it was often a backdrop to their lives. In addition, there is a general acceptance of the chaos, destruction and trauma as this is the child's world and they know no different (McHenry, 1997). Many children develop an 'immunity' to the daily events of war as they become normalised. Desensitisation, although an uncomfortable notion for many, is inevitable and although war should not be a part of a normal childhood, it is not to say that it reduced the specialness of childhood for the children growing up in these times (Sayers, 1997). 'Children with any shred of childhood left to them play, and they play what they know' (Garbarino et al, 1991, p 12). Replaying events has been theorised in a number of ways in play scholarship. Psychoanalysts saw children's play as a form of abreaction, a way of coming to terms with anxiety and fear: children use play as a medium to make sense of and take control of the world in which they live, given they are not able to verbalise their experiences in the same way as adults (Freud and Burlingham, 1943). A more recent perspective is offered by Sutton-Smith (2003), who suggests that play offers children the opportunity to keep alive primary emotions (fear, anger, sadness, happiness, shock and disgust) within the relative safety of framing behaviour as 'play' or 'as if', where such raw emotions can be held in check by the rules and ritual of the game. Similarly, Hughes (2001) suggests that children develop coping strategies through replaying events from conflict. However, both Freud and Burlingham (1943) and Hughes (2001) acknowledge that for some children, these forms of play become compulsive or stereotypical.

Van der Hoek (2005) suggests that when discussing the resilience of children or the resilience developed through childhood experiences, it is important to explore the concept from the child's perspective, first in terms of the child's own perceptions of the situation, and, second, what strategies they employ in order to cope with each situation that arises. She suggests that situations which an adult may find stressful, upsetting or fearful may be perceived by the child in a different light. The challenges which arise for adults may be less of an issue for the child. These perspectives were researched both through the literature and the participants' stories, although the latter were told from the position of adulthood and all that position carries in terms of memories of childhood.

The appropriation of the events of war into children's play during WWII is evident both in the literature and in participants' stories, for example in the collection of shrapnel, the exploration of bomb craters and bomb sites, and the role play of children which often emulated that of the Allied and Axis military. Collection of shrapnel was a popular childhood pastime during the war, mostly for boys. Shrapnel became the currency of childhood: the larger the piece or collection, the higher the status of the child among their peers (Rex, 2008). After collecting shrapnel, the retrieved souvenirs were used to make keepsakes such as brooches or to enhance the wooden model aircrafts (Veale, 2008). They were also swapped for other desirable items such as marbles and foreign stamps (Shipton, 2003).

As highlighted by Ashman (2006) and Werner (2001), the exploration of plane crash sites and observation of military air sites was popular with boys but not girls. This was true for research participants Paul and Bob who would observe the local RAF barracks to watch the spitfires come back from battle. Bob recounted a memory of an out of service Tiger Moth aircraft being delivered to his school for the children to play on saying, "They parked it in the school playground, much to the enjoyment of all the boys, they liked that sort of thing."

All of the research participants told stories that showed their courage and resilience during the war. The biggest impact on opportunities for playing highlighted by all participants were air raids, air attacks and the death of playmates. Susan, Paul and Bob all discussed traumatic experiences of the death or serious injury of their friends which occurred either through the debris of an explosion or the force of the blast: "I used to go to school with a girl and the next day she was dead. A land mine fell in her road" (Paul). Bonnie and Susan also highlighted traumatic experiences where they were shot at by German planes. Susan was travelling home through the park, on foot, during her lunch break and Bonnie was walking through the street on her way to school. Susan said, "a plane came over machine gunning. I had to hide behind a tree and would have to change sides depending on what direction it was flying from." One of Paul's responses to the traumatic experience of war was to wait by his bathroom window and say, "Get the air gun quick. If they land in our garden we'll shoot them." As Bob stated, "Your whole life changed because you just took for granted things that are absolutely outrageous now."

In addition to the direct impact of the war itself, experiences and acceptance of death, air raid and evacuation, the participants had to contend with malnutrition and disease, injuries and broken bones. Bonnie and Paul explained "A lot of kids had fleas, a lot had skin complaints and scabies and impetigo because they lacked all the vitamins." Bob also discussed the malnutrition and disease during that time, explaining that he contracted tuberculosis, losing an index finger and his right leg below the knee.

There were many similarities in terms of what and where the participants played. However, the play of Susan, Ann and Bonnie was less risky in comparison to that of Paul and Bob. Bonnie states, "Boys are dangerous creatures aren't they, they have no sense." Paul recounted the most risky play experiences by far. His accounts of play usually ended with some form of personal injury, including broken bones. Among his many tales he discussed falling in to a bramble bush he was trying to jump over and cutting his whole body, and falling off bikes: "This particular morning we came off it…it went into the air and we both landed on the deck. I broke me leg in two places…oh we was in a right state." However, Paul recounted these experiences fondly, stating that it was just boys' play.

Susan, Ann and Bonnie discussed playing 'Knock Down Ginger' in the street with their friends. Ann and Susan also recall playing a game called 'Black Man's Old Dark Scenery'. Susan explains

> "We used to get all the old coats out of the houses…you would get one [child] to cover up all the other children but some had to go and hide…you used to call out 'Alright!' and they [a child] had to come and guess who was under the coats."

Concluding reflections: What can playwork learn from accounts of wartime play?

Overall, the participants, although from varied backgrounds, had similar play experiences and opportunities for playing during WWII. Their accounts are rich in detail and although are recalled from a time of mass devastation, reflect childhoods that were often happy. Through the exploration of Kyttä's (2004) work on affordances and Nicholson's

(1971) work on the use of loose parts, it is evident that what may appear to be a chaotic, derelict or risky environment to an adult, could actually be a space rich in opportunity and affordances for play for children. The oral histories and literature review highlight the creativity of children in making use of variables and loose parts which have been discarded by adults and deemed as junk. Furthermore, although these environments were hazardous and accidents were common, such affordances and varied spaces provided opportunities for adventure and discovery, to develop attachments to peers and places, and to build emotion regulation and stress response systems, all contributing factors for resilience (Lester and Russell, 2008).

It is evident that in the East End during WWII, when left to their own devices, children were making the most of rich opportunities for play that were limited in terms of adult contact. Although wartime Britain presented a high level of life threatening danger and destruction, children still played. Where they played and what they played with was wide ranging and varied, and predominantly focused on being active, outdoors and left to their own devices.

The underpinning ethos of contemporary playwork still advocates that children and young people determine and control their own play which is freely chosen and spontaneous. The Playwork Principles (PPSG, 2005) are the ethical and professional framework describing this perspective of working with children and young people. They assert that play is 'fundamental to the healthy development and wellbeing of individuals and communities', that it is 'freely chosen, personally directed and intrinsically motivated', and that 'children and young people determine and control the content and intent of their play, by following their own instincts, ideas and interests, in their own way for their own reasons motivated'. The role of the playworker is 'to support all children and young people in the creation of a space in which they can play' (PPSG, 2005). This research shows that it is possible for children to independently find spaces that include a range of loose parts, allowing children a greater opportunity for having rich experiences of play and to freely choose and personally direct their play without the constant supervision of adults.

Although not initially intended as a focus for the research, risk and resilience featured heavily in both the literature review and the oral histories of participants. WWII was a hazardous time; however, the resilience of children during this time was remarkable. The research participants clearly expressed that although they knew that they were in constant danger, they enjoyed much of their childhoods and experienced many times of great fun and rich opportunities for playing as a result of the war. The research highlights that many children, when faced with adversity, develop coping mechanisms which strengthen their resilience (Garbarino et al, 1991; Lester and Russell, 2008). This suggests that working to the Playwork Principles to create spaces rich in opportunities for self-organised playing, with rich variables and loose parts (Nicholson, 1971), leaves space open for children to actualise FFAs (Kyttä, 2004) and associated benefits for resilience.

References

Andrews-Brown, D. (2004) 'Sixty years ago', *WW2 People's War*, BBC, www.bbc.co.uk/history/ww2peopleswar/.

Ashman, J. (2006) *Echoes from the home front: A collection of young people's World War II experiences*, Gloucestershire: South Gloucestershire Council Museums and Heritage.

Blaikie, N. (2009) *Designing social research: The logic of anticipation* (2nd edn), Cambridge: Polity Press.

Creswell, J.W. (2007) *Qualitative inquiry and research design: Choosing among five approaches*, Thousand Oaks, CA: Sage Publications.

Crotty, M.J. (1998) *The foundations of social research: Meaning and perspective in the research process*, Los Angeles, CA: Sage Publications.

Freud, A. and Burlingham, D.T. (1943) *War and children*, Oxford: Medical War Books.

Garbarino, J., Kostelny, K. and Dubrow, N. (1991) *No place to be a child: Growing up in a war zone*, Toronto: Lexington Books.

Gardiner, J. (2010) *The Blitz: The British under attack*, London: Harper Press.

Graham-White, A. (2000) 'Bombs and brambles', in M. Tymoczko and N.C. Blackmun (eds) (2000) *Born into a world at war*, Manchester: St Jerome Publishing, pp 107–9.

Holland, P. (2003) *We don't play with guns here: War, weapon and superhero play in the early years*, Maidenhead: Open University Press.

Hughes, B. (2001) *Evolutionary playwork and reflective analytic practice*, London: Routledge.

Kyttä, M. (2004) 'The extent of children's independent mobility and the number of actualized affordances as criteria for child-friendly environments', *Journal of Environmental Psychology*, 24(2): 179–98.

Lester, S. and Russell, W. (2008) *Play for a change: Play, policy, and practice – review of contemporary perspectives*, London: National Children's Bureau.

Little Bobby (2003) 'A small boy in Southwick', *WW2 People's War*, BBC. www.bbc.co.uk/history/ww2peopleswar/.

Lovet Watson, K. (2008) *Peace and War: A young schoolboy's recollections of the 1930's and 1940's: An auto-boy-ography*, Stelling Minnis, Kent: Self published.

McHenry, G. (1997) 'Children of the troubles', in L. Holliday, *Children of 'the troubles': Our lives in the crossfire of Northern Ireland*, New York: Pocket Books, pp 46–9.

Magee, B. (2008) *Growing up in a war*, London: Pimlico.

Nicholson, S. (1971) 'How NOT to cheat children: The theory of loose parts', *Landscape Architecture*, 62(1): 30–4.

O'Neill, G. (2003) *Our street: East End life in the Second World War*, London: Penguin.

PPSG (Playwork Principles Scrutiny Group) (2005) *Playwork Principles*, Cardiff: Play Wales.

Rex, C. (2008) *Doodlebugs, gas masks and gum: Children's voices from the Second World War*, Gloucestershire: Amberley Publishing.

Sark, J. (2003) 'From Sidcup to Southampton', *WW2 People's War*, BBC, www.bbc.co.uk/history/ww2peopleswar/.

Sayers, D. (1997) 'Teenage kicks', in L. Holliday, *Children of 'the troubles': Our lives in the crossfire of Northern Ireland*, New York: Pocket Books, pp 299–304.

Shipton, D. (2003) 'The Depression and World War 2: Part 3 Childhood memories', *WW2 People's War*, BBC, www.bbc.co.uk/history/ww2peopleswar/.

Smith, P.K. (2005) 'Social and pretend play in children', in A.D. Pellegrini and P.K. Smith (eds) *The nature of play: Great apes and humans*, London: Guilford Press, pp. 173–209.

Sutton-Smith, B. (1997) *The ambiguity of play*, Cambridge, MA: Harvard University Press.

Sutton-Smith, B. (2003) 'Play as a parody of emotional vulnerability', in D.E. Lytle (ed.) *Play and educational theory and practice, Play and Culture Studies, Vol. 5*. Westport, CT: Praeger, pp. 3–17.

Taylor, G. (1981) *Archive Number 5221/2*, London: Imperial War Museum.

Thompson, P. (2000) *The voice of the past: Oral history* (3rd edn), Oxford: Oxford University Press.

Tymoczko, M. and Blackmun, N.C. (eds) (2000) *Born into a world at war*, Manchester: St Jerome Publishing.

Van der Hoek, T. (2005) 'Through children's eyes: An initial study of children's personal experiences and coping strategies growing up poor in an affluent Netherlands', *Innocenti working paper No. 2005-05*, Florence: UNICEF Innocenti Research Centre.

Veale, P. (2008) *Wartime childhood memories 1939–1945*, Bungay: Norfolk and Suffolk Aviation Museum.

Werner, E.E. (2001) *Through the eyes of innocents: Children witness world war II*, Boulder, CO: Westview Press.

Westall, R. (1995) *Memories of a wartime childhood: Children of the Blitz*, London: Macmillan Children's Books.

FOUR

Adventure playgrounds and me: bringing the past into the auto-ethnographic present

Tom Williams

Introduction

This is a very personal study aimed at exploring why adventure playgrounds (APGs) have had such a fascination for me for over 40 years. It weaves a critical and narrative ethnography with an affect-based auto-ethnography (Denzin, 2006; Jones, 2008; Dewsbury, 2009), resulting in various voices and approaches: at times I am researcher, narrator and participant. The research involved an immersion in my own history with APGs aided by a process of mutual recollection via email with five participants who shared that history, (re)visiting APGs in London, Copenhagen and Berlin, and a process of observation and reflection that paid attention to my embodied and affective responses to this immersion (Dewsbury, 2009). By 'enacting a way of seeing and being' (Denzin, 2006, p 422) and through paying attention to bodily senses and sensations (Küpers, 2009) I hoped to contribute something new to articulating the significance of APGs. Four themes emerged from this iterative and intuitive process: the mindful audacity of APGs, APGs as places of drama and unspoken narratives, APGs as spaces that are alive in many ways, and the hope that arises from this process of sensemaking.

A physical and metaphorical journey

This explorative study has been for me both a physical and metaphorical journey. I move away from the 'know-and-tell dogma' (Dewsbury, 2009, p 1) of social research and instead present a postmodern, non-representational or performative approach to sociology within an embodied epistemology. The feelings from my past include physically retracing my steps and revisiting APGs to carry out in situ witnessed observations, presencing memories via email with participants and analysing a range of accumulated data including photos, diaries, drawings and rich pictures. I drew heavily on Palmer et al's (2007) narrative style in describing APG experiences, and Palmer's use of adults' memories of the 1980s to describe APGs working with 'the natural rhythms of communities' (Palmer, 2008, p 132).

> [1] "Being at the playground was very much like having a GIANT family, we would always have the best of times but would also fight, argue and fall out with each other, but not for long! Every day there would be some form of drama, but it was all a laugh really and good character building." (Participant memory, circa 1996)

I recognise that for many people in the international play sector, myself included, APGs are viewed as special places and the emotive place they hold can polarise debate about their future. I acknowledge that I make observations about APGs based on my interpretation of the literature, witnessing, memories and the experiences of my participants. These might not necessarily fit with others' perceptions or recollections. In mitigation APGs across the world are not only uniquely different, but also constantly changing in their short history in response to the next generation and external demands (Shier, 1984). The process of theming may appear to homogenise this complexity but are offered here as reflections from personal experiences and connections with the playwork sector.

From the first junk playground instigated by landscape architect CT in 1943 (Bengtsson, 1972), through a radical UK playwork philosophy in the 1970s (Hughes, 1975) to today, there is an ongoing debate about the definition of a 'real' APG. For the purposes of this study I take Conway's definition as a starting point: 'a space dedicated solely to children's play, where skilled playworkers enable and facilitate the ownership, development and design of that space (physically, socially and culturally) by the children playing there' (Conway, 2009, p 1).

For those unfamiliar with the concept I include the photo of an APG in Berlin (see Figure 4.1). I hope this image might communicate to the reader how a space co-constructed by children and adults is at variance with what a traditional children's play space might look like. It is messy and chaotic and that is the point. It becomes a contemporary child/adult statement of mindful audacity, inside and outside of societal norms and is full of heterodoxic or unorthodox possibilities.

Figure 4.1: Adventure playground in Berlin, 2013

Source: Tom Williams

The uniqueness of APGs has been commented upon by many:

- 'as old as history, as fundamental as childhood' (Mays, 1957, p 6);
- a 'revolutionary experiment' (Allen, 1972, p 8);
- APGs 'exist on the lunatic fringe of orthodox recreation' and are 'a hybrid of the strip cartoon and the junk yard' (Mays, 1957, p 5);
- 'models for a totally radical and extremely valuable form of public space' (Norman, 2003, p 8);
- 'a free society in miniature' (Ward, 1961, p 194);
- 'a new form of radical social work' (Cranwell, 2007, p 70);
- 'one of the most libertarian models for public space the world has seen' (Nuttall, 2010, p 78).

The justification for APGs' unique status and heterodoxic philosophy is summarised by British social historian and architect Colin Ward: 'That there should be anything novel in simply providing facilities (APGs) for the spontaneous unorganised activities of childhood, is an indication of how deep rooted in our social behaviour is the urge to control, direct and limit the flow of life' (Ward, 1982, p 88).

One of my first memories in my 'flow of life' is of my father, an art school lecturer and painter, dressed as a sea captain. He was painting a 30-foot pole with jam at an art college, while his students tried to climb the pole to claim the bottle of rum hanging at the top. The year was 1970 and I was four years old. His students, while possibly believing play and art were liberating forces of the New Left, also worked at a South London APG where I went with my brother and friends. My time spent playing on that APG and being in art studios with fine artists, performance and political artists is merged in my childhood memories. But those early socio-cultural experiences, where play and art were 'symbolic of a way of life and an expression of freedom' (Cranwell, 2007, p 69) had a profound effect on my subsequent interest in APGs.

While the first junk playground was being established in 1943 at Emdrup (in Nazi occupied Copenhagen) my mother was seven years old, unsupervised in war-torn Portsmouth, building dens, cooking on open fires, 'smoking old-man's-beard and teaching myself to swim in the creek'. The reader may surmise the reason APGs hold such a fascination for me is a connection with an adventurous genetic spirit. Or that my upbringing socialised me in a brand of art school recalcitrance and British self-sufficiency. But beyond the personal I believe that there is a deeper and wider, largely unrecognised narrative about APGs. Within their do-it-yourself culture and unseen magic the playful turbulence of APGs is difficult to read or understand by those not familiar or immersed in their daily complexity. APGs' stories, which have been spoken or performed over generations, contain layers of meaning difficult to capture and represent through conventional research methods.

> "There were so many stories going on…dramas, power struggles, fights, groups…they've kind of blended into a mish-mash of things…my most vivid memories are the first time I worked there…a girl called Pearl who was a sort of manic matriarch figure. She would have a group of girls around her, who maybe half liked her, half didn't and probably feared her…often only happy when a big drama was going on…I just remember her being so sweet…and then causing the biggest problems." (Participant memory, circa 1999)

'Stories are the truths that won't stand still' (Pelias, 2004, p 171)

Figure 4.2: My brother and me, 1970

Source: Tom Williams

Since those early days playing on an APG as a child (with my brother, left: Figure 4.2) my interest has grown, so my first line of enquiry was to try and understand my own lifelong fascination. I knew that many others held a similar emotional connection to these unique urban playgrounds. I felt I could better understand this connection through a shared recollection of experience with selected participants and that this could be achieved through a process of rewriting and re-presenting memories, opening them up for exploration.

My second line of enquiry was that the child–adult relationships on APGs (that I witnessed) were often, but not always, different from the societal norm of adult–child control. It was as if children's play on an APG had an intoxicating and dissenting presence that could invalidate or suspend dominant norms (Cranwell, 2003). I explored how that felt for me and the participants, during those times when adult control was temporarily or partially given up, in a potential reframing of generational power and order (Mayall, 2009).

"they [society] might not understand how wild these kids could be…they need to scream, laugh, shout, perform, and express themselves or they're going to blow up…

they don't get school or fit into that mould…they need
something else, and the APGs are a great place for them."
(Participant memory, circa 1999)

Third, the majority of my own memories of APGs had an amplified and
vivid dramaturgical quality. Not drama in a traditional sense of stage and
actors, but the stories playfully constructed by children and adults, the
moments of dramatic emotion and tension, a shared narrative integral
to everyday APG experiences. I wanted to understand whether this
was a mutual perception. I began to explore the idea of APGs fulfilling
a role as community stage where children and adults, frustrated by the
progress rhetoric (Sutton-Smith, 1997) of school and careers, came to
let off institutional steam, not only to play but to engage in a mutual
performance of cultural expression.

> "Every day was a new adventure…what I remember
> most is the constant drama, a day wouldn't go past when
> there wasn't some kind of issue…It would be unreasonable
> to say that this was all created by children…the drama was
> also coming from the staff, parents and wider community."
> (Participant memory, circa 1995)

My methodology and approach to this study is primarily based in
the established qualitative research practice of ethnography, exploring
the culture of APGs and their meaning (for me) within reflective
narratives. But the subject also fits with a relatively new approach
within ethnographic and pedagogical theories that advocate 'a writing
form that enacts a methodology of the heart' (Pelias, 2004, p 171).
Described as performance ethnography and akin to 'an act of doing'
(Denzin, 2003, p 274) it requires researcher and participants to take
risks, to act in situations where the outcome cannot be predicted,
where new possibilities are imagined and can happen, that set
free political pedagogies (Freire, 1999). The parallels between this
research methodology and a philosophy of working by generations of
playworkers on APGs is striking. It incorporates an inherently moral,
political and ludocentric view of the world.

> "There were really dramatic times, like when 9-year-
> old Billie died after falling down a hole in the road, her
> dad climbed down to hold her but she just died there. It
> was a huge funeral…and I felt a little hand holding mine

and looked down to see her little sister smiling at me."
(Participant memory, circa 1990)

My use of auto-ethnography has methodological links to narrative enquiry and oral history. These approaches are commonly used in qualitative sociology; narrative enquiry and storytelling can be powerful research methods in the interpretation of experience and meaning (Bruner, 1990). The knowledge held in stories can be relayed, stored, retrieved and performed. Auto-ethnography is now an established tool in qualitative research and is a genre of writing that displays multiple layers of consciousness, 'connecting the personal to the cultural' (Ellis and Bochner, 2000, p 738). It gives me a methodology that allows the opportunity to focus outwards on the social and cultural aspects of personal experience but also looking inwards exposing my vulnerable self.

The most welcome luxury

This is a subject that I have been immersed in for over 40 years, giving me a particular insider view. As a child of the 1970s I played on a large APG in South London that had all the anarchic features of APGs in London of the time (Heaven, 1974). When my parents moved to mid Wales I continued as a child and teenager to think about and recreate APG spaces in the freedom that the countryside afforded. As a young adult I worked on APGs in South Wales, London and south west England for over 20 years, and most recently I managed a city play service for ten years that included five APGs and new play projects based on an adventure play methodology. In 1990 I visited APGs in Aarhus and Emdrup in Denmark and what were then city farms in West Berlin. In 2013 I visited APGs all over the UK and revisited APGs in Copenhagen and Berlin. I include all of this immersive and stored data in my research process.

To be given the opportunity to study APGs for a year and examine their meaning and significance for me has therefore felt like the most welcome luxury. While I had many personal memories, conversations and photos to draw on, I realised that I needed to ask others the same questions that I was asking myself. I initially selected ten participants from a potential sample of hundreds of adults and children with whom I had shared experiences on APGs. Of these initial participants some I had remained in contact with, some I tracked down via social networking sites and some were strangers who had a connection with a specific APG. The participants needed to be willing to engage in a process of documented exchange via email. A number of initially willing participants withdrew when they realised the time and emotional commitment. Of the five participants who agreed to undertake the research process, two were playworkers with whom I had previously worked or managed, one was a child who attended an APG I worked on 20 years ago, another participant was a manager who had started on an APG, and the final participant was a colleague from the play sector. I could have sought out more participants, but for a study of this nature five participants provided ample data for exploration and analysis. All of the participants gave informed consent (in line with the research ethics guidelines of the University of Gloucestershire), were enthusiastic, and had expressed strong opinions or had good stories to tell about their experiences on APGs.

'Bringing the past into the autobiographical present' (Denzin, 2006, p 423)

Through researcher and participant exchange and a process of personal and mutual reflection I hoped to build shared accounts that captured our APG experience. The participants were given a series of questions via email based on my initial lines of enquiry. To help retrieve, replay and construct those memories and observations I answered some of the questions myself. I also asked the participants to draw rich pictures. Rich pictures were developed in soft system methodology to gather information about complex situations (Checkland, 1981).

As well as collecting and generating data with participants I carried out a series of observations at APGs in London, Copenhagen and Berlin. As an observer participating within the space I recorded my immediate reflections on what I was observing. By using a stream of conscious writing process that recognises the quality and emotion of immediate experience, I was able to reflect on my participants' data and my own thoughts about APGs. As Denzin (2006, p 423) so aptly describes it: 'In bringing the past into the autobiographical present, I insert myself into the past and create the conditions for rewriting and hence re-experiencing it.'

It was from this intuitive and reactive process while continually observing, witnessing, recollecting and recording that four thoroughly entangled themes emerged.

Drawn by a stronger narrative

The lines in this research between author and subject, fact and fiction, subjective and objective, are complex. My method, like my subject, is non-representational, looking beyond mere cognition and reliance on representing an independently existing world through language (Thrift, 2004; Dewsbury, 2009); it is a simultaneous investigation of meaning and introspective self-examination, showing how the process and product of this inquiry are inextricably linked.

My method recognises the intrinsic synthesis of mind, body and environment. Embracing the idea of observant witness that is open to other narratives (Jones, 2008), I set out to use my body directly in the field as 'a recording machine' (Dewsbury, 2009, p 5). For example, while visiting the art installation of Lars Vilks at Nimis (Figure 4.3) in Sweden in 2013, I started to comprehend the personal connection (or concoction) of creativity, childhood and bold counter-cultural statement behind my interest in APGs. While walking through the woods alone to discover this APG-like space I felt an excitement in my gut and a ludic sense of anticipation that I could recognise from my childhood. It is this somatic methodology, recognising the quality and emotion of immediate (unmediated) experience which I employ when observing.

Figure 4.3: Nimis, Sweden, 2013

Source: Tom Williams

The email exchanges with my participants comprised 12 questions across the areas of interest I had identified: making sense of why APGs were meaningful, understanding child–adult relationships, how storylines create a shared and dramatised narrative, and a socio-cultural view of APGs' significance. These email exchanges, which became extended conversations, amounted to over 16,000 words, with four themes emerging from the participants' responses. These themes then became an integral part of my visits and observations of APGs in Copenhagen, Berlin and the UK. Jones (2008) makes the case for the affinity between narrative research, artistic practice and non-representational theory (Thrift, 2004) as a way for artists and researchers to develop methodologies that are sensitive to affect. By following an emphasis on the event (Harrison, 2002), I pay attention to what is taking place in front of me, and this 'call to witness' (Jones, 2008, p 206) becomes expressed in a narrative form.

Key themes and embodied feelings

Theme 1: APG – mindful audacity in tune with the time

The 'spontaneous and unorganised' children's activity that Ward (1982, p 88) described as a benchmark of APGs' uniqueness was clearly evident on the APGs observed in London. These spaces felt once again on 'the lunatic fringe of orthodox recreation' (Mays, 1957, p 5). The APGs in Copenhagen are part of a more established (and establishment) system of socialising young Danish citizens through social pedagogy (Nuttall, 2010). They still retain the rickety child-built dens that I witnessed in 1990 and have characterised their history, but now they are predominantly constructed by Danish pedagogues who see them as important symbols of defiance.

> I am in London, the APG I am witnessing is small and intentionally chaotic, there is a maverick attention to detail, characterising an atmosphere of concentration and freedom, smoke drifts across the site, a bold statement in a city space, play structures have no pattern or form and are adorned with garish colours and road signs, a sledge hammer is used by children to smash up pallets for the fire where a vegetable curry is cooking, a child who was swearing herself tells a younger child off for swearing and then laughs…I am spotted 'what are you doing up there, are you drawing, are you police…you look suspicious!'

"APG's are different…and 'different' scares some people!" (Participant memory, circa 1993).

I am in Berlin, I witness a group of school children finish their campfire cooking lesson on the APG. While their teacher chats to the playworkers the children pick up sticks and start smashing up an old car (Figure 4.4), they go wild for ten minutes, seemingly inhabiting 'another world' and then return to school.

Figure 4.4: Adventure playground in Berlin, 2013

Source: Tom Williams

In Berlin I witnessed a culture of autonomy movements that use playful acts to engage in 'gestures of everyday resistance' (Kanngieser 2007, p 5) in response to austerity measures and a neoliberal rhetoric of scarcity. These politically unaligned movements use playful strategies to cultivate an air of fun while taking direct action such as reclaiming land for community use. They use play's indistinct and disruptive nature: by utilising play's amorphous position of being at the same time real and unreal, the protestors are able to establish 'real' gestures, which are framed as 'unreal'. These small gestures that resist, performed in a creative and playful atmosphere (combining elements of carnival, performance and irritation), make it possible for communities to create their own spaces for children.

Participants throughout the data described APGs' enduring and defiant heterodoxy and recalcitrance (Battram and Russell, 2002). The APGs that I observed retain a unique nonconformity, which, although no longer representing the bold gestures of the 1970s or Ward's 'parable of anarchy' (1982, p 114), operate a more subtle mindful audacity in tune with the time, as the examples given here show. In this way APGs 'should not be seen as a threat or disruption to adultness, not innocent wonderland, but a critique of adult(ist) society' (Jones, 2008, p 207).

Theme 2: APG – place of drama and unspoken narratives

My second theme was an exploration of those vivid and dramatic moments that are retold by my participants and witnessed by me. Lester (2008) has explored the narrative and dramatic aspects of children's play, drawing on Sibley's (1995) analysis of closed and open space, Schechner's (2003) idea of play as a transformational performance, Boal's (1995) recognition that 'children's play inherently contains dramatic tension' (Lester, 2008, p 57) and Sutton-Smith's (1997) assertion that children playing can 'pretend almost anything and connect almost anything with anything else' (Lester, 2008, p 61). Participants frequently described the experiences that remained most vivid to them. These often had a dramaturgical aspect, and offered an insight into the spoken and unspoken narratives on that APG, crossing over each other like storylines connecting children, adults, time and place.

> "The main storylines would be what brought the children down to the playground...children would arrange to meet friends, turn up on their own, on the off chance... or drawn by a stronger narrative, such as: What's happening on the playground...is anything new happening? Who's saying what about who? Is there any tension, disagreement or romance?" (Participant memory, circa 1995)

> The APG I am witnessing in London is busy with 50–60 children plus 30–40 adults, the children are playing rave music while painting. The space is shared on this day with a Christian bar-b-q playing evangelical reggae, adults are dancing in the sunshine too: "I've got many rivers to cross." I am involved in a dramatic exchange. A playworker is introduced to me "don't observe me...I'm angry"...me

laughing "I'd like to see some drama"...playworker laughing "Well you've come to the right place".

"Just jumping off the highest level of the rope swing gave you massive kudos...you feel like a god when you jump." (Participant memory, circa 1991)

An older boy swings 20ft high off the third platform and shouts "Whargone!" followed by a "Buurrpp!" and passes the swing to a younger boy nervous to go from the third platform, everyone is watching to see if he will do it for the first time, the tension builds. He finally leaps and swings but it is untidy, lacking any style or panache, but he's beaming and goes round his mates taking the praise and the boost – evoking play as a transformational performance. (Boal, 1995)

The kids were always performing...like Marcus or Pearl, who took that to its limits and couldn't stop performing and acting up...the centre of their own dramas where they wanted all the attention...and then would create situations out of their control, and often alienate themselves." (Participant memory, circa 1998)

Figure 4.5: Loose parts on an adventure playground in London, 2013

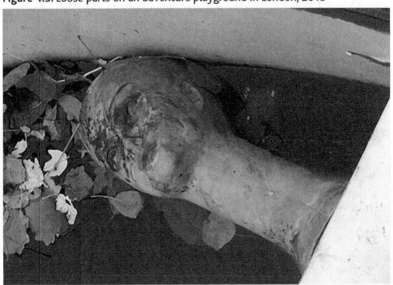

Source: Tom Williams

The use of loose parts (Nicholson, 1971) on APGs (for example, Figure 4.5) often contributes to the drama of the space. It can be possible for a child or adult who attends regularly to read the narrative within the space from the objects that are placed or left behind, to understand the stories that happened the previous day or are ongoing. Leichter-Saxby (2007, p 40) describes how APGs have obscured histories written by adults and children, built on their repetitive and playful performances; adults and children 'create a co-constructive relationship between self and place', where the writing of this narrative involves a daily 'exploration of the site, its materials and its possibilities'.

Theme 3: APGs – spaces that are alive in so many ways

In Berlin, APGs sprung up in the 1990s on the land where the wall and no-man's land divided the city. Russell (2012) describes UK APGs emerging from the bomb sites and vacant lots after the second world war as *terrains vagues*, spaces that are 'free, available, unengaged, limitless, uncertain, roving and temporary' (Carney and Miller, 2009, p 42). Participants provided descriptions of these limitless and uncertain spaces, which are complex, operating on the edge of chaos (Battram, 2008), with topsy-turvy adult–child relations, and misrule that could result in violent disruption.

> "You wanted the playground to have that energy and buzz around it, which meant it was often on the edge. It was free and wild and fun, but there had to be respect and some control." (Participant memory, circa 1999)

> The senior playworker I am observing in London is continually on the move, there is so much going on, so many children, its reached critical mass, she is an atheist liberating and distributing hotdogs from the Christian bar-b-q, talking to children and adults, she stops and with hand on heart watches a boy swing from the top platform then leads the cheers, sorts out an argument, pushes children screaming with pleasure on the tyre swing, she is the eye of the storm, the conductor of the complexity, all observed in five minutes.

> "There was just the threat of things getting out of hand...I'd look around and think, hmm I've actually lost control of this playground...but the kids would be fine, no

one was hurt…it was no longer anything to do with me… the kids had taken over…it felt important to trust them." (Participant memory, circa 1989)

Drawing on an analysis of the politics of space that was more prevalent in the 1960s and 1970s, Russell (2012) also utilises playworker narratives and the spatial analysis of Lefebvre (1991) to articulate the dialectical relationship between *conceived space*, *perceived space* and *lived space*. In Russell's application of Lefebvre's analysis *conceived space* refers to the world of playground design and adult intentions that are often imposed on a child's space. In *perceived space* Russell argues that the intuitive nature of playwork has become over-organised, outcome focused and commodified, however the constraints of Lefebvre's *conceived and perceived space* should be viewed in conjunction with his idea of *lived space*.

> "We really wanted to create these play spaces that were alive and caring…where kids could go wild and let off steam…things appeared a bit wild from the outside… but when you're in the middle of it all you can see what's going on, and have some control." (Participant memory, circa 1998)

Lefebvre's *lived space* offers opportunities to feel truly alive, to escape from and resist the domination of conceived and perceived space, 'it is the space of art, love, imagination and of course play' but also 'where resistance is experienced by others as disruption or even violence' (Russell, 2012, p 56). The constant threat of violence was a theme that ran through my participants' data and my own memories.

> "The playground was just closing so about 50 kids were all outside when the fight started. They were surrounded by all the kids coming pretty crazy for some action. I think both of them were in tears, and Cardell had the stick and chain. I put myself between the two of them and took the weapons off Cardell. He then pulled a knife out of his pocket. I didn't know what to do just standing between the two of them, with all these kids going mental around me. I said something to Cardell like, 'What will your mum say when she finds out?', and he replied with tears in his eyes 'She doesn't care'. I managed to get Junior into the building and lock the door, and try and calm him down.

Outside the crowd were baying for blood." (Participant memory, circa 1997)

Theme 4: APG – experiential meaning repaid with a sense of hope

Lady Allen of Hurtwood, a pioneer of UK APGs, said that 'the fact has to be faced that modern civilisation interferes with a hard and heavy hand in the spontaneous play of children' (Allen, 1968, p 11). She made this point over 40 years ago and yet a risk averse society continues to obtrude in children's lives (Gill, 2007). APGs' persistent ability to offer an unorthodox essence of being goes some way towards redressing this inequality. Many of the people referenced in this paper and my participants described and observed APGs as places that had significant meaning for them, and this positivity is repaid with a belief and hope that people will find a better way.

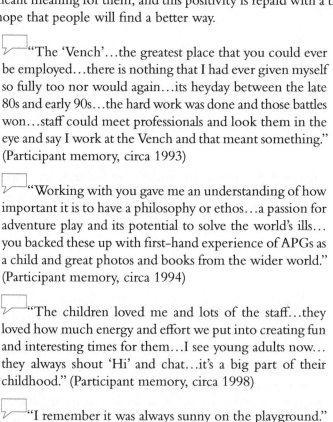

> "The 'Vench'…the greatest place that you could ever be employed…there is nothing that I had ever given myself so fully too nor would again…its heyday between the late 80s and early 90s…the hard work was done and those battles won…staff could meet professionals and look them in the eye and say I work at the Vench and that meant something." (Participant memory, circa 1993)

> "Working with you gave me an understanding of how important it is to have a philosophy or ethos…a passion for adventure play and its potential to solve the world's ills… you backed these up with first-hand experience of APGs as a child and great photos and books from the wider world." (Participant memory, circa 1994)

> "The children loved me and lots of the staff…they loved how much energy and effort we put into creating fun and interesting times for them…I see young adults now… they always shout 'Hi' and chat…it's a big part of their childhood." (Participant memory, circa 1998)

> "I remember it was always sunny on the playground." (Participant memory, circa 1997)

These open and optimistic narratives seek to represent the magic possibility and 'otherness' of APGs, by utilising an 'embodied epistemology that is enlivening, enabling, emotional, enlightening and emancipatory' (Matthews, 2005, p 272). The art school politics and civil liberties *zeitgeist* of the 1960s and 1970s added a philosophical ethos to the APG movement that still sets them apart to this day. It is this 'spirit of play' (Cranwell, 2007, p 63) that defines the idiosyncratic nature of many APGs and has imbued the lives of those closely connected with APGs. From their inception in Copenhagen to the present day, APGs have grappled with philosophical contradictions (Kozlovsky, 2008). They have maintained a flexible and adaptive public and private face (below), that makes concessions for contradictory instrumental value while allowing for a more ontological 'spirit of play' to continue.

Table 4.1: Adventure playgrounds' public and private face

Examples of instrumental contradiction		Examples of ontological spirit of play
Play as prevention		Play as freedom
Play as a leisure time activity	⬌	Play as a way of life
Play as a learning rhetoric		Play as a do-it-yourself culture
Play as a diversion		Play as acceptable destruction
APGs public face		**APGs private face**

"APGs contribute so much to society and communities that go unnoticed…a community stage to let off steam, be different, be expressive and…not be measured…not be judged…to just be yourself…it is this benefit that needs to be understood and valued." (Participant memory, circa 1986)

Conclusion

Finally let me emphasise that adventure playgrounds are no panacea or patent solution…but it has been proved that the formula of the adventure playground affords conditions for play which the town child cannot find in any other way. (Bertelsen, 1972, p 23)

My physical and metaphorical journey started as a child of the 1970s and took me through remembered and shared experiences with my participants that included the production of a series of rich pictures

(Checkland, 1981). Using drawings or pictures to think about issues is now common in problem solving and creative thinking because our intuitive consciousness communicates differently in impressions and symbols rather than words. That said I believe this participant's rich picture (Figure 4.6) is further enhanced by their words.

> "When I first started I think I really stood out at Bonneville. I was scruffy and a bit wild too! It was like going to a new country...new culture, ways of talking, attitude and ideas...which made it pretty exciting. I felt we were making a real difference in those kids' lives. It was all really positive and I felt proud to be involved, and that we were a really important part of the community...I'm not so sure that's the way we were viewed now with hindsight. The playground was often seen as a wild place where the rougher problem kids hung out." (Participant memory and rich picture, circa 1997)

Figure 4.6: Participant rich picture, 2013

Source: Research participant (photo Tom Williams)

Encapsulated in that picture and those words are many of the themes in this study, pointing to the conclusion that APGs' unique magic (for me) is attributable to their hard-fought and retained heterodoxic nature, where they retain a status as symbols of possibility. APGs' ability to change, adapt and reframe child, adult and community relations within a living space, allows for a creative and experimental dramaturgical culture to breathe and grow. The power of witnessing within non-representational theory can generate new political and ethical languages (Jones, 2008). These 'performances' are more telling and alive than academic representation within social science (Thrift, 2004). Given the difficulties of representing the chaotic complexity of APGs, my participants' memories and my observations become vivid 'non-representations' of what was seen and felt. By continuing to witness and record the narratives and stories of APGs, that include moments of mindful audacity and everyday gestures of resistance, new possibilities for children and adults are imagined, rekindling an ontological spirit that draws adventure playgrounds as enduring places and symbols of hope and freedom.

Note
[1] To help the reader distinguish between the different voices I employ the following system. A quote prefaced by a ⌐⌐ is from one of my participants, a passage prefaced by a ☁ is a witnessed reflection that I have made while carrying out an observation.

References

Allen, M. (1968) *Planning for play*, London: Thames and Hudson.

Allen, M. (1972) 'Foreword', in A. Bengtsson, *Adventure playgrounds*, London: Crosby Lockwood.

Battram, A. (2008) 'The edge of recalcitrance: Playwork in the zone of complexity', in F. Brown and C. Taylor (eds) *Foundations of playwork*, Maidenhead: Open University Press, pp 89–94.

Battram, A. and Russell, W. (2002) 'The edge of recalcitrance: Playwork, order and chaos', paper presented at *'Spirit of Play Wales Conference*, Cardiff, June.

Bengtsson, A. (1972) *Adventure playgrounds*, London: Crosby Lockwood.

Bertelsen, J. (1972) 'Early experience from Emdrup', in A. Bengtsson (ed) *Adventure playgrounds*, London: Cosby Lockwood, pp 16–23.

Boal, A. (1995) *The rainbow of desire: The Boal method of theatre and therapy*, London: Routledge.

Bruner, J. (1990) *Acts of meaning: Four lectures on mind and culture*, Cambridge, MA: Harvard University Press.

Carney, P. and Miller, V. (2009) 'Vague spaces', in A. Jansson and A. Lagerkvist (eds) *Strange spaces: Explorations into mediated obscurity*, Farnham: Ashgate, pp 33–56.

Checkland, P. (1981) *Systems thinking, systems practice*, Chichester: Wiley.

Conway, M. (2009) *Developing an adventure playground: The essential elements*, London: Play England.

Cranwell, K. (2003) 'Towards a history of adventure playgrounds 1931–2000', in N. Norman (ed) *An architecture of play: A survey of London's adventure playgrounds*, London: Four Corners, pp 17–25.

Cranwell, K. (2007) 'Adventure playgrounds and the community in London (1948–70)', in W. Russell, B. Handscomb and J. Fitzpatrick (eds) *Playwork voices: In celebration of Bob Hughes and Gordon Sturrock*, London: London Centre for Playwork Education and Training, pp 62–73.

Denzin, N.K. (2003) 'Performing [auto] ethnography politically', *Review of Education, Pedagogy, and Cultural Studies*, 25(3): 257–78.

Denzin, N.K. (2006) 'Analytic autoethnography, or déjà vu all over again', *Journal of Contemporary Ethnography*, 35(4): 419–28.

Dewsbury, J-D. (2009) 'Performative, non-representational and affect-based research: Seven injunctions', in D. Delyser, S. Atkin, M. Crang, S. Herbert and L. McDowell (eds) *Handbook of qualitative research in human geography*, London: Sage, pp 321–34.

Ellis, C. and Bochner, A.P. (2000) 'Autoethnography, personal narrative, reflexivity: Researcher as subject', in N. Denzin and Y. Lincoln (eds) *Handbook of qualitative research* (2nd edn), Thousand Oaks, CA: Sage, pp 733–68.

Freire, P. (1999) *Pedagogy of hope*, New York: Continuum.

Gill, T. (2007) *No fear: Growing up in a risk adverse society*, London: Calouste Gulbenkian Foundation.

Harrison, P. (2002) 'The caesura: Remarks on Wittgenstein's interruption of theory or, why practices elude explanation', *Geoforum*, 33(4): 487–503.

Heaven, S. (1974) *Noah's Ark – a film about Deptford Adventure Playground*, Unpublished.

Hughes, B. (1975) *Notes for adventure playworkers*, London: Children and Youth Action Group.

Jones, O. (2008) '"True geography […] quickly forgotten, giving away to an adult-imagined universe." Approaching the otherness of childhood', *Children's Geographies*, 6(2): 195–212.

Kanngieser, A. (2007) 'Gestures of everyday resistance: the significance of play and desire in the Umsonst politics of collective appropriation', *European Institute of Progressive Cultural Studies*, http://eipcp.net/transversal/0307/kanngieser/en.

Kozlovsky, R. (2008) 'Adventure playgrounds and postwar reconstruction', in M. Gutman and N. de Coninck-Smith (eds) *Designing modern childhoods: History, space, and the material culture of children*, Newark, NJ: Rutgers University Press, pp 171–90.

Küpers, W.M. (2009) 'The sense-ma®king of the senses – Perspectives on embodied *aisthesis* & aesthetics in organising & organ-isations – Or why sensing (and sense-making) makes sense and no senses lead to non-sense', *Aesthesis: international journal of art and aesthetics in management and organizational life*, 2: 33–53.

Lefebvre, H. (1991) *The production of space*, Oxford: Blackwell.

Leichter-Saxby, M. (2007) *Constructing the 'natural' child: The materiality of play, power and subversion at Evergreen Adventure Playground*, MA Dissertation, London: University College London.

Lester, S. (2008) 'Play and the play stage', in F. Brown and C. Taylor (eds) *Foundations of playwork*, Maidenhead: Open University Press, pp 55–8.

Matthews, H. (2005) 'Rising four: Reflections on the state of growing-up', *Children's Geographies*, 3(3): 271–3.

Mayall, B. (2009) 'Generational relations at family level', in J. Qvortrup, W.A. Corsaro and M-S. Honig (eds) *The Palgrave handbook of childhood studies*, Basingstoke, Hampshire: Palgrave Macmillan, pp 176–87.

Mays, J.B. (1957) *Adventure in play*, Liverpool: Liverpool Council of Social Service.

Nicholson, S. (1971) 'How NOT to cheat children: The theory of loose parts', *Landscape Architecture*, 62(1): 30–4.

Norman, N. (2003) *An architecture of play: A survey of London's adventure playgrounds*, London: Four Corners Books.

Nuttall, E. (2010) *Possible summers: Stories and reflections from the playspace*, http://possiblesummers.wordpress.com/2012/09/03/hello-world.

Palmer, M. (2008) '"The place we were meant to be": Play, playwork and the natural rhythms of communities', in F. Brown and C. Taylor (eds) *Foundations of playwork*, Maidenhead: Open University Press, pp 132–6.

Palmer, M., Wilson, P. and Battram, A. (2007) 'The playing that runs through us all: Illustrating the Playwork Principles with stories of play', in W. Russell, B. Handscomb and J. Fitzpatrick (eds) *Playwork voices: In celebration of Bob Hughes and Gordon Sturrock*, London: The London Centre for Playwork Education and Training, pp 121–38.

Pelias, R.J. (2004) *A methodology of the heart: Evoking academic and daily life*, Walnut Creek, CA: AltaMira Press.

Russell, W. (2012) "'I get such a feeling out of...those moments": Playwork, passion, politics and space', *International Journal of Play*, 1(1): 51–63.

Schechner, R. (2003) *Performance theory*, London: Routledge.

Shier, H. (1984) *Adventure playgrounds: An introduction*, London: National Playing Fields Association.

Sibley, D. (1995) *Geographies of exclusion: Society and difference in the west*, London: Routledge.

Sutton-Smith, B. (1997) *The ambiguity of play*, Cambridge, MA: Harvard University Press.

Thrift, N. (2004) 'Intensities of feeling: Towards a spatial politics of affect', *Geografiska Annaler, Series B: Human Geography*, 86(1): 57–78.

Ward, C. (1961) 'Adventure playground: a parable in anarchy', *Anarchy*, 7: 193–201.

Ward, C. (1982) *Anarchy in action: play as an anarchist parable*, London: Freedom Press.

Part Two:

Here and there, this and that: spatial and creative perspectives

Part two:

Here and there, this and that:
spatial and creative perspectives

FIVE

Dancing with strangers: observing play in an English urban square

Hattie Coppard

Introduction

Public settings are complicated places, intrinsically fluid and contested constructions within which layers of value, identity and power are continually being generated. Children and young people enter this realm cloaked in the dominant narratives of the time: the 'innocent child' and the 'anti-social' youth are common tropes through which assumptions of behaviour and identity are formulated (Gill, 2007). This study adds to the debate on the provision of a child-friendly public realm and the methodologies used to represent and interpret the elusive qualities of play. The intention is to shed light on the everyday nature of play, giving attention to an ethical sensibility (McCormack, 2003) and an understanding of the public realm as a 'collective achievement' (Massey, 2005).

Much of lived experience is transitory and gone before it can be cognitively registered; a gesture, a smile, a call to a friend are expressions of an ongoing process of interaction and response, not separate events to be analysed in isolation. It is not possible to be conscious of all things at all times: brains and bodies filter and respond to what is most compelling, taking note and filling in the gaps in order to create a coherent and workable reality, but to ignore the pre-cognitive and non-representational nature of experience is to dismiss a fundamental aspect of personal and political relations (Thrift, 2004; Horton and Kraftl, 2006; Dewsbury, 2009).

The dominance of positivist accounts of life that imply that there is a knowable world that can be revealed through rigorous and scientific methods diverts attention away from what is difficult to describe in favour of that which can be represented. If much of lived experience happens without conscious thought, then what is required are modes of enquiry that can give attention to everyday moments as they are lived. Non-representational theory (Thrift, 2008) offers promising foundations for investigating the everyday and calls for an experimentation in methodologies, capable of disrupting conventional habits of understanding and of giving attention the emergent, 'processually enactive' (McCormack, 2003, p 489) nature of reality.

This study contributes to this experimentalism by engaging with creative practitioners in a research process that takes seriously subjective and embodied ways of knowing. While it is not possible to represent any experience fully, the aim is to give attention to an 'assemblage' of 'actants' (Hillier, 2011) that create a place and moment in time in which playfulness happens. This project raises questions about methodologies used to observe and represent play that has implications for the management and design of a child-friendly public realm.

'Sensitising concepts' (Bowen, 2006) that helped shape the conceptual framework of the study include: Tim Ingold's (2007, 2011) work on lines of movement and ways of inhabiting the world; D.W. Winnicott's (1971) theory of transitional objects and the implications for play and cultural space; and Doreen Massey's (2005) notion of the public sphere as a collective achievement requiring a 'practising of place'.

The research process

Over the period of two days, a painter, a writer and dancer spent time alongside the author, giving their attention to playful behaviour and interaction of children, adults and material objects, including portable play equipment, in an English urban public square. The artists were not asked to produce a creative work but simply to observe the square, using whatever method they chose, and to report this back in some way. The objective was to engage with, rather than inhibit, their imaginative and embodied response, to tap into their interest and mode of enquiry and to examine the multiple ways of knowing the world that creative practitioners can bring to scholarly research.

The observation and communication process that each artist employed became the medium through which information and meaning were produced. The form this took included coloured lines on paper, a gesture re-enacted, a piece of prose, each of which have their own story to tell that cannot adequately be translated into academic text. While the information here is presented in the form of a linear narrative, the reality is more disparate and unresolved than this implies. This was an experiment in research methodology, offering stabs in the dark at understanding more, rather than firm conclusions.

The artists were: painter, Tim Coppard (TC); dancer, Jai-yu Corti (JYC); and writer, Chris Meade (CM). TC and CM had worked with the author previously and were familiar with the research site and the nature of the play equipment. Two preparation meetings and a test day in the square informed the format and approach of the observation sessions which took place during the summer half-term holiday. Sketches and notes made by the artists, recorded discussions, interviews with the manager of the square and a local parent, notes, photographs and videos made by the author, all collectively compose the data of the study.

Prior to the observation sessions, two meetings with the manager of the square, combined with email and telephone exchanges, ensured that the study was well understood and supported by the organisation responsible. Because of the public and constantly changing nature of the setting it was not possible to obtain the written consent of participants, who included children and young people who happened to be in the square at the time of the observation sessions. Following McCormack (2003), an 'ethical awareness' was applied and ways of communicating with and protecting the identities of participants were thought through carefully. Posters and leaflets explaining the project in easily understood cartoons and text were displayed in the square throughout the observation sessions; all of the researchers had a label with the word 'researcher' clearly displayed on their clothes. No personal or private information was gathered, no individuals were identified and to protect the identity of participants the name of the square has not been identified, nor any local landmarks or businesses. Following completion of the study, a public presentation of the research material enabled critical scrutiny and debate by stakeholders and managers of the square.

While participants are sometimes identified as 'children', 'parents', 'street drinkers', this categorisation is for ease of reference and the danger of assumptions being made based on these labels is acknowledged. So too is equating the experience of the researchers with that of the participants and descriptions of experience are referenced to make this distinction clear.

A thematic analysis technique (Bowen, 2006), in which common threads and subjects are allowed to emerge out of the data rather than being pre-determined by the research design, was undertaken. Information began to cluster around groupings of ideas and themes were coded using the QSR International NVivo (10) programme. This enabled disparate data, including drawings, notes, photographs, prose, interviews and video, to be brought together within a loose format and an initial analysis undertaken. The research findings emerged out of this process and are discussed in relation to the following themes:

- movement and presence;
- objects and imagination;
- co-existence and co-formation.

Movement and presence

In his work on lines, Ingold (2007; 2011) discusses ways of inhabiting the world and describes two contrasting modes of movement, 'transport' and 'wayfaring'. Transport is measurable and contained, defined by its function which is to move as efficiently as possible from A to B, usually along a pre-defined route and avoiding being side-tracked on the way. In contrast wayfaring is an open-ended, meandering activity, the wayfarer 'dwells' in a continual landscape, engaging with affordances encountered. For Ingold, transport and wayfaring are not simply categories of movement, but expressions of an approach to life and ways of being in the world.

TC's observational drawings of child and adult movement in the square show a striking resemblance to Ingold's (2011) descriptions of transport and wayfaring and illustrate how differently people inhabit the space. From a vantage point overlooking the square TC's concentration centred on carefully tracking the routes of children and adults and representing this as coloured lines on paper. Like Ingold's wayfarers, the children's lines can be seen to meander and weave around the space, creating skittish, multi-directional paths, engaging with affordances in the landscape and cues from other children. In contrast the lines associated with adults have an intensity and purpose that echo characteristics of transport, tending to straight paths, taking the shortest route from A to B, rarely lingering along the way, and when they do stop staying firmly in one place: "It's almost like the kids are an automatic drawing, whereas the adults are much more like they have a ruler they are going along" (TC interview).

TC describes becoming immersed in the experience of looking, slowing his own energy down as he becomes attuned, both physically and mentally to what he is observing: "I was getting into a trance-like state, entering into their world in a half conscious way…tracing movement without emotion". By simply concentrating on movement as it happened, and without associating this with any particular individual or activity, more subtle and transient qualities became apparent, such as the emotional energies and 'weights of presence' that different people possessed (TC interview).

Figure 5.1: Pathways of adult and child movements across the square

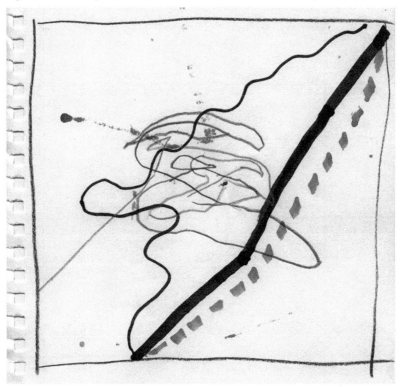

Source: Tim Coppard (photo Hattie Coppard)

Figure 5.1 describes pathways of child and adult movement across the whole of the square: the heavy black line represents an adult striding purposefully and energetically across the space, creating a dominant straight path with no stops or diversions; the more complicated and active tracks of the playing children can be seen in the lighter marks that dart back and forth, overlapping with each other; the thin black line represents the path of a child accompanying the adult and their two tracks can be seen to diverge as soon as they enter the square (bottom left) as the child loops around to briefly engage with the play equipment before rejoining the adult at the exit to the square (top right).

Figure 5.2 depicts four adults standing together chatting while their children play around them. The adult lines are clearly more stationary than the roving lines of the children, which are shown paler and dotted. The filled in shapes indicate the amount of time the adults spent in one spot: "I'd be watching and waiting for them to move and I couldn't believe how static they were" (TC interview).

Figure 5.2: Adults standing, children playing

Source: Tim Coppard (photo Hattie Coppard)

Sometimes TC would focus on two children at the same time, following two lines of direction with a pencil in each hand, picking up their speed and energy in his marks on paper. Concentrating on two children simultaneously in this way, he describes forming an awareness of an ongoing connection between them even when they were not physically close: "they would be holding hands and doing things together and then they would separate, but the slightly older girl would always be aware of what the younger boy was doing" (TC interview). TC's drawings show relationships on the move in time and space, they are not simply abstract representations of people's movement, but active manifestations of someone's looking. Drawing requires concentration and focus, the act of observation and description become united in a direct encounter of observer and observed. Ingold (2011, p 226) suggests that life's 'key descriptive practice is drawing' and urges fellow ethnographers to 'think of description in the first place as a process not of verbal composition but of line-making' (Ingold, 2011, p 224).

As a dancer JYC reads movement as expressive of internal and external emotional and physical forces. Using her own body she mirrors the actions of children and adults in order to register different ways in which children and adults move within their own bodily frame. JYC noticed how children use the whole of their body to express themselves, stretching and waving their arms around, beckoning wildly to each other, using their hands and feet to make contact with objects, enjoying the experience of balancing, jumping, expending energy. In contrast adults were less overtly expressive and more physically contained, putting their hands in their pockets, keeping their arms close to their bodies, rarely waving their limbs about, standing upright, staying in one place: "grownups don't want to do something out of the ordinary because they become self-conscious and self-critical, you can tell when the grownups are performing, then they have to make a big gesture, otherwise they keep their bodies close" (JYC interview).

The exception to this norm was a woman dancing drunkenly in the square and it was her uninhibited, dynamic and quirky movements that seemed to express a childlike energy and marked her out.

Figure 5.3: Woman dancing (top figure – detail from CM's notebook)

Source: Chris Meade (photo Hattie Coppard)

"The most kinetic and most like dance were the drinkers, and the way they were half fighting or really fighting or just dancing…and the kids were doing their own kind of movement and ballet and emotions on the equipment and around…That's something we've all picked up on, the dynamism of those two different groups co-existing." (TC interview)

The weather, time of day, comings and goings of children and adults all affected the atmosphere and polyrhythmic character of the square. JYC was alert to the rhythm and duration of people's movement and her attention was drawn to subtle changes of pace. For example, at one point she noticed an older girl who had become quite still for several moments, just staring at an object that had been knocked down by a younger child: "That moment of stillness was quite striking because there were children busy all around her, doing things, jumping…and then there was this stillness" (JYC interview).

Objects and imagination

'Play is the continuous evidence of creativity, which means aliveness.' (Winnicott, 1971, p 144)

For a child to risk reaching out beyond itself it must feel secure enough to explore the unknown. Winnicott (1971) suggests that physical objects provide a psychological extension of self that creates a transitional area of experience, between an infant's multi-sensory egocentric self and the uncontrollable reality of the external world. This is a space of possibility where the paradox of internal and external existence can be explored, in a sphere where 'reality is mouldable and meanings can be re-established' (Aitken and Herman, 1997, p 77). Geographers have taken up Winnicott's ideas, suggesting that the implications of transitional phenomena go beyond child psychology and offer an important contribution to debates around the production of space and the formation of culture (Aitken and Herman, 1997). Everyday objects, a public square, social interaction, can be understood as transitional spheres of experimentation and play, where notions of internal and external realities can mingle.

The portable play equipment in the square is regularly brought out and left outside for anyone to use. Consisting of large-scale, colourful shapes that can be moved and joined together by children, this creates a distinct and dynamic area in the middle of the space. Because the objects are loose, there is an inherent flexibility and continual-ness to the playing, with children adding to and taking away from what others have made. Toddlers and teenagers work together, lifting, carrying, combining and building structures to jump off, hide underneath, climb and balance along. Some of the structures are awkward and complex with teetering platforms, wobbly bridges, narrow entrances: "it's never like a normal thing, it always involves some daring-do, some special things that they can try…new things" (JYC interview). The unexpected and difficult nature of the equipment seems to stimulate the interaction and play, creating challenges to overcome: "this is very scientific testing, a lot of the time they find the thing that is riskiest but that still feels relatively safe, and that's why there seem to be so few accidents, it's the opposite of crazy behaviour" (CM interview).

Play happens in the mind as much as in the physical world of the player and CM saw physical action as a clue to what might be going on in people's minds: 'The boy trundling his scooter along – is he escaping from Mars?' (CM notes). In cartoon sketches and notes CM recorded transitory moments in which children and adults appeared on the edges of action, in what he described as a state of 'nearly play' (CM notes). A girl radiating happiness, a boy peeping through a hole, a man fiddling with a table tennis bat, all seemed to indicate a vague land between playing and not playing: 'When they are dragging a "noodle" about they are not entirely "here" but not in a rigid imaginary world either.' Objects seemed to create a transitional vehicle for an in-between state of 'nearly play': 'I am playing with this stuff without even noticing that I am' (CM notes).

In playing anything is possible as 'the limits of the real world are temporarily suspended and things can be different' (Lester, 2010, p 4). On one of the sunniest days of the year a group of 4–7 year olds pretend it is raining, moving objects around to create a house that they can shelter inside. After a while a child shouts out "fire!" and everyone understands that the house is on fire and they start to feed 'noodles' into the structure to represent the flames. And then the 'noodles' become fire hoses as children wave them around and point them at the 'house' while making the noise of water: "Phssshhhhh, the fire's out" (CM notes).

Meanwhile a group of older girls and boys are moving some of the larger and heavier pieces of play equipment, lifting, stretching, reaching up and physically challenging themselves as they construct a raised platform together. When the structure is complete they clamber up on top to view the square from a raised vantage point: "A slightly older kid just loved lounging on the top of there and it obviously just made him feel aaaahhhh...it was an unusual situation for an urban square that you could lounge on something soft, raised up, with people running around you" (TC, interview).

The public bench is a counterpoint to the play equipment, creating a transitional area where adults can sit in close proximity without invading each other's personal space. Families and individuals use the bench as a base, to eat food, talk on the phone, read the paper. The bench is also a hub for street drinkers, a place to congregate and linger. Adults often have an object in their hand: a drinks can, a newspaper, a mobile phone, that seems to serve a purpose beyond their obvious function, providing something to hold, to share, to identify the user. CM commented that the mobile phone enabled the person to be physically in the square at the same time as being mentally somewhere else: 'The mobile has become a toy that everyone's fiddling with all the time...they are in the space, sitting and spending time there, but they are also off out of the space, maybe playing a game or a thousand miles away' (CM notes).

Every now and then an object would appear 'out of the blue', tempting and triggering a response, for example when a plastic bag glides across the square:

> a child chases it, opens it to check there's no motor inside it, reassured he throws it and now it circles in the air, settles in a corner where the guy from the café kicks it as he passes. A girl engulfed in her coat so her hands stick out immobile, beams with pleasure as she marches up to the top of the steps and down. Now a boy joins her, he's three maybe, in baggy jeans and belt. He's just caught that plastic bag and takes it proudly to his mum. (CM notes)

The power of things to provoke behaviour, create a mood or provide a purpose, was observed throughout the two days: a bag has to be kicked, a mobile phone fiddled with, objects climbed. Bennett (2004, p 354) maintains that matter and things have an active power to affect and 'an inclination to make connections and form networks of relations with varying degrees of stability'. In contrast to the psychological role that Winnicott assigns objects, Bennett's (2010) notion of 'vibrant matter' suggests a more material, interconnected and ecological relationship that challenges conventional distinctions between beings and matter, organic and inorganic, the 'living' and 'non-living'.

While the developmental value of transitional phenomena is well documented, there has been less written about the ways in which everyday objects are a feature of social interaction and culture. Objects in the square were seen to provide purpose and identity, extend personal boundaries and enable individuals and groups to reach out beyond themselves and connect imaginatively and physically. Perhaps in an environment of constant change and flux the role of the object is to provide a sense of solidity, something stable that can be defined and acted upon. The play equipment, bench, mobile phone, plastic bag, all demonstrated a 'mouldable reality' in the hands of their users, and the square itself could also be understood as a flexible and continually evolving 'consensual transitional zone' (Lee, 2005, p 102).

Coexistence and co-formation

> Ideas of difference can come together if we are willing to be at play. (Aitken, 2001, p 176)

A public square is not simply an empty container waiting to be filled or a backdrop for action; it exists as a set of relationships and possibilities – social, emotional, material – that come and go beyond borders of place and time. This particular square is situated in a densely populated urban area, adjacent to a busy high street, across the road from a market that sells giant African snails, international mobile phones, Asian pizza. People's lives and connections stretch across continents, crossing over for a time in this local place which children and adults are able to inhabit for free.

On most days, groups of drinkers and drug users congregate in the square and the manager describes how "when it's just them in the space it can be really intimidating and off-putting" (manager interview). Against this backdrop the manager expresses her desire for the square to be more like an "outdoor living room" for the whole community, a place where everyone can feel "at home" (manager interview). Key to making this happen is to find ways of encouraging children and families to use the space and the provision of the play equipment is part of a programme of activities whose purpose is to change the social dynamic of the square: "When we have events and activities here, that completely changes the atmosphere, because there are lots of people for a particular purpose and the guys that are hanging out join in...or it keeps them quiet" (manager interview).

CM picked up on the complicated social nature of the square and the continual management and effort being made to constrain the drinkers:

"That first thing of thinking, this is nice, you put play equipment next to alcoholics and everything is fine – it's more complicated than that. Like the police coming round all the time and just taking the drinks can, not throwing them out, just constraining them a little and there are quite a lot of people there, all the time looking out onto that square." (CM interview)

The mood and atmosphere in the square changes throughout the two days, the sunshine, behaviour of adults, time of day all have an influence, but according to one parent it is the children playing which has the most effect: "People behave much better when they have the kids around. Whenever there aren't kids there is trouble…people behave differently because they don't want to give a bad example, they stop fighting, they don't shout, they even play with the children sometimes" (parent interview).

The changing nature and atmosphere in the square is reflected in CM's notes. On Friday he wrote:

It is full of very happy alcoholics; it is the perfect place to be sitting with a bottle of cider, there is an amazing range of different kinds of gangs, different genders, it feels genuinely social, people are here to meet each other, and the fact that some of them are pissed is not such a big deal.

On Saturday he wrote:

She just felt like trouble when she arrived…that kind of determination to get noticed in a self-destructive way…that edginess was much more apparent…it [the square] could easily be owned again by the drunks and the kids do get scared – not running away screaming but deciding to move away. (CM notes)

JYC found the drinking group unnerving, she felt out of place and vulnerable and her awareness of this was the starting point for her understanding: "Every time I move across that square, every move is all very deliberate, it's all very…not painful, but aware". JYC's embodied response became the record of her experience, creating a bodily store of affect that she could draw on at a later date: "It's like you are a sponge, you just soak up the atmosphere…it's just that sense of anxiety, sense of playfulness, comes into your body." She was sensitive to the emotional significance of small gestures and able to focus on and explore fleeting movements by re-enacting them: the frailty of an old man as he repeatedly turned his head to look behind him; the joy of a young child flinging out her arms: "gesture holds a whole universe for me" (JYC interview).

JYC identified an invisible territorial line dividing the square, separating the drinking group based around the bench and the children playing on the equipment. Occasionally this line would be crossed and on one occasion two women from the drinkers' group wander over to play with a young child. They both hold her hands and help her balance along the play equipment, then swing her between two objects, they bend down to the child's height and hold out their arms and one woman lifts up the child and gives her a hug, then passes her to the other woman who gives her a hug and then a kiss. The father, who had been talking to one of the stall holders, wanders over and after a few minutes picks up the child and starts to carry her away: the two women stretch out their arms in response, waving to her and blowing her kisses; and then they walk back to the drinking group, passing the table-tennis table on the way and calling out to the table-tennis players with flirtatious wiggles of their hips.

JYC commented on the mix of emotional messages that she saw being expressed in this encounter: "There was this sort of maternal longing, but it's a performance because the father was looking on and somehow they were flirting...there's always the flirting...and this is the kind of edginess that I am sensing from this group" (JYC).

This scenario illustrates something of the permissive nature of the square and the continual balancing act being played out between the different desires and needs of the participants. For much of the time children appeared comfortable and mainly oblivious to the adults around them, yet when a family replaced the drinking group on the bench and skateboarders began to practice in the middle of the square, young children began to move the lightest play equipment into other parts of the square, expanding their play territory beyond the invisible territorial line. CM was struck by the similarities between adult and child behaviour, how children would move the equipment around and build themselves a place to hang out, in much the same way that the adults were doing around the bench; "It's not like carefree children just running about frolicking, they are workmanlike, doing something quite serious" (CM interview).

Children of all ages were seen to play together, with younger ones frequently following and copying older children. At one point a young boy was drawn to where the skateboarders were practising and he began to trail the older skateboarder, watching intently as the young man jumped on and off the board doing his tricks, looking keen to have a go himself. After a while the young man stopped skating and handed him the board to try with. The young boy's technique was awkward, clumsy, full of energy: he would run towards the skateboard, leap onto it, fall off, pick himself up. He did this again and again until eventually he managed to keep his balance and stay upright for a moment or two.

JYC was curious about how the child was learning to skateboard: "Movement that requires struggle and daring is a very attractive thing for me to pick up." She was struck by how unselfconscious the young boy was and how undeterred by the possibility of getting hurt: "I was noticing how brave, he had no fear of falling, he was just really foolish." Watching the young child throw himself into this activity brought back her own memories: "I had already forgotten how I learned to skate, I had forgotten how precarious and how ruthless, that we would just go on and on...So that's how kids learn" (JYC interview). Knowledge is gained on the move, through layers of perceptual engagement and a 'creative receptivity' with one's environment (Merleau-Ponty, 2002). Through trial and error the young child learns to balance on the skateboard, building an embodied understanding of the size, materiality and scope of the action required so that eventually this becomes part of his body's schema and he no longer needs to consciously think about what he is doing.

Over the period of two days, children and adults, street drinkers and toddlers, business people and shoppers, mingled and made use of the square alongside one another. The juxtaposition of difference and the tolerance and intolerance shown is not unique; these are characteristics of city living that go hand in hand with other urban traits such as anonymity, mutual indifference and transience. It is precisely the 'thrown-togetherness' of unrelated identities coming together, creating 'the unavoidable challenge of negotiating a here-and-now' (Massey, 2005, p 140) that makes a place special. It is the ongoing, ordinary, everyday processes of getting along together that renders a place genuinely public.

Conclusion

In performative research the body is recognised as the locus of perception, emotion and sensation and central to meaning making (Dewsbury, 2000). In this study artists acted as creative receptors, using their bodies, imagination and skill to make sense of what they observed. Rather than attempting to remain objective or unaffected by their investigations they paid attention to their own emotional and imaginative response to what they were witnessing in the square. This was a 'multi-logical' research process (Bagley, 2008) in which different methods of inquiry revealed different modes of understanding through which meaning could be transmitted.

Skilful observation requires a simultaneous detachment and engagement with the subject; artists talk of evoking a state of 'un-knowing', a space of open-minded investigation in which thought and experience can merge and where no answers or conclusions are being sought (Fisher and Fortnum, 2013). Not knowing can be an uncomfortable place to be; the tendency to resolve uncertainty and to tie up loose ends is strong, yet an open-ended, indeterminate space is crucial to any creative process of inquiry (Cocker, 2013). Art practice is a 'sensitive knowledge' (Markula, 2006) and it is notable that TC, JYC and CM used words such as 'absorbing', 'trance-like' 'imagining' to describe their observation process. Placing subjective experience at the heart of the research process enabled data and meaning to emerge through an embodied and imaginative response.

Pink (2007) suggests that using multiple languages that take account of sensual and temporal knowledge may bring us closer to expressing the multi-dimensionality of experience. Although a trans-disciplinary approach of itself will not create greater understanding, experimenting with different ways of understanding may shed a different light. The perspectives and sensibilities of a dancer, a writer and a painter added a dimensionality to the study that would not have been possible from a single viewpoint: how movement was interpreted by each of the artists for example, revealed distinctly different ways of understanding how people inhabit the world. TC's drawings illustrate the different energies and weights of presence of children and adults as they move about the square; CM's cartoons and notes draw attention to a state of 'nearly-play' and the moments in between action; JYC understood movement as a language of affect, identifying the emotion contained within a gesture. The medium or nature of expression of each of the artists had its own story to tell: the re-enactment of a child's gesture is an unrepeatable performance to be experienced rather than captured in words; a drawing done freehand contains the energy and subjectivity of its maker; these are creations of the moment and descriptions of direct encounter.

Ingold (2000, p 196) describes the attentive engagement of people and their environment as an 'achievement of resonance' and suggests that the knowledgeable person is not the one with the most skills or facts at their fingertips, but the one who can identify and respond to the cues and stories in their surroundings. A 'storied' knowledge emphasises relationships rather than an end product, this is an interweaving of experience and environment and it is when your own story and others meet that meaning and knowledge are created (Ingold, 2011).

Throughout the two days of observation there was a continually shifting atmosphere in the square: at times it felt relaxed, playful, even cosy, and then there would be a tension in the air and a hovering sense of threat. The origins of these shifts in mood were difficult to decipher: the weather, time of day, personality of inhabitants, sensitivity of the observer, may all have had an influence in the production of affective atmospheres (Anderson, 2009). To give attention to the phenomenon of atmosphere one needs to 'learn to be affected by the ambiguities of affect/emotion, by that which is determinate and indeterminate, present and absent, singular and vague' (Anderson, 2009, p 77).

The inherent tension between the need for order and structure and the desire for flexibility and freedom was experienced throughout the two days. Public space is a 'collective achievement', requiring a constant practising of place, but Massey (2005, p 141) warns against the danger of romanticising ideas of free space and community, arguing that 'there can be no assumption of pre-given coherence or of community or collective identity'. An inclusive public square is one in which there is a balance of stability and freedom, where togetherness and separateness can coexist, where children and adults can feel 'at home'.

A public square is not a fixed entity but an evolving array of circumstances. As with the young boy learning to skateboard, the practice of participation required in a public setting can be bumpy and hard work, it is only when people are thrown together in a place that they are faced with the possibility of growing beyond themselves, which is 'at once a risk and a chance' (Massey, 2005, p 151). Rather than denying difference or separating people into homogeneous groupings, it is precisely the negotiation and arguing out of conflicts that creates shared understanding and makes an urban square 'public'. A free and tolerant public realm is a precious commodity and the presence of children and playfulness can be understood as an optimistic sign of health.

References

Anderson, B. (2009) 'Affective atmospheres', *Emotion, Space and Society*, 2(2): 77–81.

Aitken, S. (2001) *Geographies of young people: The morally contested spaces of identity*, London: Routledge.

Aitken, S. and Herman, T. (1997) 'Gender power and crib geography: Transitional spaces and potential places', *Gender, Place and Culture*, 4(1): 63–88.

Bagley, C. (2008) 'Educational ethnography as performance art: Towards a sensuous feeling and knowing', in P. Atkinson and S. Delamont (eds) *Sage Qualitative Research Methods* (Vol 8), Thousand Oaks, CA: Sage, pp 54–37.

Bennett, J. (2004) 'The force of things: Steps toward an ecology of matter', *Political Theory*, 32(3): 347–72.

Bennett, J. (2010) *Vibrant matter: A political ecology of things*, Durham, NC: Duke University Press.

Bowen, G.A. (2006) 'Grounded theory and sensitizing concepts', *International Journal of Qualitative Methods*, 5(3): 1–9.

Cocker, E. (2013) 'Tactics for not knowing', in E. Fisher and R. Fortnum (eds) *On not knowing: How artists think*, London: Black Dog Publishing.

Dewsbury, J-D. (2000) 'Performativity and the event: Enacting a philosophy of difference', *Environment and Planning D: Society and Space*, 18(4): 473–96.

Dewsbury, J-D. (2009) 'Performative, non-representational and affect-based research: Seven injunctions', in D. Delyser, S. Atkin, M. Crang, S. Herbert and L. McDowell (eds) *Handbook of qualitative research in human geography*, London: Sage, pp 321–34.

Fisher, E. and Fortnum, R. (2013) *On not knowing: How artists think*, London: Black Dog Publishing.

Gill, T. (2007) *No fear: Growing up in a risk averse society*, London: Calouste Gulbenkian Foundation.

Hillier, J. (2011) 'Encountering Gilles Deleuze in another place', *European Planning Studies*, 19(5): 861–85.

Horton, J. and Kraftl, P. (2006) 'What else? Some more ways of thinking and doing "Children's Geographies"', *Children's Geographies*, 4(1): 69–95.

Ingold, T. (2000) *The perception of the environment: Essays on livelihood, dwelling and skill*, Oxford: Routledge.

Ingold, T. (2007) *Lines: A brief history*, London: Routledge.

Ingold, T. (2011) *Being alive: Essays on movement, knowledge and description*, London: Routledge.

Lee, N. (2005) *Childhood and human value: Development, separation and separabilty*, Maidenhead: Open University Press.

Lester, S. (2010) Play and ordinary magic: the everydayness of play, Paper presented at the *Playwork London Conference*, London, June.

Markula, P. (2006) Body-movement-change: Dance as performative qualitative research, *Journal of Sport and Social Issues*, 30(4) 353–63.

Massey, D. (2005) *For space*, London: Sage.

McCormack, D.P. (2003) 'An event of geographical ethics in spaces of affect', *Transactions of the Institute of British Geographers*, 28(4): 488–507.

Merleau-Ponty, M. (2002*) Phenomenology of perception*, London: Routledge Classics.

Pink, S. (2007) *Doing visual ethnography*, London: Sage.

Thrift, N. (2004) 'Intensities of feeling: Towards a spatial politics of affect', *Geografiska Annaler, Series B: Human Geography*, 86(1): 57–78.

Thrift, N. (2008) *Non-representational theory: Space, politics, affect*, Abingdon: Routledge.

Winnicott, D.W. (1971) *Playing and reality*, London: Tavistock Publications.

SIX

Researching children's play and contemporary art

Megan Dickerson

Introduction

Thirty years into a significant body of work that defined what is now known as performance art, the artist Alan Kaprow wrote:

> Suppose that performance artists were to adopt the emphasis of universities and think tanks based on basic research. Performance would be conceived as inquiry...The artist as researcher can begin to consider and act upon substantive questions about consciousness, communication and culture without giving up membership in the profession of art. (Kaprow, 1993, p 177)

In 2008, Kaprow's work in artfully articulating meaningful experiences from ordinary life would inspire the development of The New Children's Museum, in San Diego, California, a space that will act as a test site of research methodologies reviewed in this chapter. Neither a children's museum nor a standard contemporary art museum, The New Children's Museum engages with contemporary artists to develop and install playful artworks for an audience of children and adults. Practitioners in such a hybrid space need tools that can go beyond the 'thick description' (Geertz, 1994) of ethnographic and positivist research positions: an approach that is closer to Kaprow's notion of the artist as researcher and inquiry perceived as performance may be of considerable value in this toolbox.

This review assembles examples of alternative research methodologies, drawn from diverse practices such as performance studies and performance art, and considers their value in mapping the complexities presented by a children's museum that also actively engages in the production of contemporary art. It may also have wider appeal for practitioners engaged in supporting children's creative and playful expressions in a variety of contexts. Understanding this hybrid museum requires research methods that emphasise diversity of experience, situated knowledge and the idea that the scientific method is just one method among many for understanding the world. It is a shift from just 'what' research explores to 'how' we undertake that research. It seeks a method of creative research and evaluation emphasising the experience of the moment that leads to the end-product, not only the end-product itself. Note that the central intent of such research is not to measure impact, although that certainly may become a bi-product of such research. The aim of the hybrid approach proposed in this review is to move beyond the 'what are children learning in children's museums?' to 'how do children and adults encounter and engage with the spaces of the children's museum?'

To do this, the chapter unfolds in three parts. The opening stage of the chapter reviews the tools that have been developed to measure the learning impact of children's museums and other play-based environments, such as preschools. It then ventures into the other half of the Museum's bicultural identity, namely the history of performative artistic practice and the still emerging field of art practice as research. This portion of the Museum's identity may be particularly important not only to this Museum but to the field in general, as more museums strategically position themselves as 'town squares' (Archibald, 2004) and examine how the connections forged through active aesthetic participation might be evaluated. The final section of the chapter explores and introduces some tentative approaches that embrace 'complexity and chaos and [attempt] to find ways to map it' (McNaughton, 2004, p 99). It marks a desire to experiment within the form of the literature review by applying performative methods in several small-scale applications over the course of three months. These research methods, many of which draw from a performative research paradigm (Haseman, 2010), were inspired by contemporary artists and their works of art.

Children's museum and early childhood research paradigms

The starting point here is a significant commonality between the children's museum world and the artworld: the work of John Dewey, whose pragmatic philosophy of democratic, progressive education (Dewey, 1900; 1916; 1933; 1938) sparked and stoked the development of the first children's museums, as well as understandings of how art can be experienced. Dewey 'preached that ideas are incomplete until they are applied and tested by being used in actual situations, and he made an effort to apply this practice to his own actions' (Hein, 2004, p 413). To some extent, the work of Dewey can be seen as influenced by positivist science, originating in the work of Comte (1864), who proposed attainable certainty through science. However, Dewey's pragmatist ideas on progressive education emphasise doing first, and then doing second, and then doing some more. Any reflection on the part of the educator happens in situ. Dewey's pragmatism maintained much of the rigour of the scientific method while also anticipating many of the concerns that fuel debate over post-qualitative work today (Lather, 2015; St Pierre, 2015).

Today, contemporary research in children's museums is largely in response to funding needs. In a survey of art, science, history and natural history museums, staff members were asked what role they saw for future children's museums (Khalsa et al, 1999). The most common response was that children's museums introduce children to museums. The second most common response was that children's museums are a site for research, development and experimentation in areas such as museum learning, family learning, interactive exhibits and schooling (Khalsa et al, 1999). However, in a literature review of existing children's museum research, Luke and Windleharth (2014) found that most studies were evaluative in nature; studies were typically undertaken on grant-funded programmes in which evaluation was required by the grant funder. In practice, the studies were descriptive; most of the research reviewed was accomplished through surveys and interviews.

The majority of research studies on children's museums has focused on the 'learning value' of museums: how museum exhibits and programmes might increase children's learning in content areas (such as basic scientific concepts). These have included measuring family talk (Dierking and Falk, 1994; Borun et al, 1995; Borun et al, 1998; Crowley et al, 2001; Crowley and Galco, 2001); measuring impact on personal motivations for visiting a museum and resulting changes in behaviour (Falk et al, 1998); and overall museum experience (White, 2013). Instruments have been developed that aim to allow researchers to better understand non-verbal as well as verbal interactions that occur between adults and children during collaborative science investigation, such as the Adult Child Interaction Inventory (ACII) (Beaumont, 2010) or reflective tracking techniques (Falk et al, 2007). Related studies have proposed methodologies for age-appropriate ways to gather information about the experiences and learning of young children in general (Massey, 1996; Greig and Taylor, 2007); in museum contexts

(Haas, 1997; Beaumont, 2010; Crowley and Jacobs, 2011; Dockett et al, 2011) and in arts-based early childhood education (Sheridan, 2007).

The children's museum context is complex in part because children very rarely visit a children's museum without an adult, typically a primary caregiver or an educator. There are a small number of studies that were designed to measure attitudinal or behaviour changes on the part of both children and adults as a result of children's museum experiences (see Kuross and Folta, 2010; Blue Scarf Consulting, 2012). However, the studies largely rely on subject self-reported data via surveys. Very few of the studies conducted in children's museums go beyond description to compare different situations or groups or to study the effects of manipulations in the learning environment.

Alternative research models that have been considered, and to some extent applied, by the children's museum field in recent years include the Reggio Emilia approach, in particular the work of Rinaldi (2006) and Vecchi (2010). Several children's museums in the United States have opened Reggio Emilia-inspired schools within their facilities, including the Portland Children's Museum; however, there is little to no published research on these environments. Educators who pioneered the Reggio Emilia philosophy also read Dewey, Piaget, Vygotsky and Bruner, just as the founders of the children's museum movement did (Hein, 2006; 2012). Reggio Emilia witnesses the meaning-making of children through documentation approaches including photography, videotaping, audiotaping, anecdotal records, note taking and collected samples of children's work (Rinaldi, 1998). Others have suggested that documenting parental interactions with their children and the school teachers can also be part of this body of daily research (Forman and Fyfe, 1998). This documentation provides a series of 'traces' (Rinaldi, 1998, p 121) that make it simultaneously possible to share the ways children and their teachers co-learn.

An approach with some similarity to Reggio Emilia is the work of Vivian Gussin Paley (1990), the researcher and early childhood educator. Paley uses storytelling and story-playing as a method for better understanding the children in her classes, work predicated on the idea that children and teachers are all actors trying to find the meaning of the scenes in which they find themselves. The story-playing of each day leads to the creation of more stories on the next day. Similar to Reggio Emilia documentation practices, Paley uses videotaping, audiotaping and notetaking to reflect upon the day's occurrences, interrogating herself through this iterative process: have I given sufficient attention to those thoughts that cannot be put into play and storytelling?

This process may allow Paley (and educators who adopt similar processes) to question what Kieran Egan (1988) calls ad hoc principles of education, assumptions that include the idea that children move from the concrete to the abstract, or, for instance, that children learn best from hands-on experiences. However, Egan argues that children have a much greater capacity for abstract thinking than we credit them; he suggests, for example, that children have very little trouble understanding the binary abstractions of Cinderella. Egan has been instrumental in introducing metaphoric theory (Egan, 1988), in which a kind of judgement shared by a group and expressed in the language of story (or myth) supersedes reflective problem solving. This is, in part, the idea that the stories we tell create meaning. Through associative and analogical thought we forge new relationships (for more aesthetic-based research approaches, see also Greene, 1995; 2001).

As demonstrated here, the majority of these methods focus on the learning potential of playful sites. This review attempts to find methods that allow practitioners the means to witness the optimism, joy, confidence, interpersonal connections and resilience that emerge in the play spaces of the children's contemporary art museum. To conclude this section before moving on to performative methods drawn from contemporary art, alternative ways of understanding children's play that may have something to offer this aim are reviewed.

Some researchers are attempting to go beyond the research practices commonly found in early childhood environments. For example, Lenz-Taguchi (2010) and Olsson (2009) put to use Deleuze and Guattari's (2004) proposal for rhizomatic thinking that moves beyond the singular, linear teleology of most theories of learning and development encapsulated in the tree metaphor (what they term 'arborescent thinking'). A rhizomatic approach focuses on process and indeterminate movement rather than predetermined end goals and pays attention to things along the way which might mean taking a different direction. The aim is to look at difference itself, as with McClure's (2013) use of colours to visually represent how children occupied more than one role at a time when they were using digital technologies to create a short film. McClure's work shows a sensitivity to new ways of 'performing' the work of research, using symbolic data (candy-coloured documents, film) as a way of attending to the relationships and movements in-between bodies and materials. This disturbs neat and fixed boundaries and binaries such as adult/child, subject/object, theory/practice and so on. Lenz-Taguchi (2010) draws on Barad's (2007) concept on intra-action to extend this: whereas interaction implies the coming together of pre-fixed entities, intra-action acknowledges that things are constantly becoming through entanglements.

A final approach, Action Research, finds its origins in the work of Lewin (1948) and is an attempt to produce a 'theory of change that emerges from the change process itself' (Friedlander and Brown, 1974, p 319). Participatory action research (PAR) even more explicitly involves the participants as co-researchers. In a recent study of an adventure playground, Lester et al (2014) adopted a PAR approach to explore how the playground is co-created by adults and children. Through storytelling, journal writing, photography and video, Lester et al (2014, p 12) are able to portray a playwork organisation as a 'collection of stories'. Appropriately to the method, the first written lines of the study acknowledge the playworkers and staff who acted as co-researchers in the study.

Art practice as research

Gray (2013) writes that the act of trying to be expertly creative – of thinking about how your end product might stack up next to someone else's end product – inhibits creativity. He quotes John Irving who, when asked whether he thinks about potential book sales while writing a book, replied 'You can't, you can't!…When you're writing, only think about the book' (Gray, 2013, p 135). Creative research and evaluation, to some, may sound like 'creative accounting', a practice that bends the rules within the letter of the law, as perhaps an evasive measure. Though a more traditional, systematic approach to literature review is resisted here, this is not to evade science but rather in part to follow the shape and content of the performative and post-qualitative research studies that are reviewed, what Haseman (2010) calls the third research paradigm, an openness to non-numeric or symbolic data as means of understanding a place or subject.

In the spirit of the museum's dual citizenship in the children's museum and art museum worlds, this review now addresses a body of methodologies termed 'art practice as research' described by Sullivan (2014, p 278) as: 'a creative and critical process whereby imaginative leaps are made into what we do not know – as this can lead to crucial insights that may change what we do know.'

He uses the metaphor of the braid to explain how the art practice as research process opens up to new knowledge and then goes deeper, only to resurface a moment later. Similarly, Leavy (2009, p 1) writes that 'arts-based researchers are not "discovering" new tools, they are carving them'.

Barrett and Bolt (2007) explore practice-based inquiry across several creative arts disciplines, focusing largely on the processes, rather than the products, of inquiry. They question what new knowledge or understanding studio-based inquiry – that is, explorations undertaken throughout the course of an artist's studio practice – can generate that could not otherwise be understood with more traditional approaches. This allows practitioners to go beyond passive reception of ideas to the generation of 'personally situated knowledge and new ways of modelling and externalizing such knowledge' (Barrett and Bolt, 2007, p 2). Barone and Eisner (2006, p 102) provide four criteria for appraising arts-based research. These include questioning if the work had an 'illuminating effect' (did it reveal things that were previously unnoticed?); encouraged 'generativity' (did it reveal new questions?); was 'inclusive' (was it able to zero in on important issues in the field?) and 'generalisable' (was it relevant to other phenomena, encouraging the reader to make more connections?). The outputs of a multiple methods (or what Law, 2004, terms a 'method assemblage') performative research design may include art installations and artist performances, but will also include exegesis: an explanation of the work. Exegesis is, 'at root, a leading or guiding out of a complexity' (Haseman, 2010, p 156).

Arts-based research is connected to the field of relational aesthetics, which, starting in the 1990s and continuing with the work of Nicolas Bourriaud (2002), has emerged as 'a set of artistic practices which take as their theoretical and practical point of departure the whole of human relations and their social context, rather than an independent and private space' (Bourriaud, 2002, p 113). It is a laboratory paradigm that brings typically studio-based practices of research and interrogation into the performance space. The artist Tino Sehgal, for instance, choreographs sculptural performances to be executed by an open call of volunteers. He does not allow photography of these works, which have included people roving massive galleries in circles coupled with timed flashes of the gallery's lighting systems and other surprises. His desire, particularly in an age of visual communication and easily accessible camera tools, is to create an aesthetic experience that exists only in the telling.

Perhaps one of the most promising methodologies that embraces this type of when-is-a-bed-not-a-bed complexity of a relational artworld is a/r/tography, in which a/r/t is an acronym for artist–researcher–teacher (Irwin, 2003; Irwin and De Cosson, 2004; Springgay et al, 2005; Springgay et al, 2008). A/r/tography is an approach that embeds research and practice, allowing for complex inquiry into love, death, power, memory, fear, loss, desire, hope and suffering, just as art may explore those same things. Irwin (2003) situates a/r/tography within the work of Deleuze and Guattari (2004) as a rhizomatic practice — that is, a constantly becoming practice with no beginning or end, that may produce offshoots in multiple directions. Irwin and de Cosson (2004, p xxiv) describes a/r/tography as an 'in-between' approach to research and a creative practice in itself. Some have gone so far as to call this hybrid notion of the artist–researcher 'scholartistry' (Knowles et al, 2008).

In contrast to the methods reviewed in the first portion of this review, a/r/tography embraces the shifting perceptions of the singular artist/ researcher/teacher and his or her journey through the complexities of an experience. This individual experience is then layered among that of other artist–teacher–researchers as they engage in a similar (but individualised) process of remaining open to in/sight: a term Irwin (2003) uses with a slash between 'in' and 'sight' in order to hold space for the unperceived in the perceived. This in/sight process, which involves being responsive to all aspects of a setting, from smells to shadows, is both aesthetic and performative. As if he or she were making a painting and committing to a particular gesture of a brush, this rhizomatic practice of following in/sights as they emerge allows the a/r/tographical practitioner to delay sense-making for a moment (or longer) in deference to a desire to honour the wonder and mystery of tacit knowledge and intuition.

A method assemblage experiment in arts-based research in a children's museum

During the preparation of this review over the course of several months, the reviewer undertook a series of investigations inspired by a/r/tography, mixed with inspiration from an existing work of art that could be termed 'relational' as a point of departure. Below is a potpourri of the traces of these non-traditional research methods.

The artwork: John Cage, 4'33" (In Proportional Notation), 1952/53

This is also known as John Cage's 'silent piece'. In 4'33" (In Proportional Notation) a pianist (or other performer or performers) sits at an instrument, starts a stopwatch, and then sits without playing the instrument for four minutes and thirty-three seconds, opening and closing the piano to mark three distinct movements. The piece attunes listeners to the sounds of the room at that moment, making the performance more of an interactive event (Badiou, 2005), turning attention from the performer to the audience, making every throat-clearing, seat-shifting and sound of passer-by more noticeable.

The experiment

The researcher chooses a location at The New Children's Museum. Once she sits down, she times a stopwatch for four minutes and thirty-three seconds and listens. She writes notes of what she hears but does not look.

Sample notes

From 4'33" in a studio space:

1. The tinkling sound of a tower of thin wooden blocks collapsing; a scream echoes from afar;
2. Recorded singing from a nearby art installation emerges like a whispered lullaby;
3. More screaming, this time more high-pitched; sound of wheels on cement (stroller?);
4. "I didn't do it! I didn't do it!" a child protesting;
5. Sound of voices over a walkie-talkie: "Bubbles is closed."

The artwork: Sol LeWitt, Wall Drawings, 1968–82

Over the course of his career, Sol LeWitt created over 100 monumental wall drawings. Each drawing exists as a set of instructions and/or a diagram. LeWitt did not physically execute the wall drawings. Instead, much as a builder would execute blueprints from an architect, a practitioner then takes these instructions and interprets them into a final wall composition, typically completed with paint, but sometimes, when the rules allow it, in other media. LeWitt (1967, p 80) wrote that 'The idea becomes a machine that makes the art.'

The experiment

Choose a space in the museum. Choose a set of instructions for a Sol LeWitt drawing. Use the wall drawing instructions as a roadmap for your visual exploration of a space. For instance, if a wall drawing calls for the delivery of colours in a specific sequence, follow that sequence. Record what you see in each place.

Sample notes

The researcher observes murals painted on the sides of *The Rain House* installation. Forty-five instructions from LeWitt's 'Color Grids Plan' guide her eyes. Two examples:

24. 'Straight Blue/Broken Blue': researcher follows a straight blue line in the mural until it stops. She records a child walking out of the play house door.

25. 'Not-straight Yellow/Not-straight Yellow': Researcher locates the nearest wavy yellow line, and follows it to a dotted yellow line. She notes the distant sound of a child's laugh.

The artwork: Yoko Ono's Grapefruit, 1964

Grapefruit is an artist's book that is a collection of instructions, or event scores. It is considered to be a significant Fluxus artwork, and itself is a hybrid.

The experiment

Follow this instruction by Yoko Ono for 'Snow Piece', 1963: Think that snow is falling.
   Think that snow is falling everywhere all the time. When you talk with a person, think that snow is falling between you and on the person. Stop conversing when you think the person is covered by snow.

Sample notes

The researcher imagines snow falling all over the gallery. The researcher watches a visitor and observes her behaviour until the researcher imagines the visitor has become covered in snow. The researcher then turns her gaze to another visitor.

The artwork: Tino Sehgal's This is So Contemporary

Tino Sehgal is a relational aesthetic artist who uses people and actions to make art rather than objects. For This is So Contemporary, at the

Art Gallery of New South Wales, three interpreters trained by the artist wear the uniforms of gallery attendants. The 'attendants' point at visitors, seemingly chosen at random, who then suddenly do a dance, waving their hands and singing "This is so contemporary, this is so contemporary!" After a moment, the visitors go back to quietly exploring the gallery.

The experiment

In June 2014, this reviewer introduced a spy game. Children approach Museum Playworkers (floor staff who wear badges and uniforms). The children then tug on their right earlobes to signal the start of the game to the Museum Playworker. The Museum Playworker then gives another secret sign (of their own choosing) and offers a challenge that utilises the space nearby. The challenge is up to the Museum Playworker; it can be full-body, small motor or any number of things. Some Museum Playworkers simply challenge kids to make the strangest noise they can and then give that noise a name. As children complete challenges, they get progressively harder. For this experiment, a Museum Playworker introduced an eyepatch, which she would give to one child in the morning. She would then instruct other children to find the child with the eye patch. The child with the eye patch was instructed to whisper "huggamugga" and then give the eyepatch to the other child.

Sample notes

The Spy Game is perhaps the most interesting of the experiments. The eyepatch itself has led to many other objects being passed from 'spy' to 'spy' in the museum. Museum Guides and child spies have also worked together to create maps of the museum's levels; planted mysterious 'red boxes' with clues hidden inside; and developed a language which only those on the inside of the game can recognise ("huggamugga" being just the beginning). Moreover, the Spy Game has become a platform for conversation and exchange among the Museum Guides, who leave notes for each other in the locker room to share new challenges. Recently, the Museum Guides have introduced hand-drawn maps of each level, on which they write new challenges and record strange or unusual experiences. Through this, others learned the story of a ten-year-old boy with autism who, while visiting with his grandmother, played the game for five hours. The Museum Guide who spoke with the grandmother recorded on the map the story of how the boy, according to the grandmother, had never been so engaged in a public place in San Diego and that they would be coming back to play again.

Conclusion

Sullivan (2006, p 19) states that the art research response to the positivist science question of 'If you don't know where you are going, how will you know when you get there?' is this: 'If you don't know where you are going, then any road will take you there.' Following the work of the zen(ish) monk and artist Allan Kaprow that began this chapter, this can also be expressed through the words of zen philosopher Suzuki (1926, p 24), who writes:

> Before a man studies Zen, to him mountains are mountains and waters are waters; after he gets an insight into the truth of Zen through the instruction of a good master, mountains to him are not mountains and waters are not waters; but after this when he really attains to the abode of rest, mountains are once more mountains and waters are waters.

Perhaps, by using a potpourri of research methods, we seek defamiliarisation: a way of seeing then unseeing then seeing again. It is close to Gallagher's (2011) contrast between the dramatic theatre spectator and the epic theatre spectator. The dramatic theatre spectator, like the deductive researcher, looks for confirmation of values or what they suspect is true (I weep when they weep; I laugh when they laugh). The epic theatre spectator experiences work as a contrarian (I laugh when they weep), and through this defamiliarisation, may find a different sense of the moment. There may be no deeper truths, but we will only find them by not seeking them.

Though there are existing research methodologies for artistic practice, and many methods for examining children's learning, there are few approaches that merge the two in such a ludocentric way. A new hybrid creative research method, brought into being, would enable practitioners to document the verbal and non-verbal actions and interactions that take place in museum spaces, allowing a mapping of connections between people and objects. This review is an attempt to cull the existing methodologies and find shared reverberations, perhaps leading to a multiple method approach tailored to the specific contact space of the museum. This approach might be termed 'ludo-artographic.' Though still subject to some degree to the credibility test of research, an experimental, method assemblage approach fits the spirit and mission of the organisation. By approaching research as artists, the practitioners at The New Children's Museum may get closer to Kaprow's (1993) vision of performance conceived as inquiry. Through zen(ish) performative research, practitioners open themselves to complexity as well as create traces that can then generate new complexity: a goal, to some extent, of contemporary art practice itself.

References

Archibald, R. (2004) *The new town square: Museums and communities in transition*, Walnut Creek: AltaMira Press.

Badiou, A. (2005) *Being and event*, London: Continuum.

Barad, K. (2007) *Meeting the universe halfway: Quantum physics and the entanglement of matter and meaning*, Durham, NC: Duke University Press.

Barone, T. and Eisner, E. (2006) 'Arts-based educational research', in J.L. Green, G. Camilli and P.B. Elmore (eds) *Handbook of complementary methods in education research*, Boston, MA: American Educational Research Association, pp 95–110.

Barrett, L. and Bolt, T. (2007) *Practice as research: Approaches to creative arts enquiry*, New York: Tauris and Co.

Beaumont, L. (2010) *Developing the Adult Child Interaction Inventory: A methodological study*, Washington, DC: informalscience.org.

Bishop, C. (2004) 'Antagonism and relational aesthetics', *October*, 110: 51–79.

Blue Scarf Consulting (2012) *Storyland: A trip through childhood favorites*, Summative evaluation report of findings, Minnetonka, MN: Minnesota Children's Museum.

Borun, M., Cleghom, A. and Garfield, C. (1995) 'Family learning in museums: A bibliographic review', *Curator*, 38(4): 262–70.

Borun, M., Dritsas J., Johnson, J.I., Peter, N.E., Wagner, K.F., Fadigan, K., Jangaard, A., Stroup, E. and Wenger, A. (1998) *Family learning in museums: The PISEC perspective*, Philadelphia, PA: The Franklin Institute.

Bourriaud, N. (2002) *Relational aesthetics*, Paris: Les presses du reel.

Comte, A. (1864) *Cours de Philiosphie Positive*, Paris: Balliere.

Crowley, K. and Galco, J. (2001) 'Family conversations and the emergence of scientific literacy', in K. Crowley, C. Schunn and T. Okada (eds) *Designing for science: Implications for everyday, classroom and professional science*, Mahwah, NJ: Lawrence Erlbaum, pp 349–67.

Crowley, K. and Jacobs, M. (2011) 'Building islands of expertise in everyday family activity', in G. Leinhardt, K. Crowley and K. Knutson (eds) *Learning conversations in museums*, Mahwah, NJ: Lawrence Erlbaum, pp 333–56.

Crowley, K., Callanan, M., Jipson, J., Galco, J., Topping, K. and Shrager, J. (2001) 'Shared scientific thinking in everyday parent–child activities', *Science Education*, 85(6): 712–32.

Deleuze, G. and Guattari, F. (2004) *A thousand plateaus: Capitalism and schizophrenia* (2nd edn), trans. B. Massumi, Minneapolis, MN: University of Minnesota Press.

Dewey, J. (1900) *The school and society*, Chicago, IL: University of Chicago Press.

Dewey. J. (1902) *The child and the curriculum*, Chicago, IL: University of Chicago Press.

Dewey, J. (1916) *Democracy and education: An introduction to the philosophy of education* (1966 edn), New York: Free Press.

Dewey, J. (1933) *How we think: A restatement of the relation of reflective thinking to the educative process*, Boston, MA: D.C. Heath.

Dewey, J. (1938) *Experience and education*, New York: Collier Books.

Dierking, L.D. and Falk, J.H. (1994) 'Family behavior and learning in informal science settings: A review of the research', *Science Education*, 78(1): 57–72.

Dockett, S., Main, S. and Kelly, L. (2011) 'Consulting young children: Experiences from a museum', *Visitor Studies*, 14(1): 13–33.

Egan, K. (1988) *Primary understanding*, New York: Routledge.

Falk, J.H. Moussouri, T. and Coulson, D. (1998) 'The effect of visitors' agendas on museum learning', *Curator*, 41(2): 106–20.

Falk, J.H., Reinhard, E.M., Vernon, C.L., Bronnenkant, K. Heimlich, J.E. and Deans, N.L. (2007) *Why zoos and aquariums matter: Assessing the impact of a visit to a zoo or aquarium*, Silver Spring: Association of Zoos and Aquariums.

Forman, G. and Fyfe, B. (1998) 'Negotiated learning through design, documentation, and discourse', in C. Edwards, L. Gandini and G. Forman (eds) *The hundred languages of children: The Reggio Emilia approach to early childhood education*, 2nd edn, Norwood, NJ: Ablex Publishing Corporation, pp 239–60.

Friedlander, F. and Brown, L.D. (1974) 'Organization development', *Annual Review of Psychology*, 25(1): 313–41.

Gallagher, K.M. (2011) 'In search of a theoretical basis for storytelling in education research: story as method', *International Journal of Research and Method in Education*, 34(1): 49–61.

Geertz, C. (1994) 'Thick description: Toward an interpretive theory of culture', in M. Martin and L.C. McIntyre (eds) *Readings in the philosophy of social science*, Cambridge, MA: MIT Press, pp 213–32.

Gray, P. (2013) *Free to learn*, New York: Basic Books.

Greene, M. (1995) *Releasing the imagination: Essays on education, the arts, and social change*, San Francisco, CA: Jossey-Bass.

Greene, M. (2001) *Variations on a blue guitar: The Lincoln Center Institute lectures on aesthetic education*, Williston: Teachers College Press.

Greig, A. and Taylor, J. (2007) Doing research with children, Thousand Oaks, CA: Sage.

Haas, N.T. (1997) 'Project explore: How children are really learning in children's museums', *Visitor Studies Today*, 9(1): 63–9.

Haseman, B. (2010) 'Rupture and recognition: Identifying the performative research paradigm', in E. Barrett and B. Bolt (eds) *Practice as research: Approaches to creative arts enquiry*, New York: IB Tauris.

Hein, G. (2004) 'John Dewey and museum education', *Curator*, 47: 413–27.

Hein, G. (2006) 'Progressive education and museum education: Anna Billings Gallup and Louise Connolly', *Journal of Museum Education*, 31(3): 161–74.

Hein, G. (2012) *Progressive museum practice: John Dewey and democracy*, Walnut Creek, CA: Left Coast Press.

Irwin, R.L. (2003) 'Towards an aesthetic of unfolding in/sights through curriculum', *Journal of the Canadian Association for Curriculum Studies*, 1(2): 63–78.

Irwin, R.L. and de Cosson, A. (eds) (2004) *A/r/tography: Rendering self through arts based living inquiry*, Vancouver: Pacific Educational Press.

Kaprow, A. (1993) *Essays on the blurring of art and life*, Berkeley, CA: University of California Press.

Khalsa, G., Steuert, P. and Sykes, M. (1999) 'Learning from each other: Children's museums and the museum field', in N.F. Gibans and B.K. Beach (eds) *Bridges to understanding children's museums*, Cleveland, OH: Mandel Center for Nonprofit Organizations, Case Western Reserve University.

Knowles, G., Promislow, S. and Cole, A. (eds) (2008) *Creating scholartistry: Imagining the arts-informed thesis or dissertation*, Halifax: Backalong Books.

Kuross, E. and Folta, S. (2010) 'Involving cultural institutions in the prevention of childhood obesity: The Boston Children's Museum's GoKids project', *Journal of Nutrition Education and Behavior*, 42(6): 427–9.

Lather, P. (2015) 'The work of thought and the politics of research: (Post) qualitative research', in N.K. Denzin and M.D. Giardina (eds) *Qualitative inquiry and the politics of research*, Walnut Creek, CA: Left Coast Press, pp 97–117.

Law, J. (2004) *After method: Mess in social science research*, Abingdon: Routledge.

Leavy, P. (2009) *Method meets art: Arts-based research practice*, New York: Guilford Press.

Lenz-Taguchi, H. (2010) *Going beyond the theory/practice divide in early childhood education: Introducing an intra-active pedagogy*, New York: Routledge.

Lester, S., Fitzpatrick, J. and Russell, W. (2014) *Co-creating an adventure playground (CAP): Reading playwork stories, practices and artefacts*, Gloucester: University of Gloucestershire.

Lewin, K. (1948) 'Action research and minority problems', in G.W. Lewin (ed) *Resolving social conflicts*, New York: Harper and Row, pp 201–16.

LeWitt, S. (1967) 'Paragraphs on conceptual art', *Artforum*, 5(10): 79–83.

LeWitt, S. (1975) *Color Grids. Set of forty-five etchings*, 27 x 27 cm, New York, NY: Parasol Press.

Luke, J. and Windleharth, T. (2014) *The learning value of children's museums: Building a field-wide research agenda, a landscape review*, Washington DC: Institute of Museum and Library Services.

McClure, M. (2013) 'The monster and lover-girl: Mapping complex relations in preschool children's digital video productions', *Studies in Art Education*, 55(1): 18–34.

McNaughton, G. (2004) 'The politics of logic in early childhood research: A case of the brain, hard facts, trees and rhizomes', *The Australian Educational Researcher*, 31(3): 87–104.

Massey, C. (1996) 'Listening to young children: Assessment and research techniques for very young visitors', *Visitor Studies*, 8(1): 82–9.

Olsson, L.M. (2009) *Movement and experimentation in young children's learning: Deleuze and Guattari in early childhood education*, London: Routledge.

Ono, Y. (1970) *Grapefruit: A book of instructions and drawings by Yoko Ono*, New York, NY: Simon and Schuster.

Paley, V.G. (1990) *The boy who would be a helicopter*, Cambridge, MA: Harvard University Press.

Rinaldi, C. (1998) 'Projected curriculum constructed through documentation: An interview with Lella Gandi', in C.P. Edwards, L. Gandini, and G.E. Forman (eds) *The hundred languages of children: The Reggio Emilia approach – advanced reflections*, Greenwich, CT: Ablex, pp 113–25.

Rinaldi, C. (2006) *In dialogue with Reggio Emilia: Listening, researching and learning*, New York: Psychology Press.

Sehgal, T. (2014) *This is so contemporary*, performance, Kaldor Public Arts Projects, Art Gallery of New South Wales, Sydney, 6–23 February.

Sheridan, K. (2007) 'Studio thinking in early childhood', in M. Narey (ed) *Making meaning: Constructing multimodal perspectives of language, literacy, and learning through arts-based early childhood education*, New York: Springer, pp 71–89.

Springgay, S., Irwin, R.L. and Wilson Kind, S. (2005) 'A/r/tography as living inquiry through art and text', *Qualitative Inquiry*, 11(6): 897–912.

Springgay, S., Irwin, R.L., Leggo, C. and Gouzouasis, P. (eds) (2008) *Being with A/r/tography*, Rotterdam: Sense Publishers.

St Pierre, E.A. (2015) 'Practices for the "new" in the new empiricisms, the new materialisms, and post-qualitative inquiry', in N.K. Denzin and M.D. Giardina (eds) *Qualitative inquiry and the politics of research*, Walnut Creek, CA: Left Coast Press, pp 75–96.

Sullivan, G. (2006) 'Research acts in art practice', *Studies in Art Education*, 48(1): 19–35.

Sullivan, G. (2014) 'The art of research', *Studies in Art Education*, 55(4): 270–86.

Suzuki, D.T. (1926) *Essays in Zen Buddhism*, first series, New York: The Buddhist Society.

Vecchi, V. (2010) *Art and creativity in Reggio Emilia: Exploring the role and potential of ateliers in early childhood education*, New York: Routledge.

White, R.E. (2013) *The power of play: a research summary on play and learning*, Minnetonka, MN: Minnesota Children's Museum, www.childrensmuseums.org/images/MCMResearchSummary.pdf

SEVEN

Play and value: determining the values of a nature play setting

Linda Kinney

Introduction

The mission of many zoos and aquaria is to inspire people to make a difference in the conservation of wildlife and wild places and provide opportunities for families to connect with nature. For many families, nature play can begin at accredited zoos and aquaria (AZA), affording AZA institutions the possibility to become leaders in their community for the nature play movement (Ogden, 2015). Zoos and aquaria are beginning to feature outdoor play spaces within their institutions, although they are diverse in their design and approach to nature play. The zoo play setting in this study was designed specifically to support nature play by offering a rich and varied play environment intended to appeal to all ages. The play setting aims to engage the senses, inspire exploration, encourage risk taking and support openness and change. It is a place of difference within the zoo, providing opportunities for running, climbing, building forts, making mud pies, splashing in a stream, or just messing about.

Extensive research speaks to the benefits and value of play, outdoor environments and managed play provisions for children, their families and community (Hart, 2002; Louv, 2005; Chawla, 2006; 2007; Kuo, 2010). Managed play provision can enhance and extend play opportunities by being an example of what might be possible in public spaces of all shapes and sizes (Beunderman, 2010) and provides circumstances for adults to take a supportive role, allowing children to play as freely as possible. However, in supporting free play, tensions can develop between those who encourage the openness of play and those who believe that children's play should be tightly managed or outcome based. Less literature explores the organisational management of a large institution and the perceived values of a segregated space for play within the organisation (like a zoo). This study focuses on an organisation's stakeholders (zoo management and staff) by exploring their opinions on the purpose and value of a nature play setting within a zoo in the United States.

Supporting openness and change

Many adults think of a play space as an adult-designed play environment often identified with other terms such as playground or play setting, implying a dedicated and segregated environment for play, with specific physical design features. But as Ward (1979) notes, children will play anywhere and with anything and playing is determined by more than its physical setting. A play space is co-created through the relational movements between bodies, materials and affects and it is these interconnections that are fundamental to the realisation of emerging play possibilities. Playing is creative, open and constantly evolving and can be seen as an indeterminate emergent system (Keene, 2000), with the potential to create new spaces, springing up almost anywhere. As Lindquist (2001, p 21) points out, 'playfulness can appear wherever agency and intentionality open space'. Thus, the open-ended possibilities of playing extend the understanding of what makes up a space for play (Harker, 2005). Consequently, an adult designed play environment must be sensitive and responsive to conditions which enable children to co-create and shape their worlds rather than follow adult determined agendas (Lester and Russell, 2008). However, many large organisations, like zoos, can be governed by specific rules and regulations, agendas and expected ways of being.

The purpose of this study was to examine the ways a play setting within a zoo is understood as a segregated space for both play and learning and the tensions that are created by the conflicting values of stakeholders. The research focused on capturing and assessing the opinions of the stakeholders on the purpose of a play setting within a zoo. It drew on Beunderman's (2010) adaptation of Holden's Cultural Value Triangle (2006) to consider the value of adult staffed play provision. This adaptation highlights the multiple and often contested value attributed to the nature and benefits of play provision. Beunderman argued that good quality staffed play provision creates a surprising complexity of value and increases the opportunities for rich and varied play, especially those forms of play that are often controlled or limited in public places or institutional settings. Having a more comprehensive understanding of differing values and tensions becomes a vital component in managing and advocating for the creation of an environment that is sensitive and responsive to children's play.

The genesis of a nature play environment

The 'nature' play setting where the study took place is a mix of designed elements and naturally occurring flora, fauna and geologic features, characterising those nooks and crannies many children often access: 'areas in and around neighborhoods, construction sites, playgrounds, wooded areas and vacant lots' (Vadala et al, 2007, p 8). However, the terms 'nature' or 'natural world' are used in many contexts. They are highly complex and come with multiple and often contested meanings. The idea that there is a 'nature' that is external to the human has attracted a great deal of criticism which recognises that body, mind and environment are thoroughly enmeshed and cannot be distinguished as separate categories of experience; the environment is not 'in the head' or 'out there' (Bateson, 1973, cited in Ingold, 2011, p 171). The mind is embodied and embedded in the world and there are mutual, reciprocal and intimately entwined feedback loops among and between these levels of organisation (Lester and Russell, 2008). However, as Clayton and Opotow (2003) point out, how we define or view nature as a society is in large part due to our relationship with it. The human/ nature duality still retains considerable influence in the approach to a nature play setting, and certainly informed the design aesthetic of the setting investigated in the study. The 'nature' of this play setting is described as the nature that is encountered on a daily basis and provides opportunities for children to engage with the natural elements (rocks, boulders, trees, shrubs, dirt, water, flowers, etc) located within the setting. Humans encounter nature every day, and it should be seen as an interactive agent that can show itself in both subtle (weeds pushing through the cracks in a sidewalk) and not so subtle (violent storms) ways (Čapek, 2010). Nabhan and Trimble (1994) suggest that many naturalists start their journeys on ditch banks and empty lots – in open yard space just beyond the backyard fence.

The reasoning behind using nature play as a vehicle for connecting children with nature was a response to the emerging literature on children's diminished opportunities for contact and associated benefits from being in nature (Hart, 2002; Kellert, 2002; Karsten, 2005; Louv, 2005; Mayer et al, 2008; Sobel, 2008; Skår and Krogh, 2009; Moore, 2014). Although much of the research focuses on wilderness or partially wild areas (Ewert et al, 2005; Thompson et al, 2007; Ramey, 2010), a theme running throughout the literature points to children's attraction to natural and green areas whether it is a park setting, the back yard or pockets of green throughout neighbourhoods. Numerous studies reaffirm children's preference for natural locations, for example, Sobel's

(2002) exploration of children's den- and fort-making and Moore's (1986) ethnographic study of children from urban areas.

The zoo play setting is often described as a nature playground which may be characterised as an outdoor playscape that is physically varied and affords opportunities for diverse play (climbing, digging, den-building). However, the definition of a natural playground continues to be ambiguous and can be defined as areas that incorporate the surrounding landscape, where children play with natural elements or nature inspired hardscape structures. The design of the play setting also recognised adult influence on children's perception and appreciation of the natural world and this informed the development of a programme that fosters children's love of nature and maintaining a 'sense of wonder' through mentoring, co-exploring and sharing experiences in nature (Carson, 1956; Chawla, 2006; 2007; Ramey, 2010).

Although the play setting is designed to support playing children, its value for the majority of zoo staff continues to be in its ability to connect children with nature. In design terms, it is an immersive, naturalistic exhibit that draws the visitor in and keeps them engaged, blending recreation and education, which follows the current trend in zoos and aquaria (Shettel-Neuber, 1988; Davey, 2006). Thus, the play setting can be described as a nature play and learning space as defined by Moore (2014, p 5):

> A designated, managed location in an existing or modified outdoor environment where children of all ages and abilities play and learn by engaging with and manipulating diverse natural elements, materials, organisms, and habitats through sensory, fine motor and gross motor experiences.

While conservation education programmes in zoos continue to move away from producing *desired outcomes* to creating *new patterns of behaviour* (Ogden and Heimlich, 2009), allowing children to play freely in their own way is often misunderstood as an important method of engaging children. During free play, children's play responses can be interpreted as chaotic. If adults see their role as one of control and do not understand the complexities of play, their goal will be to constrict the range of responses to ones that are more easily managed.

Zoo vs game reserve: managing the play setting

The zoo's play setting is often referred to as the institution's 'habitat for kids' or the 'kids' exhibit'. It is an area designed to invite children in to play, to engage with the environment, or as one staff member states, "an exhibit for thousands of primates". While physical boundaries exist, the boundaries for play are quite loose. Dedicated staff who have an appreciation of playwork and associated Playwork Principles (PPSG, 2005) are responsible for day-to-day operations. Their everyday practice or management style considered from an animal care perspective may be akin to creating a game reserve, an area where endangered animals can live out their lives in the most natural way possible. It is managed in a way that supports the play process, allowing children the opportunity to follow their own unique ideas and intentions and support the range of behaviours that accompany playing children, while maintaining the integrity of the space (Lester, 2015). In this context, the play staff act as game reserve wardens, acknowledging the wide range of behaviours and accompanying emotions as the natural state of the playing child. This style, with minimal intervention and simple rules, is conducive to the emergence of co-created play spaces. Having a variety of loose parts (Nicholson, 1971) further supports this approach, promoting flexibility, open-endedness and dynamic social interactions which together encourage creative engagement with the environment as well as one another (Moore, 1977).

However, these roles and practices take place in an organisational structure in which senior managers have a broad educational remit and find that the unpredictability of playing children can often be uncomfortable. They perceive the role of the play staff as one of control, order and supporting learning, an approach that is more akin to staff acting as the zoo keeper who takes care of the animals and establishes very clear boundaries for the animal's protection (Lester, 2015). The zoo cannot fully replicate a natural habitat and tends to be a highly controlled space, where children's playful behaviours repeatedly encounter boundaries (Lester, 2015). If the play staff acted as zoo keepers, children playing at and pushing the boundaries (physical and emotional) would be checked by staff responses requesting children to 'play nicely' or listen quietly and learn something about nature. Children will always seek those opportunities to test the controls set for them, and play staff as zoo keeper often reciprocates with 'didactic practice' (Sturrock et al, 2004, p 83) which attempts to correct what appears to be wayward and atypical, eliciting compliant behaviour that is believed to be in line with developmental psychology's 'ages and stages' mandates (Sturrock et al, 2004).

The play staff in the zoo's play setting are, however, responsive to what is happening as children play rather than following a pre-established set of rules and codes. The character of the setting is in a constant state of flux according to what is taking place at any given moment. Therefore, a wider range of play behaviours is accepted as the boundaries are continuously pushed, played around and often widened. Looking at an either or approach (game reserve or zoo) is a binary relationship and does not fully represent this ever-changing movement. Taking a game reserve approach, the play staff recognises the complexities of children's play with the overall intention to continually provide an open and playful 'game reserve' which may often be in conflict with expectations of accountability, designated outcomes and fixed boundaries that tend to control children's play, creating a 'closed' space' (Sibley, 1995, cited in Lester, 2010).

The zoo play setting was designed as a place for children to play and the play staff has a huge stake in its continued availability as a play setting. However, there are others who have invested in its success and it is also important to identify these stakeholders. Recognising and exploring their diverse views is essential to the setting's continued success, since their participation, influence and understanding of why the zoo is supporting play can influence important decisions such as funding, staffing, maintenance renovations, policy formulation and implementation. As such the findings from the study provide a valuable resource for developing an advocacy strategy.

Assessing the value of the play setting: designing an approach

The focus of the research was to capture and assess the opinions of the stakeholders on the purpose and value of having a play setting within the zoo. Each stakeholder has different views of the world created through their upbringing, education, career and social connections. Crotty (1998) posits that different people, even when experiencing a simultaneous phenomenon, may construct meaning in diverse ways. Perceptions of children's relationship with the natural world, understandings of the nature and value of children's play and the purpose of the zoo are different, creating multiple perspectives of the purpose and value of an outdoor play setting situated within a larger organisation. This study attempts to understand the meanings of people's realities from their point of view and aims to generate a more comprehensive understanding of the differing values placed on the play area. This understanding can serve as a tool for managing the complexities of operating a designated space within the zoo that supports the play process. As such, the study was best suited for a qualitative research approach using semi-structured interviews with key stakeholders. This was enhanced by the use of a wider survey across a range of diverse roles within the zoo.

An initial stakeholder analysis was carried out to identify the stakeholders (those most likely to affect and be affected by having a play setting at the zoo) to 'develop a strategic view of the human and institutional landscape, and the relationships between the different stakeholders and the issues they care about most' (Golder and Gawler, 2005, p 1). The analysis revealed that children are obviously a major stakeholder in what happens in the setting and while they have considerable influence in shaping the everyday activities in the setting, they have less power in the more strategic operations of the zoo. The research intended to include observations of how children were using the space alongside parent/caregiver surveys to assess their perceptions of the setting. This was not possible due to the fact that during the timeframe of the study, the setting was closed due to rescheduled renovations. However, the ongoing observational practices of play staff offer rich evidence that children value the setting as a place to play. Given this, the primary focus for the study was influential members of the zoo staff, identified as senior management, education staff, general zoo staff and zoo volunteers. These have a major stake in the success of the play setting as a recreational space, a site that supports the zoo's conservation education mission and the commercial success of the zoo.

Having obtained participants' voluntary informed consent, in line with the research ethics guidelines at the University of Gloucestershire, semi-structured interviews were carried out over a two-month period and transcribed verbatim. For consistency, the researcher was the only person who interviewed the range of stakeholders and transcribed recordings. The questions for the interviews revolved around perceptions of the value of having a play setting at the zoo; the philosophy behind the setting; and challenges of incorporating a play setting within a zoo. These broadly coincided with the general staff and volunteer survey questions carried out during the same period. As part of the interview, participants were given a small dry erase board and asked to draw mind maps. In this case, the central topic was the play setting and the mapping was used to gather a richer understanding of participants' thoughts, ideas and connections (Buzan, 1995). Kinchin et al (2010) suggests that mind maps can help unravel the complexities of the research question by focusing on participants' perceptions. Figure 7.1 shows an example of an interview question and mind map created during the interview process. Data were collected from six senior managers and the play setting coordinator, who manages its daily operations. For the purpose of this chapter, senior staff will be identified as A, B, C, etc. Participating zoo departments included: A Design; B Horticulture; C Play Setting Team; D Visitor Services; E Animal Collection; F Director's office; G Education.

Figure 7.1: Example of mind map and interview question

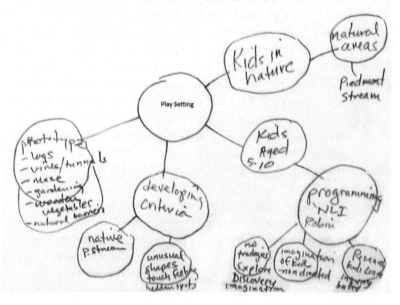

Source: Research participant (photo Linda Kinney)

The purpose of the zoo-wide survey was to gather insight from a broad range of stakeholders. All zoo employees and volunteers were invited to take an online survey. A link to the survey was sent to staff through an organisational email and to volunteers through the volunteer email network. The survey contained seven questions: four of the seven questions were closed questions which were categorical in nature; the remaining three questions were open-ended. Research questions targeted the philosophy behind the play setting; its congruence with the zoo's mission; participants' perception of its purpose and value; challenges associated with the play setting; what stands out about the play setting; what changes are needed, if any, at the play setting; and the three words participants would use to describe the play setting. One quarter of the staff responded which was both adequate and encouraging since employees rarely respond to a non-mandated survey. This response could be an indication of the strong feelings associated with having a nature play setting with the zoo.

Emerging values of play at the zoo

After the transcriptions were complete, the text was broken down into manageable and meaningful segments (Attride-Stirling, 2001). Listening to the interview recordings while looking over each participant's mind map (and situating the mind maps against the transcripts) gave further insight into their thought processes. Examining the mind maps also afforded the opportunity to see if any new relationships would be revealed. There was quite a bit of diversity between the maps; ranging from a relatively simple spoke form to a complex sprawling free form network (see Figures 7.2 and 7.3).

Figure 7.2: Simple spoke map

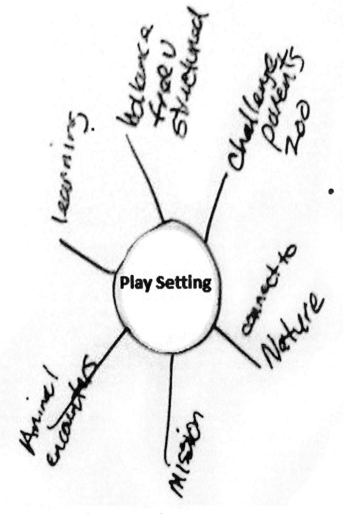

Source: Research participant (photo Linda Kinney)

Figure 7.3: More complex map

Source: Research participant (photo Linda Kinney)

During the interviews the mapping process sparked many new ideas and memories; and even though some maps looked less complex, it did not mean that the content was less rich. The maps served as a useful means of recall, providing a non-traditional way to capture 'unique memories' (Legard et al, 2003, cited in Wheeldon and Faubert, 2009). Once the themes were determined a matrix was developed to illustrate the connections across categories. While reviewing the interviews, differing stakeholder perceptions of the play setting's importance and benefits began to emerge and this was further refined by returning to Beunderman's (2010) model and categorising according to the three main values attributed to children's play and play settings, namely intrinsic, instrumental and institutional values. Findings will be discussed using these three themes in the next section.

Intrinsic value: 'a place to play'

'Intrinsic values are the values that relate to the subjective experience of culture intellectually, emotionally and spiritually' (Holden, 2005, p 9). These values are difficult to measure and sometimes hard to articulate. Beunderman (2010) suggests that intrinsic values are tied to the subjective experience of play and difficult to express as outcomes; however, they emphasise positive freedoms that empower human beings to live a fuller life, beyond the instrumental expectations of society.

Staff observations in the setting demonstrated children were playfully engaged with the environment (taken to mean the physical landscape, materials, other children and adults) and often did not want to leave the area, even at their parent's urging to visit the remainder of the zoo. The children were playing for the sheer joy of it, and for the most part, were free from adult direction and control. They valued playing for its own sake. The play staff also created intrinsic value through their support of the play process and providing a rich variety of opportunities for playing. Staff and volunteers, including senior staff also recognised and valued the opportunity for children to have fun and play at the zoo, but they attributed the greatest value of the play setting as a vehicle for discovery and learning about nature. Several participants described much of the zoo experience as rather passive: "It is a different aspect of something else along with the other experiences – instead of looking at stuff, it is doing stuff…hands-on; playing" (Participant G).

What stood out most for the participants who had observed playing in the setting was seeing children fully engaged with their surroundings and taking ownership of the play environment.

Instrumental value: connecting children with nature

For Holden (2006, p 16) instrumental value can be described as 'the ancillary effects of culture, where culture is used to achieve a social or economic purpose'. This kind of value tends to be captured in outcomes. An example would be using nature play to build an environmental ethic. All participating staff felt the greatest value of the play setting was in the benefits gained through environmental education programmes. They were in agreement that the play setting was designed to introduce children to nature or teach them about the natural environment. All interviewees viewed the play setting as a place that provided opportunities for environmental exploration; developing empathy for animals; and fostering a love of nature with the shared purpose of building future conservationists. Everything described above can happen when children play outdoors, but senior managements' perceptions of the value of children engaging in nature play focused on the adult's role in implementing meaningful facilitation/programming. Participant A's comment neatly summed up the responses:

> "I see the setting as fitting into the zoo's mission to encourage the love of nature; to value the natural world and eventually to become conservationists themselves: to become aware of the bigger picture, eventually, gradually, that is what this playing outside and the whole experiential nature of the setting is."

The primary idea that emerged from the analysis was that the play environment is a rich, textural environment designed to immerse children in nature. Connected to its physical design was the importance of adult guided programming. Several participants voiced concerns for the need for meaningful facilitation. Participant E felt that the play staff should teach environmental messages:

> "I know that if we don't have a facility like that [a place to teach kids environmental messages] and we are going to rely on kids just wandering around the park [zoo] with their families to absorb those messages – it probably won't happen very well, although...I do know that it can work from personal experience to engage these kids."

Play in the setting was primarily viewed in the context of play and learning. Participant F acknowledges that some children will run into the setting and build forts; however, the interviewee suggests that others will need help, pointing out that careful consideration should be given to the messages and kind of play introduced. Participant F also felt that having structure in the setting may be needed to help them become comfortable with playing more freely. What is striking here is that during the interviews, childhood memories of playing were sentimental accounts of the staffs' (or their children's) time playing outside either alone or with friends. Although they drew the conclusion that these experiences were instrumental in developing their love of the environment, they did not address the complexities of experiences throughout a lifetime that shapes who we are.

The survey revealed that zoo staff perceptions of the play setting's purpose are consistent with the senior management opinions revealed through the interviews. *Learn about nature* received the greatest number of responses; *play in nature* and *explore the outdoors* ranked a close second; and *just for fun for kids* was ranked fourth. The percentage rating across Strongly Agree, Agree, Neutral, Disagree or Strongly Disagree showed that zoo staff also agreed with senior staff that having a nature play space was in alignment with the zoo's mission. The volunteers who responded to the survey also agreed that the purpose of the play setting was to connect children with nature. Volunteers were also concerned that the play setting lacked a strong animal presence and that parents' buy-in was needed to allow children to stay and play. The volunteers also tended to corroborate the management and staff views that having a nature play setting for children was an asset to the zoo.

Institutional value: the institution's stake in a nature play setting

The final major theme relates to institutional value or the 'processes and techniques that organisations adopt in how they work to create value for the public' (Holden, 2006, p 17). In the context of supporting play, these values relate to the policies and everyday practices organisations adopt to create play opportunities (Beunderman, 2010). Therefore, this connects to the policies and procedures which the zoo adopts to provide a fun, recreational experience for park visitors, including the organisation's support of the play setting and its staff.

The zoo is a popular destination for families and a great deal of time and money is spent on finding ways to provide a wide range of experiences for visitors by hosting special events, exhibits and promotions. A nature play setting contributes to this as an 'added value,' and therefore it is important to senior management that visitors enjoy their time in the play setting. Senior staff also recognise the importance of generating public trust not only in the institution as a fun, safe, family oriented place to visit but as an organisation that cares about the community and in the case of the zoo, the environment.

Using the Value Triangle to capture the values of the play setting illustrates the different perceptions of purpose and value of having a nature play space at the zoo. Finally, all participants were asked to sum up the play setting in three words. The words that occurred most often were *play*, *fun*, *nature* and *educational*. However, the volunteers offered a wide range of responses when they were asked to choose three words to describe the setting. Word choices ranged from *fun*, *awesome*, *educational* and *natural* to *supervised mayhem*, *non-educational*, *tear it down* and *a waste of tax-payers' money* revealing that misunderstandings of the value of play at the zoo still exist among many of the institutional stakeholders.

There are limitations to this study, notably the lack of a more rigorous examination of the survey results; the need to include all stakeholders in the study (however, due to construction at the play setting, the nature of the study changed to focus on the institution's stakeholders); and the difficulty of drawing the mind map while talking. Nevertheless, it is possible to discern the complex ways in which diverse stakeholders value the provision of a separate environment for play within the zoo. However, as Beunderman (2010) points out, although all three forms of value matter and are often in tension with each other, without intrinsic value the other two will be diminished.

Conclusion

The study highlighted the different attribution of value from diverse stakeholders. Although the setting supports opportunities for play, it is also situated within a zoo, which includes conservation education as part of its mission. For both the zoo and the play setting, continuing public support is important for their success but, following Holden (2004), this will only come about if ways can be found to express how institutions create value.

Developing a better understanding of why 'connecting children with nature' is important and the importance of play in children's lives could lead to the understanding that there is value to children playing on their own terms as well as participating in environmental education programmes. Holden (2004) points out that tensions will always exist, and in addition to recognising the tensions, it is important to feel the emotions behind them. Understanding the needs of the stakeholders, listening to them and respecting their different viewpoints can lead to healthier relationships and work environments. Additionally, a better understanding of play could lead to exploring children playing at the zoo beyond designating segregated spaces for play.

Within communities around the world and throughout time, adults have designed playgrounds for children. Hart (2002) points out that building a segregated space for children began with the social and moral goals of the reformers who believed that children were being improperly socialised. So looking beyond a segregated space for children to play, there may be an opportunity to consider how the zoo itself may be a playful environment (for both adults and children). Children are the major stakeholder of the zoo's nature play setting and should be considered a major stakeholder for the entire zoo. If they are to be considered equal citizens within the zoo community, then they should have an equal opportunity to navigate the zoo playfully: to find special kid *pass throughs*, climb a rock, find a secret path, discover hidden treasures and anticipate what might be around the corner.

Returning to the metaphor of zoos and game reserves, the play setting's staff must operate in both zoos and game reserves. Zoo management will invariably push the boundaries inwards while the play staff and playing children will continue to resist and push back. Like playworkers, the play setting's staff must stay focused on the playing child while at the same time acknowledging other perceptions. Children will always be playing with the boundaries as they explore a wide range of emotions and play types:

This playing at the boundaries gives rise to wonderful and 'aweful' forms – as explored through children's development of peer friendships, their pretend play and associated languages and rituals, the folklore of children and their relationship with place. Such cultural forms and expressions are features of game reserves (Lester, 2015, p 233).

References

Attride-Sterling, A. (2001) 'Thematic networks: An analytic tool for qualitative research', *Qualitative Research*, 1(3): 385.

Bateson, G. (1973) *Steps to an ecology of mind: Collected essays in anthropology, psychiatry, evolution and epistemology*, London: Paladin, Granada.

Beunderman, J. (2010) *People make play: The impact of staffed play provision on children, families and communities*, London: National Children's Bureau.

Buzan, T. (1995) *The mind map book* (2nd edn), London: BBC Books.

Čapek, S. (2010) 'Foregrounding nature: An invitation to think about shifting nature-city boundaries', *City and Community*, 9(2): 208–24.

Carson, R. (1956) *The sense of wonder*, New York: Harper and Row.

Chawla, L. (2006) 'Learning to love the natural world enough to protect it', *Barn*, 2: 57–78.

Chawla, L. (2007) 'Childhood experiences associated with care for the natural world: A theoretical framework for empirical results', *Children, Youth and Environments*, 17(4): 144–70.

Clayton, S. and Opotow, S. (eds) (2003) *Identity and the natural environment: The psychological significance of nature*, Cambridge,MA: Massachusetts Institute of Technology Press.

Crotty, M. (1998) *The foundations of social research: Meaning and perspective in the research process*, Thousand Oaks, CA: Sage.

Davey, G. (2006) 'Relationship between exhibit naturalism, animal visibility and visitor interest in a Chinese Zoo', *Applied Animal Behaviour Science*, 96(1–2): 93–102.

Ewert, A., Place, G. and Sibthorp, J. (2005) 'Early-life outdoor experiences and an individual's environmental attitudes', *Leisure Sciences*, 27(3): 225–39.

Golder, B. and Gawler, M. (2005) *Cross-cutting tool: Stakeholder analysis*, World Wildlife Fund, http://wwf.panda.org/what_we_do/how_we_work/programme_standards.

Harker, C. (2005) 'Playing and affective time-spaces', *Children's Geographies*, 3(1): 47–62.

Hart, R. (2002) 'Containing children: Some lessons on planning for play from New York city', *Environment and Urbanization*, 14(2): 135–48.

Holden, J. (2004) *Capturing cultural value: How culture has become a tool of government policy*, London: Demos.

Holden, J. (2005) *Valuing culture in the southeast*, London: Demos.

Holden, J. (2006) *Cultural value and the crisis of legitimacy*, London: Demos.

Ingold, T. (2011) *The perception of the environment: Essays on livelihood, dwelling and skill*, London: Routledge.

Karsten, L. (2005) 'It all used to be better? Different generations on continuity and change in urban children's daily use of space', *Children's Geographies*, 3(3): 275–90.

Keene, A. (2000) 'Complexity theory: The changing role of leadership', *Industrial and Commercial Training*, 32(1): 15–18.

Kellert, S. (2002) 'Experiencing nature: Affective, cognitive and evaluative development in children', in P. Kahn and S. Kellert (eds) *Children and nature: Psychological, sociocultural and evolutionary investigations*, Cambridge, MA: Massachusetts Institute of Technology Press, pp 117–52.

Kinchin, I. Streatfield, D. and Hay, D. (2010) 'Using concept mapping to enhance the research interview', *International Journal of Qualitative Methods*, 9(1): 52–68.

Kuo, F. (2010) *Parks and other green environments: Essential components of a healthy human habitat*, Ashburn, VA: National Recreation and Park Association.

Legard, R., Keegan, J. and Ward, K. (2003) 'In-depth interviews', in J. Ritchie and J. Lewis (eds) *Qualitative research practice: A guide for social science students and researchers*, Thousand Oaks, CA: Sage, pp 138–69.

Lester, S. (2010) *Managing and supporting playwork practice workbook*, Gloucester: University of Gloucestershire.

Lester, S. (2015) *Play cultures and children's communities workbook*, Gloucester: University of Gloucestershire.

Lester, S. and Russell, W. (2008) *Play for a change – play, policy and practice: A review of contemporary perspectives*, London: National Children's Bureau.

Lindquist, G. (2001) 'Elusive Play and its relation to power', *Focaal – European Journal of Anthropology*, 37: 13–23.

Louv, R. (2005) *Last child in the woods: Saving our kids from nature deficit disorder*, Chapel Hill, NC: Algonquin Books.

Mayer, F.S., Frantz, C.M., Bruehlman-Senecal, E. and Dolliver, K. (2008) 'Why is nature beneficial? The role of connectedness to nature', *Environment and Behavior*, 41(5): 607–43.

Moore, R. (1977) 'The environmental design of children-nature relations: Some strands of applicative theory', in *Children, nature, and the urban environment: Proceedings of a symposium-fair*, General Technical Report NE-30. Upper Darby, PA: US Department of Agriculture, Forest Service, Northeastern Forest Experiment Station, pp 206–13.

Moore, R. (1986) *Childhood's domain: Place and play in child development*, London: Croom Helm.

Moore, R. (2014) *Nature play and learning places: Creating and managing places where children engage with nature*, Raleigh, NC: Natural Learning Initiative and Reston, VA: National Wildlife Federation.

Nabhan, G. and Trimble, S. (1994) *The geography of childhood: Why children need wild places*, Boston, MA: Beacon Press.

Nicholson, S. (1971) 'How NOT to cheat children: The theory of loose parts', *Landscape Architecture*, 62(1): 30–4.

Ogden, J. (2015) *Family nature clubs and you toolkit: Zoos and aquariums connecting families to nature*, Association of Zoos and Aquariums, www.aza.org/nature-play/#AZA_Toolkit_FamilyNatureClubs.

Ogden, J. and Heimlich, J.E. (2009) 'Why focus on zoo and aquarium education?', *Zoo Biology*, 28(5): 357–60.

PPSG (Playwork Principles Scrutiny Group) (2005) *The Playwork Principles*, Cardiff: Play Wales.

Ramey, L. (2010) 'Rekindling memories of yesterday's children: Making the case for nature-based unstructured play for today's children', *Journal of Sustainability Education*, 1(1): 228–54.

Shettel-Neuber, J. (1988) 'Second- and third-generation zoo exhibits: A comparison of visitor, staff, and animal responses', *Environment and Behavior*, 20(4): 452–73.

Sibley, D. (1995) *Geographies of exclusion*, London: Routledge.

Skår, M. and Krogh, E. (2009) 'Changes in children's nature-based experiences near home: From spontaneous play to adult-controlled, planned and organised activities', *Children's Geographies*, 7(3): 339–54.

Sobel, D. (2002) *Children's special places: Exploring the role of forts, dens and bush houses in middle childhood*, Detroit, MI: Wayne State University Press.

Sobel, D. (2008) *Childhood and nature: Design principles for educators*, Portland, ME: Stenhouse Publishers.

Sturrock, G., Russell, W. and Else, P. (2004) *Towards ludogogy, parts I, II and III. The art of being and becoming through play*, Sheffield: Ludemos.

Thompson, C.W., Aspinall, P. and Montarzino, A. (2007) 'The childhood factor: Adult visits to green places and the significance of childhood experience', *Environment and Behavior*, 40(1): 111–43.

Vadala, C.E., Bixler, R.D. and James, J.J. (2007) 'Childhood play and environmental interests: Panacea or snake oil?', *The Journal of Environmental Education*, 39(1): 3–18.

Ward, C. (1979) *The child in the city*, Harmondsworth: Penguin.

Well, N.M. and Evans, G.W. (2003) 'Nearby nature: A buffer of life stress among rural children', *Environment & Behavior*, 35(3): 311–30.

Wheeldon, J. and Faubert, J. (2009) 'Framing experience: Concept maps, mind maps, and data collection in qualitative research', *International Journal of Qualitative Methods*, 8(3): 68–83.

EIGHT

Your space or mine? Play in out of school clubs

Rebekah Jackson

Introduction

The origins of this study are rooted in a desire to explore adults' design intentions for environments for children's play. Through observations it was evident that there were many complex pressures that affect the design of such environments and this study seeks to examine the context or 'how and why' behind the adult design process and whether playwork interventions work to maintain these design intentions.

There are accepted fundamental writings and theories that underpin the development of a playwork approach in the UK (for example, Sturrock and Else, 1998; Brown, 2003; Hughes, 2003; 2012). However, there is little research that explores the ways in which playwork theory informs practice. While contemporary research into children's play embraces an increasing inter-disciplinary approach (see for example Fagen, 2011; Woodyer, 2012), few published works in playwork utilise recent theorising; there remains a persistent gap in academic literature which examines the ways in which playwork understandings and practices support or constrain environmental conditions for children's play. This is particularly noticeable in the UK context of 'out of school care' where research is limited and generally focuses on the economic value of provision for supporting adults into the labour market or enhancing children's social skills or educational attainment (see, for example, Barker et al, 2003; Wikeley et al, 2007). While out of school care may be ascribed, following Beunderman (2010), with important instrumental and institutional value, little attention has been given to the ways in which settings recognise and support the intrinsic value of play (see Smith and Barker, 2000a; 2000b; Smith, 2010; and Kane, 2015 for exceptions). As Beunderman (2010) asserts, it is this intrinsic value, that is, the freedom, fun and enjoyment associated with playing, that gives rise to potential instrumental and institutional benefit and as such must be the primary focus for playwork provision. Given this, the overall intention of this study was to provide practice-based research into the phenomenon of constructions of space in play settings. The intention in this small-scale case study is not to generalise, rather it is to suggest ways in which we can pay greater attention to the everyday and particular actions of playworkers to better understand the complex processes involved and how they may inhibit or support conditions for playing.

The aim of this study, therefore, was to explore the everyday practices, habits and routines of playworkers in an afterschool club in the northwest of England (hereafter the 'ASC') and the ways in which these help shape children's lived experience within the setting. Of key interest is the relationship between espoused playwork intentions for the design of a play environment and what happens in practice. In doing so, it draws on a number of interrelated concepts drawn from the field of children's geographies that suggest spaces are not fixed containers for action or a background against which humans carry out their interactions, but are actively produced by the ongoing encounters between adults, children, materials, movements, affects, imaginations and so on (Massey, 2005; Horton and Kraftl, 2006). A 'play space' does not pre-exist its formation but is co-created and emerges from the prevailing conditions. In this sense, playing may be seen as an open-ended process that appears in unpredictable ways.

As the ethical foundations for playwork practice, the Playwork Principles (PPSG, 2005) articulate that 'play is a process that is freely chosen, personally directed and intrinsically motivated'. In elaborating this, the Playwork Principles suggest that the primary purpose of playwork is to create an environment with children where they can play. This would imply that practitioners have an appreciation of the complexity of spatial productions that exceeds simple cause–effect relationships which often reduces design to the physical arrangement of materials to effect certain types of play. Following Kyttä (2004) this produces a field of promoted action in which, for example, the arts and crafts table, the dressing-up area or quiet corner are intended to foster specific play behaviours.

While spaces are always in the process of being produced and are open to all sorts of possibilities, they are also imbued with power relationships, and dominant forces (in this case generally the adults) have considerable influence in shaping the possible movements and encounters within the setting. Relationships between adults and children are an entangled flux of interactions and relations, and it is these interactions which constantly tip the balance of power in favour of one or the other party with a resulting impact on children's use of space (Gallacher, 2005). The intention here was to pay closer attention to these entanglements and how they produce environments that might be more or less open to moments of play emerging.

Designing an approach

In designing this study, it was important to recognise not only the relationships and entanglements that co-produce spaces for children's play but also the complex relationship between playwork theory and practice. A traditional divide maintains that theory is logical and valid while practice is disorderly (Lenz-Taguchi, 2010). Practice is often judged against apparently remote and objective concepts, but in fact everyday encounters and interactions in a play setting are always producing and re-producing 'theory'. The intention here was to examine practitioner understandings and ways in which ideas, values and beliefs are enacted in practice. It recognises that 'There is no objective truth waiting for us to discover it. Truth, or meaning, comes into existence in and out of our engagement with the realities in our world' (Crotty, 1998, pp 8–9). Such meanings are not fixed but constantly shifting; ideas and actions cannot be isolated from the complex contexts in which they are formed. Attention, thus, is drawn towards the multiple material and discursive influences both within and outside the setting and their effects on everyday practices. In recognition of this an in-depth case study approach was selected. This methodology for research allows the 'researcher to study contemporary phenomena in a real-life setting, where boundaries between context and phenomenon tend to be blurred' (Gibbert and Ruigrok, 2010, p 712). A qualitative case study approach also allows the researcher to reveal interrelated and contingent phenomena and observe the complexity of the process of designing children's play spaces. Case study research draws on a range of methods in a *bricoleur* manner (Hyett et al, 2014) and is both descriptive and exploratory. The afterschool club where the study took place responded to a call for participation sent to a network of providers with whom the researcher had previously worked. An initial meeting was held where the study was introduced and voluntary informed consent obtained from eight of the 15 staff members (not all of whom work each day), in line with University of Gloucestershire's guidelines for ethical research. The primary methods developed for this study were:

- initial face-to-face, semi-structured interviews with the playwork team, in order to begin to untangle the power relations and provide context to the analysis and to examine the playworkers' understanding of their role and the use of space within the setting;
- the interviews were followed by a period of observations within the setting, focusing on playwork design, interventions and interactions;
- follow-up interviews with staff to discuss observations of practice were carried out after observation notes had been compared with interview recordings to analyse how observed practice related to the playworkers' statements of intent. In these interviews participants were asked to consider how existing practices, both those observed and those discussed, may be supporting or constraining children's use of space and how the ways in which children's contributions to the production of space, including everyday and minor contestations of adult intentions for space, were affecting them as practitioners;
- throughout the process participants were asked to keep a reflective diary using Hughes' (1996) intuition, memory, experience and evidence (IMEE) model as a structure for reflection and to provide reflective material for discussion at the final interview stage of the project. The intention of this was to promote more reflexivity in practice and to expose any gaps between espoused theory and 'theory in use' that develops from habitual ways of working with children (Palmer, 2003). Palmer (2003) suggests that playworkers should consider and challenge the gap between espoused theory and 'theory in use' and whether either or both match their day-to-day practice.

The afterschool club that took part in this study is based on the edge of a large town in Cheshire and is one of the multiple childcare services offered from birth upwards. It operates across two mobile buildings with a canopy covered walkway between them. One of the buildings is used as a nursery during the day, and the other is used by the preschool-aged children during school hours and by the out of school club outside school hours. The buildings offer access not only to their own enclosed play area to the front of the buildings but also to the extensive school playing fields to the rear and they are able to use the multi-use games area once it is no longer needed by the school. The afterschool club is registered with Ofsted (the registration and inspection authority for care services for children and young people and for education services in England) and provides up to 80 places for children each day. The youngest children in the out of school club (4- and 5-year-old children) have a 'base' in the nursery building and the older children have a 'base' within the out of school building. The staff team have all achieved a nationally recognised vocational qualification at Level 2 or above. Three of these are Playwork qualifications with the remainder holding Higher Level Teaching Assistant qualifications or Early Years Education qualifications. The staff team had completed training on the Playwork Principles (PPSG, 2005) among other short courses.

Analysis of the data is presented here across the following interrelated themes: shared space; designing space (routines, habits and competing values); everyday interactions (supporting or constraining children's play); and power.

Your space or mine? Sharing space(s)

A theme across a number of interviews was the difficulty faced by the playworkers when sharing space between themselves and the other childcare sessions run during the day. Staff explained that there is limited time between childcare sessions, and the ritual tasks such as collecting children, staff change over, and the dual use of space does not afford sufficient time for the playworkers to reshape the environment before the children come in. One playworker explained:

> "We just set it up as we always have. There isn't time for anything else. By the time you've come in, found out who you're collecting (from school) and got your register you have to be over at the school. When you get back the kids just pick up wherever they left off. There's no need for us to set anything different up, if the kids want something then they know where to find it. Any changes we make, we do as the session goes on but of course you have to remember that we have to get it back into shape before 6pm when we finish."

There are a number of conflicting pressures on the adults in the setting that affect their ability to support the production of a place for children to play. The overwhelming pressure described by the staff interviewed was the need to meet the regulatory requirements of their Ofsted registration which enables them to operate. The setting holds registration from 3 years of age upwards and a large number of children that attend the setting are under 5 years of age. This necessitates the setting demonstrating that is adheres to both the Early Years Foundation Stage (EYFS) and the Childcare Register requirements. The staff identified difficulty in prioritising the Playwork Principles over their particular understanding of the EYFS requirements. In the nursery room, the room design is typical of an environment maintained by adults with the intention of supporting the learning and development of young children. There are clearly labelled resource boxes on low level shelving; defined role-play and activity areas, such as mark making; an adjacent sleeping room; and a reading area with cushions and beanbags. Within this space, the playworkers demonstrated different approaches in their practice than in the other 'afterschool' room. In the 'nursery' room, playworkers were observed to be more didactic in their interventions (Russell, 2008) than when the same playworkers were observed with a different group of children in the 'afterschool' room.

The interactions between adults and children appeared less playful and more directive in nature, and the children's ability to navigate the environment was generally more restricted. For example, where older children in the afterschool room were observed subverting the pre-ordained structure of the space by taking action men figures outside, it was seen by the playworkers and accepted. In the nursery room, children were directed to return toys to the right baskets and were not permitted to remove books from the reading area. Such a tightly controlled sense of order in the nursery room by the playworkers resulted in an adult dominated 'closed' space (Sibley, 1995), a strongly defined environment with clear boundaries, where people adhere to and aspire to accepted norms and values. Within closed spaces, 'fitting in' is maintained through the rituals, rules, hierarchy and dominance of one actor (or group of actors) over another and in this case the children's agency as co-creators of the space was significantly limited.

Designing space: routines, habits and competing values

It is recognised that there are times when adults need to be present in places where children play in order to support children in staying safe, dispel parental fears and to satisfy legal requirements. The Playwork Principles (PPSG, 2005) promote the primacy of the play process over other adult agendas, focusing the role of the adult on supporting the creation of an environment where children can play, advocacy, and a considered approach to intervention. Play and playwork theory also recognises that children do not need adults to play as all children have an intrinsic play drive (Sturrock and Else, 2005). The Playwork Principles (PPSG, 2005), as an accepted framework for practice, encourage playworkers to interact with children in a way that is supportive of the playing child, recognising that playing is unpredictable, emergent and uncertain. This requires playworkers to be flexible, responsive and dynamic in their interactions with children, focused on supporting the creation of an environment in which children can play (Lester and Russell, 2008), and remaining in balance with the things that happen in a playwork setting that are not 'play' but which might contribute to a 'playful feel'.

Newstead (2009) argues that although the language used to describe playwork is shared with other professions, a playwork methodology is unique, in that the key elements that define it as a way of interacting with children all link to relationships. Massey's (2005) concept of space is valuable here in recognising that space is always co-produced by encounters and interactions between heterogeneous 'agents' including humans, imaginations, materials and so on. Massey explains that spaces are constantly being produced and never 'finished' and as such they exist in the realm of possibility. An afterschool club by its very nature of being a playwork setting is designed to be open to playful possibility; children's play is not necessarily ordered and rational and settings operating in line with the Playwork Principles are supportive of the emergence of irrationality and disorder, or differently ordering, of bodies and materials to re-create and re-shape space. The habits, routines and everyday interactions of playworkers are vitally important in establishing the 'feel' of the setting and conditions in which children can co-create play spaces.

Observations undertaken when ritual tasks were being completed highlighted how the adults held the balance of power over design of the space in order to fulfil an adult agenda with consequent impact upon children's use of space. Snack time in this setting was observed to be firmly within the control of the adults. One member of staff routinely takes charge of 'rolling snack' where children come to the table when they are ready rather than there being a set time for all children to eat at once. Consequently, the snack tables are a permanent feature of the environment. It was observed that children are not allowed to play at the table, a rule which is enforced by the staff member who supervises them. Children were not permitted to bring toys to the table and playful behaviours were discouraged. The supervising playworker justified this approach during an interview:

> "parents (like to) know how much they've had to eat and there are so many of them to get through we have to make sure there isn't too much messing around. We don't really have the space to get them all sat down in one or two gos so we have to do it like this but it's definitely no messing or we'd never get through them all!"

Needing to complete the routines of the session, such as a 'rolling snack time', is a pressure felt by staff that in turn not only affects the design of the space but also diminishes the power children have to play across all spaces and at all times, drawing the adult away from their playwork role with the primary focus of supporting children's play frames (Sturrock et al, 2004).

Everyday interactions: supporting or constraining children's play?

Given what has been said about space and play, it may be suggested that planning or designing a space where children can play requires adults to pay attention to and question the routines, rituals and habits developed within day-to-day practice and to examine whether the 'everydayness' of 'how we do what we do' supports or constrains children playing. A closed space seeks to predict and order possible behaviours. For example, by rigidly implementing a planned programme of activities, adults may unwittingly limit the possibility that the environment affords the playing child (Kyttä, 2004). This undervalues an appreciation that children's play is influenced by multiple complex, interwoven factors and may play with and against the adults' intentions.

In contrast to the identification of 'closed spaces', Sibley (1995) identifies weakly defined 'open spaces' that are fluid and flexible and have not been named or defined therefore offering possibility and novelty. Play is emergent, and as such planning for play becomes more about supporting the emergent and indeterminate nature of play rather than following a 'blue print' of a perfect play space. Sibley's notion of open space sits comfortably with this; designing a play space is less about planning a timetable of activities and more about cultivating the conditions in which moments of play might emerge, which might, paradoxically, include 'activities' offered in the knowledge that these may be taken in any direction, forming part of creating conditions for play. Rather than a focus on ensuring that every child has a turn at the arts and crafts table and making sure that the prepared activities meet each area of learning and development, attention is turned towards qualities of an open space.

Thus a setting that fosters children's play should be one which offers the potential for change, to be modified, adapted or deconstructed via a wide range of movable resources, props, materials and structures. Gibson's (1979) concept of affordance refers to what the environment offers for the individual, and can be useful when considering the interrelationship between playing children and the environment.

Gibson suggests that affordances, or 'possibilities' for playing, arise from the interaction between the physical environment and the individual's interests, motivations and desires. Kyttä (2003; 2004; 2006) develops this further to consider the social and cultural aspects of actualising affordances, through proposing three fields of action. A field of constrained action limits actualisation either physically or through social and cultural prohibitions. The field of promoted action promotes actualisation. Children will seek to enlarge the field of free action, which sits in between and overlaps the fields of constrained and promoted action. Playful use of space can be affected in a multitude of ways, for example, through physical, cultural and organisational constraints and by direct interventions by adults. While playworkers cannot create fields of free action (since this would render it a field of promoted action), skilful playwork practice can extend children's actualisation of environmental affordances, supporting emergent play in more open and flexible spaces by encouraging and supporting children to act and move freely towards a 'field of free action'.

Through their longstanding relationship with the children, the staff interviewed said that they know what tends to be popular with the children and things that children are likely to enjoy. When asked further about how they then used what they know of the children's interests to shape the afterschool club's design, they discussed the equipment, toys and resources that they routinely set out to cover the kinds of activities that the children like to do. It is this knowledge which provides the 'continuous' environment in the club, aimed towards those activities that the staff team know will be successful and are always available. While the notion that the staff plan for successful activities might suggest that there is limited understanding of the play process represented in day-to-day practice, it is also important to recognise that the staff may also offer activities in the knowledge that the resources may be used in any number of ways by the children. The 'activity' itself may represent a field of promoted action; while the children may engage with this they may also seek a field of free action, and if conditions are right, play will emerge in a largely unpredictable manner.

There are numerous tensions and ambiguities in this process that counter adult presumed cause–effect relationships. During interview, the owner of the setting detailed how after attending a training course the staff team reviewed the environment and created some private semi-permanent teepee dens from sheer fabric which provided some secluded spaces for children. Drawing on Kyttä's (2004) taxonomy, these dens are promoted fields of action created by the adults as a result of their collective reflections. The idea of ready-made dens suggests that adults want to provide for specific play forms yet these have become a favourite space within the club. The staff who work in the preschool during the school day have also noticed the younger children playing in them too. The owner recalled that the preschool children often search under the cushions in the den to find any items that the older children may have left over or hidden at the end of the out of school club session and this provides much fascination and amusement for the children when they do find the remains of the older children's play. This serves as an example of how the older children may resist the adult requirement to spend some time tidying up toward the end of the session and potentially maximising their play time while also further subverting the adult order of where toys are kept within the club. While the adults appear to find the shared use of space an added difficulty for them in completing their tasks, this does not appear to have had a negative impact on the children's playful use of space. Drawing again on Kyttä's (2004) fields of action it is interesting to note that while promoted and constrained fields of action often collude to limit children's playful desires, there are occasions when adult promotions, such as the teepee in the above example, may lead to children creating fields of free action, or the co-creation of a 'play space' from the promoted use of space.

Gallacher's (2005) study examining the geography of a toddler room in a nursery establishes that the children's understanding of the rules allow them to create a vibrant 'peer culture underlife' entwined with the official organised world created by adults. Through the children's exploitation and identification of the gaps and weaknesses in the adult design, they carve out alternative play spaces away from the adult gaze which lead the adults to reshape and reassess their technologies of control to attempt to restore order. An example of this at the ASC was demonstrated when children were playing with the adult imposed boundary to the edge of the playing field. The two boys were observed jumping over the narrow path that winds around the outer edge of the playing field. The path is used as the outer boundary of the playable space and the two children were jumping in and out of the permissible area and were not stopped by the adults. When questioned why she did not intervene, she felt that it was not really breaking the rules and that the children were not going to come to any harm by what they were doing. She further explained that the boundary had been defined by the adults not the children and that it was not strictly enforced by the adults, so children test the boundary regularly and staff would often patrol the boundary by walking along the path. Amit (2003, cited in Leverett, 2011, p 19) suggests that while children are not necessarily able to exert direct control or influence over the use of a space, they still exert their will by making and remaking spaces at a micro-level thorough exerting a form of indirect 'tactical agency'.

Power

The issue of power and control over space is constantly negotiated by everyday movements and actions. The following example highlights a more deliberate process of rearranging the setting. During interviews staff discussed the rationale for creating the environment and the development of the older children's lounge area. They had spent time talking to the children about the play opportunities in the club environment and children expressed dissatisfaction. The staff recognised that only a handful of children used the computer room and that it was largely empty during the sessions. In response the staff decided to create an area predominantly for the older children where they could relax, chat and chill out after school, and created 'The Lounge'.

It was observed that The Lounge has been marked out as under the control of the children by a sign on the door stating that it is for *'Years 5 and 6 only...knock to come in.'* Staff as well as other children knocked and waited for permission to enter, supporting the children to retain power over this space. The same adults who appeared sufficiently preoccupied in their practice with concerns for children's safety resulting in segregation of the youngest children, do not appear to share the same prevailing concerns for the safety of the children within this space and this affords the children to draw out some freedom from the adult gaze.

The children who use this space have created, with some oversight from the playworkers, a set of rules for its use. A playworker explained that the children know that the adults "keep an eye on them through the windows, but we do want to give them their own space and some privacy as they are old enough now," and went on to explain that "it was the children who put up the sign on the door, we just didn't have the heart to take it down. Unless it gets really bad in there, I suppose we'll leave it up and play by their rules."

Of note here are the different adult perceptions of what children across the age groups deserve in terms of privacy and supervision when using the respective spaces and how this has allowed a particular group of children to wrest an element of control back from the adults. The adults believe that they are allowing children some privacy and that they ultimately retain control and in doing so afford the children the luxury of self-regulation within a co-constructed set of rules and boundaries.

Furthermore, they believe that they have retained the ability to re-instate adult control. This may well be true, and the children may feel differently, but what is clear is that the children know how much they can 'get away with' before the adults will intervene, and this balancing of power and control and sense of 'playing by the rules' just enough from both sides, seems to be what makes this sharing of power work on this occasion.

Smith and Barker's (2000a; 2000b) study of play in afterschool provision found that most of the play activities on offer were planned by adult staff and represented 'an example of the inequitable distribution of power between children and adults inherent to the vast majority of clubs' (Smith and Barker, 2000a, p 248). This raises an important question, as noted by Palmer (2003, p 180) who asks 'how many playworkers will express the need for children to have flexible environments to support their play and then practice in ways that restrict children's experience of the environment?'

While many of the playworkers interviewed said that they remembered looking at adult interventions into children's play as part of their training, and again recognised that playwork is an approach where "we as adults are more hands off", they demonstrated practice that was not congruent with principles of their training nor with the way they described how their practice should be. Almost all of the staff in this study had achieved a qualification in playwork, which under the National Occupational Standards (SkillsActive, 2010) cover 'working with children to create play spaces' and 'reflect on and develop practice', suggesting that the gap between the espoused theory and the theory in use is significant. A further observation that serves to demonstrate the gap between theory and practice was when three boys were pulling the large parachute along outside with it trailing behind them like a tail. A group of girls ducked under the tail of the parachute and ran along underneath it and after a short while they collapsed in a heap with some children under the parachute and some on top. A few children tried to roll themselves up in the parachute while there were others underneath. A member of staff shouted over to children on the floor telling them to "Get up. You will tear the parachute. Come and play a proper game nicely," and was seen to move the children off the parachute and begin a traditional parachute game. The noise level dropped and most of the children ebbed away. One could be heard being told to go away as they were not playing the game correctly. The adult in this example intervened in the children's play in a way which ended with no children playing with the parachute. Rather than supporting children's playful behaviour in this example, the adult intervention was not congruent with the playwork training that she had received, nor was it in line with the way in which, as a staff team, they talked about their job role.

Conclusions and closing thoughts: story-telling and reflections on practice

Spaces are products of human interrelationships, habits and rituals, materials and symbols, as well as the physical properties of the space (Massey, 2005), and when taken together these elements contribute to the 'feel' of the space. In this out of school club, the 'feel' of the space is somewhat contradictory. Some spaces are 'playable' and the children exert their tactical agency (Amit, 2003) and subvert adult control and design intentions, as shown with 'The Lounge', jumping over the outside boundary and the dens where children hide toys that should have been put away. Some spaces, like the nursery room and snack tables, become less playable by nature of the way the playworkers exert control through their interactions with the children.

Children live in very different worlds from adults and adults can only presume to know and therefore make guesses about what children require in the environments they are planning for their use (Thomson, 2007). This study has shown that it is important when adults are intending to create spaces that support children's play to not only consider the physical environment but also the messy, dynamic and complex interrelationships that make up the ongoing feel of the play setting. This involves paying more attention to the ways in which bodies, things, imaginations, movements and so on, the dimension of things being and existing at the same time (Massey, 2005), are productive of playful fields of free action. Space is imbued with stories, memories and shared history. Spaces only become play spaces when children play in them and as such to create a play space is more than having fun toys and appropriately sized furniture. It is about adults supporting a playful feel to a space. Letting things slide and bending the rules, hiding and discovering toys across age groups, deliberately not seeing something through a partially covered window all contribute to the shared multiplicity of connections between adults and children being playful or not. The degree to which the above support or constrain children's behaviour is what playworkers should focus their reflections and stories on in order to determine whether a space 'works' rather than a taken-for-granted notion of what has always worked here. The practice-based theory that is produced through the cycle of story-telling and re-telling is important in order to embed the Playwork Principles holistically into the everyday routines, habits and ritual that are entangled within the fabric of a play space. Playworkers need to subject their everyday practice to critical account in order to ground their practice within playwork theory, produce new theory from practice and to reflect upon whether their playwork understandings and practices support or constrain environmental conditions for children's play.

References

Amit, V. (2003) 'Epilogue: Children's places' in K.F. Olwig and E. Gulløv (eds) *Children's places: Cross cultural perspectives*, London: Routledge, pp 236–44.

Barker, J., Smith. F., Morrow, V., Weller, S., Hey, V. and Harwin, J. (2003) *The impact of out of school care: A qualitative study examining the views of children, families and playworkers*, DfES Research Report RR446, London: DfES.

Beunderman, J. (2010) *People make play: The impact of staffed play provision on children, families and communities*, London: National Children's Bureau.

Brown, F. (2003) 'Compound flexibility: The role of playwork in child development', in F. Brown (ed) *Playwork theory and practice*, Buckingham: Open University Press, pp 51–65.

Crotty, M. (1998) *The foundations of social research: Meaning and perspectives in the research process*, London: Sage.

Fagen, R. (2011) 'Play and development', in A. Pellegrini (ed) *The Oxford handbook of the development of play*, Oxford: Oxford University Press, pp 83–100.

Gallacher, L. (2005) '"The terrible twos": Gaining control in the nursery?', *Children's Geographies*, 3(2): 243–64.

Gibbert, M. and Ruigrok, W. (2010) 'The "what" and "how" of case study rigor: Three strategies based on published work', *Organizational Research Methods*, 13(4): 710–37.

Gibson, J. (1979) *The ecological approach to visual perception*, Boston, MA: Houghton Mifflin.

Horton, J. and Kraftl, P. (2006) 'Not just growing up, but going on: Materials, spacings, bodies, situations', *Children's Geographies*, 4(3): 259–76.

Hughes, B. (1996) *Play environments: A question of quality*, London: Playlink.

Hughes, B. (2003) 'Play deprivation, play bias and playwork practice', in F. Brown (ed) *Playwork theory and practice*, Buckingham: Open University Press, pp 66–80.

Hughes, B. (2012) *Evolutionary playwork and reflective analytic practice* (2nd edn), London: Routledge.

Hyett, N., Kenney, A. and Dickson-Swift, V. (2014) 'Methodology or method? A critical review of qualitative case study reports', *International Journal of Qualitative Studies on Health and Well-being*, 9, www.ijqhw.net/index.php/qhw/article/view/23606.

Kane, E. (2015) *Playing practices in school-age childcare: An action research project in Sweden and England*, Stockholm: Stockholm University.

Kyttä, M. (2003) *Children in outdoor contexts: Affordances and independent mobility in the assessment of environmental child friendliness*, PhD dissertation, Helsinki: Helsinki University of Technology.

Kyttä, M. (2004) 'The extent of children's independent mobility and the number of actualized affordances as criteria for child-friendly environments', *Journal of Environmental Psychology*, 24(2): 179–98.

Kyttä, M. (2006) 'Environmental child-friendliness in the light of the Bullerby Model', in C. Spencer and M. Blades (eds) *Children and their environments: Learning, using, and designing spaces*, Cambridge, UK: Cambridge University Press, pp 141–58.

Lenz-Taguchi, H. (2010) *Going beyond the theory/practice divide in early childhood education: Introducing an intra-active pedagogy*, London: Routledge.

Lester, S. and Russell, W. (2008) *Play for a change – play, policy and practice: A review of contemporary perspectives*, London: National Children's Bureau.

Leverett, S. (2011) 'Children's spaces', in P. Foley and S. Leverett (eds) *Children and young people's spaces: Developing practice*, Milton Keynes: Open University Press, pp 9–24.

Massey, D. (2005) *For space*, London: Sage.

Newstead, S. (2009) *Playwork and the Early Years Foundation Stage*, Eastleigh: Common Threads Publications.

Palmer, S. (2003) 'Playwork as reflective practice', in F. Brown (ed) *Playwork: Theory and practice*, Buckingham: Open University Press, pp 176–90.

PPSG (Playwork Principles Scrutiny Group) (2005) *The Playwork Principles*, Cardiff: Play Wales.

Russell, W. (2008) 'Modelling playwork: BRAWGS continuum, dialogue and collaborative reflection', in F. Brown and C. Taylor (eds) *Foundations in playwork*, Maidenhead: Open University Press, pp 84–8.

Sibley, D. (1995) *Geographies of exclusion: Society and difference in the west*, London: Routledge.

SkillsActive (2010) *Playwork National Occupational Standards*, London: SkillsActive.

Smith, F. and Barker, J. (2000a) 'Contested spaces: Children's experiences of out of school care in England and Wales', *Childhood*, 7(3): 315–33.

Smith, F. and Barker, J. (2000b) '"Out of school", in school: A social geography of out of school childcare', in S. Holloway and G. Valentine (eds) *Children's geographies: Playing, living, learning*, London: Routledge, pp 245–56.

Smith, H.H. (2010) *Children's empowerment, play and informal learning in two after school provisions*, PhD thesis, London: Middlesex University.

Sturrock, G. and Else, P. (1998) *The playground as therapeutic space: Playwork as healing (The Colorado Paper)*, Sheffield: Ludemos Press.

Sturrock, G. and Else, P. (eds) (2005) *Therapeutic playwork reader 2, 2000–2005*, Sheffield: Ludemos Associates.

Sturrock, G., Russell, W. and Else, P. (2004) *Towards ludogogy parts I, II and III: The art of being and becoming through play*, Sheffield: Ludemos.

Thomson, S. (2007) 'Do's and don'ts: Children's experiences of the primary school playground', *Environmental Education Research*, 13(4): 487–500.

Wikeley, F., Bullock, K., Muschamp, Y. and Ridge, T. (2007) *Educational relationships outside school: Why access is important*, York: Joseph Rowntree Foundation.

Woodyer, T. (2012) 'Ludic geographies: Not merely child's play', *Geography Compass*, 6(6): 313–26.

NINE

Co-creating spaces on an adventure playground: using participatory action research as an approach to continuing professional development

John Fitzpatrick and Bridget Handscomb

This chapter discusses the use of participatory action research (PAR) as an approach to reflective playwork practice and continuous professional development (CPD) for people engaged with children's play and playwork. The research took place on Homerton Grove Adventure Playground (HGAP) managed by Hackney Play Association (HPA) and based in Hackney, an inner city borough of London, UK (see Figure 9.1). It explores the conceptual framework and processes brought to this small-scale research project and the ensuing co-production of ways of thinking and acting with 'play'. Key themes include co-investigation, reflective playwork practice, dialogue, mapping, story-telling and working with meaning. The overall intention was to explore the ways in which playworkers at the playground make sense of and give meaning to their practice in designing and maintaining an environment for play. Working collaboratively with members of the play and playwork team at the University of Gloucestershire (UoG), the adventure playground team explored current articulations of design intentions and practices drawing on a range of conceptual approaches and tools alongside their working experiences. This brought a critical and reflective lens to the production of the Adventure Playground (AP), its everyday rhythms, routines and habits, and the ways in which adults and children co-create play spaces. It also brought opportunities to experiment with approaches that could deepen understandings of play and playwork practice in a variety of situations from training courses to conference workshops leading to more relevant and reflective approaches to adults working with children's play.

Figure 9.1: The playground

Source: Cecilia Divizia

The idea of working together with practitioners and academics on a project to develop shared knowledge and understanding had been emerging over a period of time. A number of both serendipitous and planned events had led towards creating the conditions whereby a partnership project connecting research, learning, theory and practice could begin. These were:

- Two senior staff members had studied at the UoG on the graduate and post-graduate play and playwork programmes.
- Collaborative approaches and working relationships as partners had already been forged through shared ventures in the development of learning, theory and practice in playwork including planning and delivering workshops, conferences and particularly through the Playwork London and UoG collaboration on the 'Thinking About Play' programme.
- HPA had recently become responsible for managing HGAP following a period of difficulties, and staff and trustees were keen to use a variety of analytical tools to review and develop what was offered in this established setting introducing a fresh perspective within a new framework.

These histories, relationships and encounters are mentioned early in the research story because they have particular significance and resonance. First, the need to recognise the fertile ground that was already prepared and its value in creating conditions whereby the seeds for open, flexible, participative, innovative and challenging work could grow. Second, the relevance of situational and relational contexts emerged as a recurring theme within the research project.

Initial exploratory discussions helped to identify a broad research focus and a commitment to working flexibly, inductively and intuitively within a simple framework while using shared underpinning principles as the overarching methodology. The core questions that informed the research focused on how children at play use space and how playworkers make sense of and give meaning to their practice in designing and maintaining a space for play. There was a shared curiosity to understand more about how the setting of an adventure playground affects, and is affected by, the children, adults and materials, plus a particular interest in the methodology of recording, analysing and reflecting on playwork practice. A full report of the research, *Co-creating an Adventure Playground (CAP): Reading playwork stories, practices and artefacts* (Lester et al) was published in 2014.

The development of the research project and its focus was negotiated between HPA and the UoG and implementation was led by the Playwork lecturers from the UoG, Stuart Lester and Wendy Russell, with support from John Fitzpatrick as Research Assistant from HPA who holds a Postgraduate Certificate in Play and Playwork from the UoG and is also a Playwork Assessor and Tutor within the HPA's Training and Assessment Centre. Opportunities to meet with playworkers and to introduce methods and approaches for collection of practice data were managed by Bridget Handscomb, the Play Development and Training Manager for HPA, manager of the playwork team at HGAP and graduate of the Playwork degree at the UoG.

Some research questions were identified to frame the project while seeking to retain sufficient flexibility to enable the co-investigators to influence lines of enquiry throughout the action research period. These were:

- What value does an action research approach to professional development have for playwork practice?
- How might theoretical concepts of the playful co-production of space in an adventure playground inform practice?
- What can be learned to inform policy development and shared practices at HGAP and with other adventure playgrounds?

The project started with two learning and development days for the full research and the playwork team. The programme was designed to ensure that the purpose, approach, methods, possibilities and constraints of this project were explored and participants were able to develop their understanding of what it would entail prior to giving informed consent.

This opportunity for dialogue threw up many questions and helped to clarify the reality of PAR in practice. Understandings of what it meant for the playworkers in the dual role as co-researchers as well as being research participants were evolving. Given the flexible and explorative nature of using PAR methods the issue of consent in relation to children, families, staff and the organisation was examined and debated in depth initially, then throughout the project and far beyond the active investigative research stage. In fact, after initial consent was given by everyone involved early in the project it was later revisited and adapted in order to meet changing wishes.

The research project was fully and actively supported by the HPA's staff team and trustees with particular support from Nicola Butler, HPA's Director. The playwork team were crucial to the research activities and to ongoing reflective practice and learning. The authors would like to acknowledge each individual and their invaluable contributions and give special recognition to Sarah Wilson and Eniola Odebunmi.

There were many discussions about the importance of exploring and capturing perceptions, perspectives, feelings, attitudes and emotions while also gathering data that could be described as factual or objective. How can what happens in a space – movements, routines, dynamics, tone, playfulness, and imaginations – be captured and then understood? How can the issues of limited time and opportunity to either write or discuss experiences be navigated? The challenge of being open and creative to using a diverse range of sources and methods for gathering information and making experiences visible to others was considered and all participants contributed ideas on potential artefacts, records and opportunities for capturing some sense of what happens. It was in these 'encounters between these practices marked by collective, intense and unpredictable experimentation' that 'new things may be born' (Olsson, 2009, p 104).

One of the approaches used was to gather documentary artefacts in as many forms as possible through a process described by Dahlberg and Moss (2005, p 107) as making 'practice visible'. This included writing, recording, mapping, sketching, audio, photos and video as ways to capture and describe what happens on the playground. In collecting these artefacts, the intention was not to find solutions to problems as it was impossible to plan or predict findings. Rather, small moments of playfulness were captured, and in exploring these many meanings and understandings emerged. An ambition was to try to draw out as much as possible from what, on the surface, might seem to be tiny and trivial moments. 'Underneath the large noisy events lie the small events of silence' (Deleuze, 1994, cited in Olsson, 2009, p 120).

The approach that emerged as the research progressed reflected a more rhizomatic quality influenced by the work of Deleuze and Guattari (1987). This approach avoids the more obvious cause and effect and linear progression of 'tracing' (reproducing more of the same in an attempt at accurate representation), aiming instead for 'mapping' (looking for lines and entry points that are new or unknown) (Leafgren, 2007). The team did not confine themselves to structured ways of thinking or approaching the research questions looking for a beginning, middle and end. They pulled at questions like bits of yarn to see where it took them and to where 'meaning making [was] a struggle full of contradictions and ambiguities' (Dahlberg et al, 1999, p 110). Through a series of discussions drawing on experiences, knowledge, observations, stories and reflections, a possibility space was created where multiple understandings were produced. These discussions were recorded and transcribed. 'Meaning does not come from seeing or observing alone; meaning is not lying around in nature waiting to be scooped up by the senses, rather it is constructed. It is produced in acts of interpretation' (Steedman, 1991, p 54).

This process of construction, deconstruction and reconstruction is ongoing. It happens in solitary moments yet even more so in dialogue and through questioning and shared explorations. The research project gave everyone time to talk, focus, interrogate and rethink their observations and experiences. This balance of internalised reflection, externalised expression and creating new meanings was a feature of the meetings that held the threads together. There were many possible ways of thinking and acting as illustrated in this conversation:

PW1:   It is a very difficult thing to do trying to describe what it is we do. There is something intangible about the way you work and what happens here doesn't readily lend itself to being captured.

PW2:   It is about co-production, you don't create this space for children and then children come in and do what you intend but this space is open for children and adults and collectively you work together to produce a space where kids can play – it takes us away from 'us' and 'them' to see it as a collective – and if so there is a better chance of seeing a collective sense of production as opposed to an individual 'we're here' providing a service for children.

PW1:   I think it does come back to an awareness of your presence in the space and the relationships – it is really subtle and unpredictable (taken from discussion transcript).

A more detailed account of the stages and methods used to gather and analyse data is given in the published report, although at this point it may be interesting to consider why some of the methods used worked better for some people than others. As adult educators, as well as playworkers, it is important to deepen understandings of different styles and preferences for thinking about, sharing, investigating and making practice visible. It is a challenge for people to develop methods that capture and record what playworkers do. Like trying to catch a bar of soap in the bath, it is slippery and elusive. The approaches cultivated the need to be realistic, relevant and practicable within the constraints of daily practice.

All of the research participants were given access to the UoG Moodle system, an interactive internet based platform. This allowed photographs, maps, stories and blogs to be posted and shared. Although some used Moodle very little, most added one or two postings and used it to read others' stories and prompts. Some added audio recordings and photos and one wrote regular blogs and posted stories. Here is an example:

> I was 'it' on and off all day. I could never catch any of the children despite my best efforts. After a while the children decided they wanted to up the difficulty of the game by making it a team game. I got a team mate, T. We were always 'it' still. Further rules developed as we played. Because the game was now more challenging the children brought in the rule that 'home' was when the two members of a pair were together. My team mate came up with lots of clever 'pincer movement' type strategies. The game ended with a stalemate with both sets of pairs trying to tag each other while both sets of pairs were together so everyone was 'home'. (Taken from Moodle)

These stories were often a spark for starting discussions or a useful anchoring point for working through shared meanings together. All of the team expressed themselves through discussions and these were probably the most fruitful and participative method used. On the whole everyone seemed to be productive, focused and creative in dialogue, but what needs careful consideration is that the capturing of evidence from this, either through audio–recording with transcripts (time-consuming and labour-intensive) or through contemporaneous note-taking summarising points (danger of losing detail, emotional content and more subtle nuance), creates challenges for keeping records.

In this group a shorthand developed resulting in some specific terms taking on a whole set of meanings creating cornerstones for defining the territory being explored. When 'the chairs' were mentioned it called to mind an ongoing dialogue based on meanings beyond those that can be captured in language about a particular period of time, individuals, groups, dynamics, emotions and feelings where a shared understanding operated. This illustrates the concept of a community of practice, described by Wenger-Trayner and Wenger-Trayner (2015, p 1) as 'groups of people who share a concern or a passion for something they do and learn how to do it better as they interact regularly'. This definition includes groups who are both consciously and unconsciously learning from each other. It is what the playwork team, the wider partnership of organisations and networks can offer. The importance of being part of such groups to support learning, develop meanings and deepen understanding is a vital part of professional development and something the team is keen to promote.

An important element of working together was the recognition that each individual engaging in the research brought their own multiple and varied characters into the shared space and time which formed the process of this work. These aspects of personality that co-exist within each individual come from other histories, spaces, teams, learning experiences, traditions and ancestries beyond the immediate. They were manifested in the responses, stories, perceptions, assumptions and emotions expressed throughout the emerging investigations and dialogues. This meant paying attention to working in ways that were respectful of different life and work experiences, feelings and perspectives while being willing to question and explore more deeply one's own and others' expressions about the work.

One of the earliest exercises the participants did together was to bring their own remembered and individually drawn maps of the playground to create a shared picture of the whole space. There was extensive discussion of what went where and attempts to draw something that in some way represented the physical environment. The end product would probably be recognisable to anyone who visits the playground although some parts would only make sense with a bit more explanation. What was far more enlivening than any attempt at accurate representation was the sharing of stories of what happened in the space and how people felt about particular spaces. Features from the landscape were plotted together with the emotions and experiences associated with those spaces. The significance of the playground cat's presence, to have or not to have a tuck shop, histories of what other staff or children not present now had said or done around the site, the weather and seasonal impact, the archaeology of the playground, legends of what was dug up and what used to be there, descriptions of how certain things resonated with personal childhood memories, feelings and emotions connected to both good and bad events and situations – this and much more was brought to the table (see Figure 9.2).

Figure 9.2: Mapping the playground

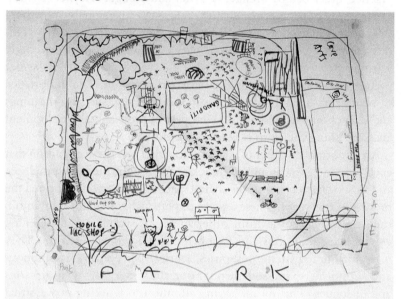

Source: John Fitzpatrick and Bridget Handscomb

What we have here are the physical features of the landscape – and last week we were beginning to talk about – through photographs – more than the physical features – the memories, experiences, senses, emotions that went with photos – even though you played 'it' there is so much more happening – all the messing around that is so difficult to capture but it is such an important part of being in that space – looking at ideas of mystery, legibility, complexity and coherence. The playground as a collection of stories – while each selected one, there are multiple stories – good/bad/everyday stuff that starts to reveal what happens here. We had a discussion around technical aspects of maps – as a representation of the physical features of space – and a landscape invested with emotions, experiences, etc and that it is both of these not either/or (taken from discussion transcript).

A focus of the research was on different ways of thinking about space. The playground is constantly being formed and re-formed by the relationships between the children, the playworkers, the space and the objects within that space. Change any one of those things and it has an impact on the others. This recognition contributes to greater understanding and interpretation of Playwork Principle 5: 'The role of the playworker is to support all children and young people in the creation of a space in which they can play' (PPSG, 2005).

Spaces are always produced through encounters (Massey, 2005). They are always in the process of being made, continually open to possibilities and transformations; the ongoing productions offer the chance to reconfigure relationships, to think and be different. 'Space is not a mere thing but rather a set of relations between things' (Lefebvre, 1991, p 83).

> The adventure playground is not just a physical but also a relational space, produced by the performances of everyday and ordinary experiences, habits, routines and their accompanying sensations, emotions, meanings, movements and actions. It is, by its very nature, an environment in which children and adults are thrown together, and have to get on together. (Lester et al, 2014, p 6)

The team explored the language that was used when describing the playground. Should 'space', 'place' or 'environment' be used, or is there another way of talking about it? Words such as 'place' and 'space' are used all the time but they have ambiguous meanings. Massey's definition of space as always in the process of being made struck a chord. It captures the transient nature of children's play. The movement and flow and chance encounters children have with each other, the playworkers, the landscape, objects and loose parts (Nicholson, 1971). Massey (2005, pp 11–12) sees space as 'open...there are always connections yet to be made...[it is] of loose ends and missing links'.

Tuan (1997, p 6) asks us to think of 'space that allows movement... and each pause in movement makes it possible for location to be transformed into place'. The playground can hold significant meaning for the children who go there with strong bonds built over periods of time. Cresswell (2004, p 12) describes place as 'space invested with meaning in the context of power'. For children, who experience being treated as 'other', with little control over their lives, time and space, the playground can be a place of which they are a part and it is a part of them. They become the insiders and experience a shift in power dynamics and identity. There is a rhythm of life and everydayness in what happens on the playground. The children who come regularly both form and are part of the traditions and rituals of the playground. They know where the ropes are and how to attach them, the bordering rules on the swing, the hose you can use on the water slide and who can use the toaster in the kitchen. They have a familiarity with the people and the space. Conversely, those 'who do not know the routine will appear clumsy and "out of place" simply through the non-conformity of their bodily practice' (Cresswell, 2004, p 34).

Being involved in a small-scale research project in partnership with both a practice-based and academic organisation has helped clarify the team's thinking and approach as playworkers and educators. The importance of questions rather than answers, nonsense and vagueness as opposed to sense and certainty and the process of learning rather than some concept of teaching to a pre-determined product or outcome has been greatly reinforced. The journey that started through asking those initial questions, was itself launched from many previous explorations and has already led to new expeditions.

> The staff have got to know each other. We have looked at reflective practice, ideas, childhood memories, also it has brought staff together – when we started this process we were new – we were still starting to get to know the playground, the children – and I feel like this process has given us the chance to analyse the playground, its features, children, how each works, what it stands for – for example we started by looking at areas – the sand-pit, the skateboard area, the hut, the taxi – and how every child influences the playground. We have been experimenting alongside the children and the playground – moving things about. We have been writing things down, observations, what are negative/positive experiences. It is ongoing and we have turned the page over now – it is like a new chapter because there are new children now. (Taken from discussion transcript)

Since this research project, HPA has worked with an artist, Cecilia Divizia, to continue the idea of capturing use of space, movement and mapping of children at play in HGAP. The process of having an independent non–playwork witness creating maps and seeking to record actions using visually creative methodologies helped develop new ways of seeing (see Figure 9.3). Cecilia's skill in drawing, photography, notating and observation helped raise new questions and develop resources for future research. Her endeavours to work with the team from her own distinct discipline and not in her first language showed real persistence and flexibility. In many ways Cecilia has often asked questions for clarification that have helped everyone to explore aspects of the work in a far more rigorous and complex way than would have happened if meanings were based on assumed understandings.

Figure 9.3: Artist's mapping

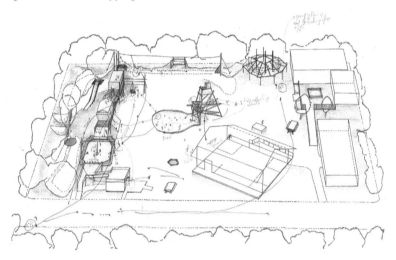

Source: Cecilia Divizia

As the research progressed the team extended the inquiry into ongoing practice and further questions emerged:

- Where should we observe from, can we hear and how is our presence felt?
- What impact does observation and recording (of all kinds) have on children, play and space?
- What do we call particular spaces so we can understand each other?
- What do the children call places and why? What meanings are suggested through names?

- What language or art can capture the mood, movement, feeling, connection between and ambience of a time or place?
- What differences are there between listening to sounds, story-telling, viewing pictures, reading words, physically experiencing actions or spaces in helping us make meaning of it?
- How can we help others to benefit from the learning experienced through doing research?
- How can we continue an inquiring and investigative approach despite pressures on time, money and hegemony for answers and outcomes?

This process of focusing on questions is a conscious departure from the notion that learning is the search for the right answers which are pre-determined. 'The intention is to study and make meaning from actual practice, recognizing that in fact there may be many meanings or understandings, not attempt to reduce what is going on to fit preconceived categorical criteria' (Dahlberg et al, 1999, p 109).

PAR has helped to validate and renew commitment to an approach to education and reflection in playwork that the team holds dear. This is to avoid a technical approach that playworkers should be trained to meet assessment or performance criteria and be taught techniques for competency. The authors' longstanding view is that playworkers have been poorly served by packaged and prescriptive training programmes that over-simplify complex ideas. Attempts to teach theories and concepts without adequate dialogue and with little or no ownership of their application in practice from playworkers themselves have successfully alienated and disillusioned many or led to delusions in others. 'The focus of work with pedagogical documentations must be on the processes of learning, not knowledge or goals to attain. Moreover learning must be treated as impossible to predict, plan, supervise or evaluate according to predefined standards' (Olsson, 2009, p 117).

The team has been reminded of the importance of exploring, investigating and developing shared meanings through reflection and team discussion and has become far more focused on questions rather than answers. Simply following the line of inquiry 'What if…?', enables ideas to emerge, challenges the practice of doing things the way they always have been done and offers more to playwork than a playwork trainer suggesting that there is a blueprint for how to do the job.

At a number of recent workshops the authors asked people to work in teams to consider pictures of children playing that depicted differing risk. The teams were asked to place the pictures on a continuum depending on how comfortable they felt with what they saw, from least to most comfortable. The discussions that ensued were manifold and encompassed sharing experiences from childhood, playwork, adulthood, parenting and from different roles and places. Usually there were one or two pictures that teams could not agree on or it was clear that either the more dominant personalities or those with the most risk averse attitudes had influenced the final positioning of those pictures. There is not a right or wrong answer and the exercise, rather than resolve what playworkers should do, throws up many avenues for investigation from what can we learn about team work to what would happen if we stopped children from doing everything that any adult was uncomfortable with.

Another exercise invited teams to complete a puzzle as quickly as possible. Each team was given pieces that make up a picture that is unsettling because it is made up of many different pictures taken of the same setting from a slightly different angle at a slightly different time (see Figure 9.4). The idea came out of the research project experience that there are many different perspectives, histories, ways of seeing and being in this space that are all part of the picture. We wanted to introduce the concept of diffraction as distinct from traditional forms of reflection. Reflection implies an accurate mirror image; Barad (2007) suggests the optical metaphor of diffraction, which happens when a wave hits an obstacle or is slit, producing different patternings. Applied to data analysis, '[a] diffractive reading of data through multiple theoretical insights moves qualitative analysis away from habitual normative readings toward a diffractive reading that spreads thought in unpredictable patterns producing different knowledge' (Mazzei, 2014, p 742).

This exercise was used to explore reflective playwork practice and to recognise it as dynamic, taking place over time, multi-layered and multi-various with diverse perspectives. The photos have stories attached to them. Play spaces are produced and generated over a period of time and the space is complex for staff and children. Bodies and movement, personalities and feelings, light and dark, quiet and noise all add differences to the pictures shared. People are asked to consider the whole picture and the many parts of it – multiple play frames, the space in between people, movement, atmosphere, own play memories and anything that emerges.

The philosophy of using these methods in learning situations is about supporting playworkers to take part in a community of practice, having conversations, experiencing, thinking, exploring, examining, experimenting, continuing the enquiry and deepening understanding – not problem-solving. Experience and insights are highly valued, more

Figure 9.4: Diffractive jigsaw of the playground

Source: John Fitzpatrick and Bridget Handscomb

so than the hierarchy of hard data or espoused theory. As Lindeman (1926, pp 9–10) says in his exploration of education: 'the resource of highest value in adult education is the learner's experience. If education is life, then life is also education. Too much of learning consists of vicarious substitution of someone else's experience and knowledge'.

Schön (1983) also recognises the difficulties of applying rigid or elitist concepts of espoused professional knowledge when the 'situations of practice are inherently unstable'. He goes on to describe a context where a body of knowledge is constantly increasing, expectations of society vary widely according to fast moving events and change: 'The situations of practice are not problems to be solved but problematic situations characterised by uncertainty, disorder and indeterminacy' (Schön, 1983, p 16).

Practitioners have a reflective conversation with a situation that should be treated as unique and uncertain – a probing and playful 'exploratory experiment' is taking place (Schön, 1983, p 147). The practitioner needs to be aware of their own 'move patterns' and themselves functioning as agent and participant with potential benefit and reflex reactions. This is a vital part of the self-knowledge which reflective playwork practice should embrace.

The importance of body and mind sensations, self-awareness and how things 'play through us' (Sturrock et al, 2004, p 31) were, and still are, frequent explorations in discussions both during the research project and more generally. This extract from one meeting gives context to the relationship between body, space and mind:

> You could substitute production for creation – the co-creation of space and it would mean possibly the same thing. That's how play happens – it is co-created – not an individual thing – always created with something – imagination, other bodies or something else – always an act of co-creation. If we see play as this, it slightly disturbs other ways of thinking about play – the idea that play is freely chosen, personal directed, intrinsically motivated isolates the player – to me – this whole idea that I am making a choice – perhaps doesn't quite work like that – a lot of playing is spontaneous, largely pre-cognitive, pre-thought – looking at examples of walking down the street and breaking out in skipping moves – PW1 sharing recent example of outburst of this – that first skip is not 'I think I will start skipping now and then you start skipping' – it just seems to be your body taking over and leading it – and then you think. (Taken from transcripts)

Some of the tools and methods experienced through PAR continue to be used to encourage exploration and discussion within training sessions. This is a simple short record of an observation with a map that was used to help playworkers develop ideas around mapping, representation of playing and questioning (see Figure 9.5).

It captures the flow of movement of two girls aged about 8 over a period of 20 minutes. Alongside the map is a narrative that describes what the observer saw, where the girls went and at certain times what was overheard. It describes the girls in constant motion running in between and up and down the wooden structures, ducking under the zip wire, climbing up the towers and scrambling over nets and up and down the ramps. The observation concludes with one of the girls collapsed on the ground in the long grass as though she was dead. The other girl stood over her trying spells to re-awaken her and then a younger boy came over and said "I killed one death eater!" These are the questions generated by one group of playworkers on a HPA playwork qualification course 2015:

Figure 9.5: Observation map

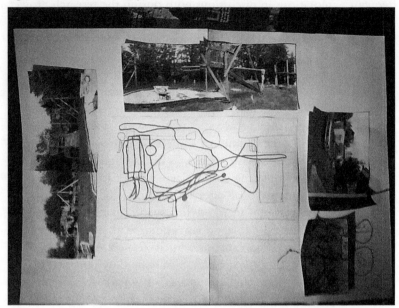

Source: John Fitzpatrick and Bridget Handscomb

- Was it one big game or small games that overlapped? Are different games and frames joining up and merging?
- Is it real or imaginary or both? What is a 'death eater'? How important is it that we know about children's cultural references?
- Was the boy's "I killed a death eater" input at the end of observation notes an extension (cue), a stop (annihilation) and was there a return?[1]
- What happened before and after the play observed?
- Does the narrative follow set rules from external sources? How much do children change known stories and roles within them when playing?
- Were other children involved at other times and how? What were the interactions with others?
- How aware are children of each other's play frames and narratives?
- Did it happen in this way because of the space? Does the play theme happen elsewhere (bedrooms, school, street, park, etc)?
- What impact does the space and environment have on the play?
- Do play types[2] seem to be constantly adapting and changing? In what ways do children elaborate, develop and return to narratives?
- Is there a 'boys versus girls' element to the play? Have I brought this in from my own play and life experiences?

- What values and preferences do I bring to bear on observations? Do I like this type of play? How do my own thoughts, feelings, values, preferences, experiences of playing, etc affect my playwork?
- Who were the goodies and baddies in the play? Does that change? What teams and bonds are going on?
- What have I assumed? How far can we know what is going on? Can we guess?
- Is this game carried on from another time or place or with other players?
- Are children playing multiple characters in the narrative?
- Was there a need to intervene? What does it say about me that maybe I wanted to intervene? What would have happened if someone had intervened when they pretended to collapse?

Within the daily work at HPA and with other colleagues the team carries on building the repertoire of methods and deepening understandings of play and playwork. Some playworkers have found the reflection model developed by Moon (1999) and applied to practice by Else (2014) useful as it is simple enough to remember yet encompasses some of the complexity explored here:

- noticing
- making sense
- making meaning
- working with meaning
- transformative learning.

Hughes (2012) developed the IMEE model (intuition, memory, experience and evidence) to help playworkers increase their understanding of play and environments. These ideas helped to extend playwork thinking, encouraged attentiveness and deepened connections between emotional and bodily sensations when reflecting. The sector needs to build on these examples and continue to develop more creative methods for supporting a kind of rigorous and specialist reflection that resonates with playworkers. Recognising the limitations of reflective approaches that are locked into a linear model of progress and starting to develop methods that support an endeavour of continuous enquiry is an important shift towards an exploration of the multi-layered and diverse world of play and playwork.

After the research project had ended the playwork team shared some thoughts on what the experience had meant to them.

PW1:   It's like you do your qualification and you learn about reflective practice, and health and safety, and children and you know about different age groups and play types. And then once a person's got their qualification, they think, that's it, I've got it now, I'm in work. But from this project, where it's still an ongoing thing, we're still using a lot of theories, putting it into practice, we're still reflecting, so it's like, it's an ongoing learning experience, it's ongoing learning, we're always developing, that's what I feel.

PW3:   It's true, actually, I hadn't thought about it like what you're saying. It's like the research project kind of gave us the tools to find the learning in our everyday practice. It's true, so instead of just reflecting at home about what kids were doing, possibly, and how they might have used space, it's much more about reflecting together about you, you in the space, and kids and you, and you and things and space, and learning from that, and that being an ongoing process.

PW1:   Yeah, it doesn't stop there.

PW3:   ...rather than playwork being a course. There's no full stop.

PW2:   There's no full stop after playwork.

PW1:   There's no full stop after playwork [laughter]. (Taken from discussion transcript).

The research project has helped the team to expand their knowledge, increase their observational skills, adopt and develop data collection and evidencing methods, make sense and create new meanings about play and playwork, become more articulate and confident in advocating for play as well as identifying new possibilities and extending repertoires of play responses, provocations and playwork actions.

  The authors have been exploring understandings of what reflective playwork practice is for many years now and feel that this experience as co-investigators in PAR has been really valuable in widening and deepening their knowledge and application of reflection. The starting point for undertaking reflection has come from a wider and more general professional context informed by a tradition of using psychological models and perspectives linked to external and technical statements of quality. These usually focus on individual and organisational development and can lead to a confusion about the purpose of the reflective endeavour and an emphasis on evaluation, identification of deficits, needs analysis and quality audits. In some ways this creates an environment and approach of pathologising children's play and playwork where the focus is on problems and remedies, rather than exploring a deeper understanding of meanings.

Playwork theories and concepts can become taken for granted, self-evident, unquestioned and seen as the only right way to think and act, rather than being understood as just one possible way of thinking and acting. The research project worked 'on the border of our knowledge, in between knowing and not knowing', and as Olsson (2009, p 189) points out 'that's where everything happens'.

Notes
[1]   Elements of the play cycle as described by Sturrock et al, 2004
[2]   Hughes, 2006

References
Barad, K. (2007) *Meeting the universe halfway*, Durham, NC: Duke University Press.

Cresswell, T. (2004) *Place: A short introduction*, Malden, MA: Wiley-Blackwell.

Dahlberg, G. and Moss, P. (2005) *Ethics and politics in early childhood education*, London: Routledge.

Dahlberg, G., Moss, P. and Pence, A. (1999) *Beyond quality in early childhood education and care*, London: Routledge.

Deleuze, G. (1994) *Difference and repetition*, trans. Paul Patton, London: Athlone Press.

Deleuze, G. and Guattari, F. (1987) *A thousand plateaus*, trans. Brian Massumi, Minneapolis, MN: University of Minnesota Press.

Else, P. (2014) *Making sense of play: Supporting children in their play*, Maidenhead: Open University Press.

Hughes, B. (2006) *Play types: Speculations and possibilities*, London: London Centre for Playwork Education and Training.

Hughes, B. (2012) *Evolutionary playwork and reflective analytic practice* (2nd edn), London: Routledge.

Leafgren, S.L. (2007) *Reuben's fall: A rhizomatic analysis of disobedience in kindergarten*, Walnut Creek, CA: Left Coast Press.

Lester, S., Fitzpatrick, J. and Russell, W. (2014) *Co-creating an adventure playground (CAP): Reading playwork stories, practices and artefacts*, Gloucester: University of Gloucestershire.

Lefebvre, H. (1991) *The production of space*, trans. D. Nicholson-Smith, London: Blackwell.

Lindeman, E.C. (1926) *The meaning of adult education*, New York: New Republic.

Massey, D. (2005) *For space*, London: Sage.

Mazzei, L.A. (2014) 'Beyond an easy sense: A diffractive analysis', *Qualitative Inquiry*, 20(6): 742–46.

Moon, J.A. (1999) *Reflection in learning and professional development: Theory and practice*, London: Kogan Page.

Moon, J.A. (2006) *Learning journals: A handbook for academics, students and professional development*, London: Kogan Page.

Nicholson, S. (1971) 'How NOT to cheat children: The theory of loose parts', *Landscape Architecture*, 62(1): 30–4.

Olsson, L.M. (2009) *Movement and experimentation in young children's learning: Deleuze and Guattari in early childhood education*, London: Routledge.

PPSG (Playwork Principles Scrutiny Group) (2005) *Playwork Principles*, Cardiff: Play Wales.

Schön, D. (1983) *The reflective practitioner: How professionals think in action*, Farnham: Ashgate Publishing.

Steedman, P.H. (1991) 'On the relations between seeing, interpreting and knowing', in F. Steier (ed), *Research and reflexivity*, London: Sage, pp 53–62.

Sturrock, G., Russell, W. and Else, P. (2004) *Towards ludogogy, parts I, II and III. The art of being and becoming through play*, Sheffield: Ludemos.

Tuan, Y. (1977) *Space and place*, Minneapolis, MN: University of Minnesota Press.

Wenger-Trayner, E. and Wenger-Trayner, B. (2015) *Communities of practice: A brief introduction*, http://wenger-trayner.com/wp-content/uploads/2015/04/07-Brief-introduction-to-communities-of-practice.pdf.

TEN

Children, mobile phones and outdoor play

Chris Martin

Introduction

This chapter examines the relationship between children and mobile phones in their outdoor play, using singular instances from an adventure playground in south west England. It is influenced by new materialist theories (Bennett, 2010a; Coole and Frost, 2010) and posthuman geographies (Whatmore, 2002; Castree and Nash, 2006; Änggård, 2015) that seek to acknowledge the vitality of material things and decentre the human as an organising force apart from 'nature'.

Drawing on these foundations, the chapter examines the affordances (Gibson, 1979; Heft, 1988; Kyttä, 2003) offered by mobile phones for instigating and maintaining play. It does this by looking at the relationships between human and non-humans as complex and emergent assemblages or 'ad hoc groupings of diverse elements' (Bennett, 2010b, p 23) in which there is no central locus of control and agency is distributed. Suggesting agency as a collaborative force overcomes traditional subject/object, nature/culture binaries to draw more detailed attention to the nuanced ways in which certain formations, which might be referred to as moments of playing, come about. As such, the chapter examines instances where children and mobile phones combine to create playful occasions. These observations act as exemplars (MacLure, 2010) and are revealing in their own right; they are not intended as a basis for formulating theories or generalisable conclusions. The detailed exploration of the ways in which bodies and materials assemble and their affects activates the relationality of each event. Each example is a singular and apparently everyday moment, but as Horton and Kraftl (2006, p 262) argue, 'banal, low-key, everyday, easily-overlooked things matter to everyone, everywhere, and perhaps especially during childhood'. Given that much of life is lived in the everyday, to ignore the mundane and banal is to ignore a huge chunk of life. These commonplace experiences of childhood live on into adulthood and even affect adult responses; indeed it is to these experiences that humans return to in times of difficulty and stress (Horton and Kraftl, 2006).

The following, from the researcher's reflective log, illustrates how bodies, movements and materials can casually entangle in everyday ways.

> Two 12-year-old girls were standing outside in the playground's upper area. They were deep in conversation, one of them had her phone out and was texting while they talked. They both paused on several occasions while the one girl texted. I observed them for a few minutes but couldn't hear their conversations and their body language didn't provide clues. They sent and received texts several times as well as playing music through the phone's speaker. The episode lasted under five minutes, and then they walked away.

This was an everyday occurrence with hidden detail; a unique production of time and space that created a singular assemblage; remove any element and this would have altered. The phone afforded social interaction with an unknown (to the researcher) other and without the phone, or signal, this element disappears. Remove the phone's ability to play music and the shared mood, the half smiles and glances alter the formation. Introduce rain, or loud children running past, and the assemblage and its affordances change.

There are considerable methodological challenges in paying attention to these relational formations, such as looking at how they cohere, fall apart and reform, and which elements should be examined and included. In addition, the role of the researcher, also a playworker on the site, is looked at as having an impact on and becoming a part of each assemblage, with the dual function additionally offering affordances for play (or not play) through the playworker's very presence, attitudes and actions. The notion of insider/outsider and clinical, objective research falls away to be replaced by a messier approach that reframes 'the research encounter as performance [and] causes us to deconstruct the notion of hierarchical relations between researcher and researched, adults and children' (Woodyer, 2008, p 352).

Attempting to describe what happened within an assemblage and to identify the actants and affordances meant that judgements needed to be made, necessitating that some would not be identified and/ or included. The delineation of starting and stopping points of each assemblage were always arbitrary and depended on the researcher's skill in reading the situation and to external elements: calls on the researcher from colleagues or other children, cries or loud noises which needed investigating, or (welcome) cups of tea delivered randomly by teenage volunteers. As such, this project was the start of an experimental attempt to go beyond ways of accounting for play that would tease things apart to examine individual human actions on often presumed passive objects. It pursues a relational methodology that pays attention to things-in-the-making to 'catch some of the realities we are currently missing' (Law, 2004, p 2). Methods have been provisional and the research became as much (if not more) about exploring the methodology as seeking to answer pre-established research questions.

Slip-sliding the approach

Children at play are always part of an ongoing process of assemblage; even the solitary playing child interacts with an environment, material objects, words, ideas or imaginary actants. Each element affects and is affected by each other, only coming together at a specific point in time and space in a time-limited grouping in which elements enter, leave, and change over time, sometimes emerging considerably altered. Agency and power are spread unequally rather than located solely in the human, and no part has 'sufficient competence to determine consistently the trajectory or impact of the group' (Bennett, 2010b, p 24). Assemblage thinking opens up the possibility that not only the child is able to issue a play cue; a 'lure or invitation from the child to the surrounding environment to join in play productions' (Sturrock and Else, 1998, p 15), but that other actants can also do so. Indeed, this chapter argues that a play cue can be understood as part of an assemblage. This does not diminish the affective power of the child or propose that non-human actors possess intentionality. Nor does agency presuppose intentionality (Bennett, 2010b): agency is always a collective force within an assemblage. It acknowledges the importance of and kinship with non-human materiality, moving away 'from a determinist mode of thought in which one entity – biological or social – is seen as the driving force of understanding' (Woodyer, 2008, p 350). Displacing humans from the role as repository of divinely granted power also raises the profile of other, non-human actants and the environment.

The term environment itself has perhaps suffered from overuse and been burdened with a myriad of meanings; certainly in the minority world this term is often conflated with ideas of the natural environment and nature, itself a contested concept (Whatmore, 2002; Ginn and

Demeritt, 2008). Indeed nature, argues Ingold (2011), is often seen as what is out there, separated from humans. This chapter considers humans and other organisms as inseparable from environment; one does not exist in isolation from the other, both are continuously brought into being through entanglements. From this point of view an adventure playground is a hybrid environment composed of the organic, material and socio-cultural, located not only in geographical space but also in digital space, and where diverse actants converge, assemble and diverge in ever changing assemblages.

Affordances and affect

Constructing 'children as links in heterogeneous assemblages' (Woodyer, 2008, p 350) draws attention to ways in which various actants affect and are affected by each other, and what affordances they offer. Gibson (1979, p 127) suggested that 'the affordances of the environment *are what it offers the animal, what it provides or furnishes, either for good or ill'* (emphasis in the original). Examining the potential functional qualities of an object or environment, rather than static form, provides very different insights into analysing behaviour, and therefore affordances 'are its *functionally significant* properties considered in relation to an individual' (Heft,1988, p 29, emphasis in the original). This chapter argues that this relationship is not, however, a simple subject/object binary, but needs to be seen collectively, where each element is mutually affective and dynamically involved in co-creation of a 'process', which on some occasions might be recognisable as playing. The relationality of affordances, which 'breaks the subject–object division and re-presents the transactional idea of the inseparably intertwined nature of the person – environment relationship' (Kyttä, 2003, p 47), is also a key concept influencing this research. Kyttä goes on to suggest that any environment has a limitless number of potential affordances but not all of these are perceived or actualised, since 'The qualities of an individual, as well as his or her current intentions, and other social and cultural factors determine which affordances out of all potential affordances the individual perceives in different situations' (Kyttä, 2003, p 55).

Mobility is also a crucial aspect of actualising affordances as 'without possibilities for mobility, active perception of environmental affordances through the use of one's own body is impossible' (Kyttä, 2003, p 105). Bodies are thus constantly alert to the possibilities that any environment presents for producing beneficial states of being and such states are always the product of relational entanglements with other bodies, movements, imaginations and materials, which in this context specifically includes considering the affordance of mobile phones in children's everyday ways of getting-on at the playground. However, while this study does highlight mobile phones, it should be stressed that this focus is not to privilege mobile phones over all the other active constituents of playful formations.

The spaces of mobile technology

Extending ideas from the previous section, the idea of space as a fixed container for action becomes untenable; it is always a lively production of relationships/assemblages between heterogeneous materials (Massey, 2005); space is dynamic and ever-changing, always open to the future. This includes digital and material space which, rather than being two distinct entities are 'concurrently entwined and experienced for a particular person in a particular instance' (Madge and O'Connor, 2005, p 4). Technological advancements such as voice activated commands, fingerprint recognition, sophisticated haptics and wearable technology promise to further alter the relationship between the human and personal technology, suggesting even greater hybridity and blurring of the boundaries between the digital, material and human.

The mobile phone exemplifies this blurring and has 'become a central cultural technology in its own right' (Goggin, 2006, p 2), playing an increasing role in the everyday lives of children (Bond, 2010; Mascheroni and Ólafsson, 2014). It is estimated that in the UK 48 per cent of 8–11 year olds have mobile phones, rising to 87 per cent among 12–15s (Ofcom, 2011), and across the EU many children acquire their first mobile phone by the age of 8 and their first smartphone before they turn 9 (Mascheroni and Ólafsson, 2014). Smartphones have added an extra dimension by enabling mobile access to the internet, affecting the quality of children's online experiences (Mascheroni and Ólafsson, 2014). Children and mobile phones have given rise to numerous discourses, and key themes in both popular and academic conversations include safety, health and learning (Waterman, 2010; Wood et al, 2011; Sandercock et al, 2012); the roles phones play in children's social interactions and construction of self and culture (Bond, 2010, 2013; Goggin and Hjorth, 2009; Haddon, 2013); and how children use them to negotiate permissions with parents and increase mobility (Pain et al, 2005; Ling, 2007; Kullman, 2010).

Methodology and methods

An ethnographic approach was chosen, and some of the exemplary accounts included in this chapter are moments which are brought to attention through what might be termed 'accidental ethnography' to signify the unplanned ways in which they emerge; there is no forewarning and no deliberation other than anticipatory readiness to be open to the possibilities that the world presents (Bennett, 2004). As with other research methods, this form of playful apprehension can be developed and refined through practice; bodies can learn to be attentive and form an enchanted attachment to the world, a form of receptive and generous ethical sensibility towards other things and bodies (Bennett, 2001). While moments of insight arise from chance encounters that cannot be controlled, they can be recorded using a range of media (Fujii, 2014).

Paper log sheets were prepared to document observations and follow-up casual interviews, and the researcher's mobile phone prepared for voice notes and recordings. Recording tools were designed as much as an aide memoir as an absolute record, as observations were expected to be transitory and interviews fragmentary. While this was sound in theory, the reality was very different. Observations happened in an ad hoc fashion and many instances of mobile phone usage were observed, often from the corner of the eye while the researcher was *en route*; or breathless teenage volunteers would announce that so and so had just been spotted using their mobile, resulting in, from an orthodox research perspective, disjointed data collection. This, however, did reflect the messiness of play; in this case not just that of the human players but also the non-humans. Reflecting this messiness, the methodology and methods are therefore less concerned with being slick in order to pay more attention to the textures and intricacies churning throughout the assemblages (Law and Urry, 2004; Stewart, 2007). All of the observation sheets were filled in after the incidents took place, some of them a number of hours afterwards, challenging the researcher's memory. Use of the phone as dictaphone proved to be difficult due to interruptions and background noise, and the researcher additionally often became self-conscious while using the phone for this. A reflective log was, however, particularly invaluable capturing embodied experiences and provided far richer material than the observation or interview sheets, due to additional reflexive time.

As the researcher is also a playworker on the site, the study acknowledges the likelihood that this combined role would influence the formation and dynamics of the assemblages in addition to offering affordances as an actant, and indeed the playworker as affordance was a major player in one of the instances recorded. The Playwork Principles (PPSG, 2005), the ethical basis underlying the profession, state 'For playworkers, the play process takes precedence', and the dual role necessitated sensitivity towards this as well as being conscious of any tensions between the roles. The two are not incompatible; playworkers are continually attentive and responsive to children's movements, with the intention of not using one's power and position to affect the emergence of playful assemblages in potentially harmful ways. The researcher was very conscious that for the children, playing was more important than the research, and this necessitated a time lapse between many of the observations and their recording. Additionally, the researcher waited until the play frames where children were using phones had finished before he interviewed them, but in all of the instances where the researcher went to do this they had disappeared and the opportunity was lost.

Data gathering took place over the three days the playground was open during autumn half term 2013. On the final day, concerned that observations and interviews were not providing enough data, the researcher actively asked children about mobile phones irrespective of whether they had been seen using them onsite or not, or if they even had one, and this generated additional data, particularly around off-site use of devices. The research was approved by the University of Gloucestershire's Faculty Research Ethics Panel and adhered to the playground's safeguarding policies. Children had the option of participating or not in the interviews and were asked to confirm their assent if they were interviewed.

Mobile phone use in context: the adventure playground

Fieldwork took place in a long-established adventure playground on a former railway siding, occupying a 3.5-acre enclosed site in the middle of a housing estate in a rural market town in south west England. Trees dominate, a combination of smaller species and towering pines reaching 60–70 feet in height. There are a few small open sections, and beaten paths wind through the trees and brambles, interspersed with simple wooden play structures and picnic tables.

Materiality and physicality are crucial elements in the playground; children play in and through their bodies, they run, laugh, fall down and climb trees. Den or 'base' building is the primary activity, and children, who generally work in self-selecting groups frequently containing one or two young teenage volunteers, use hammers and saws independently to build often ambitious structures. Mass running and chasing games are also extremely popular as are campfire-cooking sessions. Children are free to come and go as they please and many attend the playground regularly, spending most of the day there when it is open. The affective atmosphere of the playground exerts a powerful effect, filled with exuberant non-technological, non-human actants, ranging from the scent-bearing pines swaying in the breeze, to tiny insects chattering among dried twigs. The scale of the site itself exudes power and presence; the tall trees dwarf playing children and the wind and rain bear no heed to human playfulness. It is in this context that mobile phones – tiny, fragile objects – enter and seek to affect.

Mobile phone use at the playground

How phones were used varied according to the type of activity and the combination of actants. With the more physical activities such as base-building or chasing games, phones played a more passive role and were treated as protected objects; prone to breakages, loss or being covered in mud. When the play was more sedentary or conversation-based, phones played a much more active role and their more sophisticated functions were more likely to be used. Since each instance contained a variety of actants in unique assemblages, analysing the instances posed its own challenges, and each were analysed slightly differently, bearing in mind the epistemological position, which is to examine each example as singular and therefore containing its own unique formations and so not amenable to being addressed by universal methods or concepts.

The first stage in the data collection was to discover the major actants that constituted each assemblage, and indeed to describe the assemblage itself. Actants recorded were those perceived to exert the greatest effect in the assemblage, while acknowledging that agency is not an individual possession, and here the limitations imposed by the methods and the situation acted to limit the number that could be recorded. From the point of view of this research, the trigger for recording observations was noticing a mobile phone in use, accepting that this is an artificial marker and that not all instances of usage would be observed or would indeed be the focus of attention. The end point was more clear-cut, generally when participants moved away or stopped doing what they were doing. It must be stressed that all through the research period children were predominately playing without using mobile devices; they were running, banging nails into bits of wood, inventing games and shouting at each other. While the instances of mobile phone usage are highlighted in this study, they were just another element of the rich play woven into the children's playground lives.

In the observations, interviews and general questioning it became apparent that all children considered mobile phone usage to be normal, a viewpoint supported by contemporary studies (Livingstone et al, 2014; Mascheroni and Ólafsson, 2014). Not all children owned phones or brought their phones to the playground, however, and some of them equated iPods with phones as they performed a number of identical functions, such as social networking (when linked via Wi-Fi), taking photos and playing music. Although texting was the most popular form of using the phone to communicate, this and the use of phones to talk to people did not appear as important as other functions, such as using the phones to tell the time or to take photos. Children did talk about their phones, either to show off their capabilities if they had a smart phone, or to regale with tales of accidents that had befallen them. Many of the phones were hand-me-downs, suffered cracked screens, and none had protective cases. Conversations around credit, or lack thereof, were widespread.

The most common uses observed in the playground are given below. This is not a definitive list or an attempt to quantify and prioritise observation data.

- Texting
- Speaking on the phone
- Playing games
- Taking photographs & video
- Showing photographs & videos to others
- Playing music
- Phone as status symbol – showing off
- Phone as conversation item
- Watch/clock/stopwatch
- Accessing media (for example, YouTube videos)
- Phone as personal/valuable object for chasing
- Pretending to be busy or have friends
- Fighting boredom
- Accessing information (for example, Googling)
- Negotiating with parents
- Social networking

While each instance was unique in itself and demonstrates the complex ways phones were introduced into everyday play, what unifies them is their mundaneness. However, two instances stood out for their complexity and extended timeframe. The following example, from the reflective log, is one particular playful moment.

> Three 11-year-old girls were taking it in turns to go on the zip wire, and they asked me to push them. They each had phones, which they gave to each other to look after while they took their turn since they explained they didn't want to lose or damage their phones. After they had all had their turns they decided I should have a go, so I gave my phone to one of them to look after – mostly out of interest to see what they would do. My phone is an iPhone, while not the latest model but still a smart phone and a desirable and valuable object. They wanted to know which model it was and asked for my password, which I refused, playfully, to give them. After my go on the zip line I asked for my phone back but they refused and ran off laughing so I chased them round the playground, dodging around trees and jumping streams. This went on for about ten minutes with me never quite managing to catch up with them and them laughing and me pretending to be fierce. I finally caught up and after negotiation was given my phone back and the frame ended.

There are a number of actants in this assemblage (and potentially many more unobserved and unrealised), who actualise affordances as well as offering them. The humans were the most energetic actants, the three girls affording being chased, passing and throwing the phone from one to another, and taunting the playworker. The willing playworker afforded a chasing function, with the added thrill of the risk of imposing 'adult-ness' and attempting to stop play. The trees provided a barrier to dodge around and hide behind; the zip wire the initial impetus behind the emerging assemblage, offering a moving–down–ness as well as speed and a sense of danger. The phone itself played an active role as the focus of play, affording the possibility of it being dropped or damaged, with the attendant consequences. As an object of value it added an additional sense of potential transgression of boundaries, with the possibility that the game might turn out 'not to be ok' and straying into what Kyttä (2003) describes as the *field of constrained action*, in which actualising certain affordances are discouraged.

Other actants offered their own unique affordances. The stream afforded jumping over and the risk of slipping/getting wet/dropping the phone into; muddy patches afforded dodging around jumping over and sliding through, with the attendant risk of slipping, falling, or getting muddy. Paths, open spaces, brambles and thick undergrowth all contributed their own affordances, as did time, affording sufficient time for play to run its course and mild weather, which was one of the major players, as without this the assemblage would have been completely different.

The qualities of the phones changed dynamically throughout the assemblage. Starting as status symbols, the girls compared their phones' various functions and histories and they became tokens of friendship and trust when they looked after each other's, yet the introduction of the researcher's phone changed the dynamics. The girls' phones receded in importance while the qualities of the researcher's phone were explored and the researcher's relationship with it and them as boundaries of acceptability – what they could get away with – were probed and established. Once this relationship was provisionally determined it changed again when the researcher asked them to keep the phone safe while he went down the zip line. Issues of trust had to be re-examined as did the affordances offered by the researcher and his phone, the control of which offered far more (or different) options for play than a peer's phone. The point at which they refused to return the researcher's phone and started the chasing game was a pivotal moment. The phones as things had affect and exerted agency even without any technological function being utilised. The qualities of the physical environment, the trees, paths and streams contributed to the physicality of the chase and their qualities dominated the game in the latter stages.

The next scenario was another extended observation, and was observed by another playworker and verbally recounted, adding an additional actant. A boy and a girl, boyfriend and girlfriend, both aged 11, had a combined text/spoken conversation, first standing outside the hut, and then transferring inside as rain started. Although the example started outside, the comparative peace and quiet, comfort and shelter inside offered more attractive affordances for delving deeper into the conversation. What is also interesting is the suggestion of a ghostly third person, almost as if previous conversations and the mixture of texting and spoken conversation gave rise to an ethereal actant. The two sat side by side on a sofa, interspersing texts with conversations and as the playworker reported:

> "But the phone was the focus, or whatever was on it, the game or the text or the picture. Instead of initiating a new conversation, they were building on what they'd done

virtually, so probably they'd done loads and loads of texting and actually face to face they'd build on that rather than starting again."

> Boy: "Have you seen this? Have you still got all my texts?"
> Girl: "Do you remember when you sent this?" (Referring to text message).

They were concentrating on the phones, not looking at each other and not making any eye contact. The playworker said she thought "It was easier to talk through whatever it was they were doing" and that "the conversation was kind of third-hand; it was almost as if there was another person in the room". After this had been going on for a while they put the phones away and spoke face to face. The playworker continued to observe and noted that:

> "Another 11-year-old girl, who was a friend of the two, came along and took the girl's phone and started doing things with it. Later I realised the second girl had her own phone, but it wasn't as whizzy, so she wanted to use the first girl's phone, because it did more."

Situated realities

Play itself has also been described as 'a child's way of creating an alternative or virtual reality' (Lester and Maudsley, 2007, p 12). In their everyday interactions with mobile technology children create social network groups, upload photos and other content, share thoughts and ideas and indeed become content creators rather than just passive users. They do this actively, 'as moral interpreters of the worlds they engage with, capable of participating in shared decisions on important topics' (Mayall, 1994, p 8).

Observed instances illustrate the everydayness of mobile phone usage. Children's casual, skilled use of their phones, almost as if they were an extension of themselves, suggests more of an embodied knowledge than a cognitive one. This skill results from constant practice, and engagement in the mundane activities offered by phones contributes to this as well as accessing their more sophisticated functions. Woodyer (2008) suggests that meaning is contained in an embodied relationship between instrument and body; it is tacit, difficult to articulate and represent. The routines and habits of phone use are acquired over time and with practice. As the researcher is an avid phone user and experienced playworker it is possible to make some inferences by drawing on personal embodied 'knowledge' of being a competent practitioner, which Woodyer (2008, p 355) describes as 'acquiring familiarity with "local" knowledge and practices...we can fill in gaps in meaning with (embodied) information'.

Livingstone (2002) suggests new technology sits on top of old rather than replacing it. This was reinforced by the researcher's observations; children still wrote notes to each other rather than automatically texting and drew pictures of each with pencils as well as taking photographs. On no occasion in the observations was it obvious that mobile phones were replacing other objects used in play or that they encouraged more sedentary behaviour, within the confines of this limited research. When a stick was the most appropriate object, this was used; shouting across the playground was still the easiest form of communication if the recipient was in earshot; and throwing pebbles at objects was highly popular. When the phone offered qualities that were beneficial to the play frame, these were used to contribute additionality, such as playing music or taking and sharing photographs.

While this chapter's research was small in scope it suggests areas for further exploration. Time precluded examination of power issues from playing a larger part in the study, however closer examination of the relative power that ownership of phones and expertise in their use bestows as well as collective use could provide insights, as could examining how this might shift the playworker/child power balance. Adventure playgrounds are adult-run spaces for children, and on the playground in question both playworkers and children have co-created a cultural atmosphere over the last few decades, largely based around the idea of outdoor, non-technological play, which has its own assemblages and affordances. Investigating whether adventure playgrounds promote a particular sort of play, one in which use of mobile phones is 'the wrong sort of play' and whether children introducing mobile phones challenge and subvert this would add significantly to the understanding of playworkers' attitudes to phones and generational issues.

Conclusion

Examining different instances of mobile phone use via the concepts of assemblages and affordances has proved valuable in offering a different perspective on children's relationship with their environment. By sidestepping binary positions such as nature/technology and looking at how children and other 'things' around them form together in an assemblage, it becomes clearer how different actants possess and exert collective agency. The decentring of the playing child brings other elements into sharper focus, offering an ecological perspective that includes a greater examination of and respect for the non-human.

This chapter attempts to recognise the entanglement of multiple components that assemble to produce a unique formation, imbued with power relationships and a collective agency to generate a moment of vibrancy – what we might represent as 'play'. It also brings to the foreground the challenge of accounting for these formations since the tendency is to break things apart into separate components and attribute subject/object, cause/effect relationships. Within the approach developed in this study to consider each actant in isolation would however be an epistemological contradiction. The challenge is therefore how to develop methods that are sensitive to relationships, movements, entanglements and processes yet are able to explore actants in sufficient detail without being 'distorted into clarity' (Law, 2004, p 2). This chapter's methods have been provisional and the research became as much about playing with these and examining the methodology as seeking to answer pre-established research questions.

The playwork sector's definition of play as 'freely chosen, personally directed and intrinsically motivated' (PPSG, 2005) grew out of practice and theory developed in the largely non-technological, outdoor focused adventure playground movement of the 1970s, and the author suggests the value of digital technology in play may meet with scepticism. Mobile digital technology is part of children's everyday lives and for playworkers to treat it only as a negative is to disregard how children are playing and indeed create an updated perspective of the idealised model of 'child as innocent'. A re-visioning of playwork practice itself may be needed to take account of changing times and ideas and develop a more relational methodology that pays attention to things-in-the-making to 'catch some of the realities we are currently missing' (Law, 2004, p 2).

The examples in this chapter show children using technology in their everyday lives and everyday play, and offer one tentative path for exploring such methods. The children's mobile devices have not supplanted use of non-digital technology, such as sticks and pencils, but they show a sophistication in choosing what to use and how to use it, and for what ends, affording them an increased palette of objects and spaces for play.

References

Änggård, E. (2015) 'How matter comes to matter in children's nature play: Posthumanist approaches and children›s geographies', *Children's Geographies*, 14(1): 77–90.

Bennett, J. (2001) *The enchantment of modern life: Attachments, crossings, and ethics*, Princeton, NJ: Princeton University Press.

Bennett, J. (2010a) 'A vitalist stopover on the way to a new materialism', in D.H. Coole and S. Frost (eds) *New materialisms: Ontology, agency, and politics*, Durham, NC: Duke University Press, pp. 47–69.

Bennett, J. (2010b) *Vibrant matter: A political ecology of things*, Durham, NC: Duke University Press.

Bennett, K. (2004) 'Emotionally intelligent research', *Area*, 36(4): 414–22.

Bond, E. (2010) 'Managing mobile relationships: Children's perceptions of the impact of the mobile phone on relationships in their everyday lives', *Childhood*, 17(4): 514–29.

Bond, E. (2013) 'Mobile phones, risk and responsibility: Understanding children's perceptions', *Cyberpsychology: Journal of Psychosocial Research on Cyberspace*, 7(1).

Castree, N. and Nash, C. (2006) 'Posthuman geographies', *Social and Cultural Geography*, 7(4): 501–4.

Coole, D.H. and Frost, S. (eds) (2010) *New materialisms: Ontology, agency, and politics*, Durham, NC: Duke University Press.

Fujii, L.A. (2014) 'Five stories of accidental ethnography: Turning unplanned moments in the field into data', *Qualitative Research*, 15(4): 525–39.

Gibson, J.J. (1979) *The ecological approach to visual perception*, Boston, MA: Houghton Mifflin.

Ginn, F. and Demeritt, D. (2008) 'Nature: A contested concept', in N. Clifford, S. Holloway, S. Rice and G. Valentine (eds) *Key concepts in geography*, London: Sage, pp. 300–11.

Goggin, G. (2006) *Cell phone culture: Mobile technology in everyday life*, London: Routledge.

Goggin, G. and Hjorth, L. (eds) (2009) *Mobile technologies: From telecommunications to media*, Abingdon: Routledge.

Haddon, L. (2013) 'Mobile media and children', *Mobile Media and Communication*, 1(1): 89–95.

Heft, H. (1988) 'Affordances of children's environments: A functional approach to environmental description', *Children's Environments Quarterly*, 5(3): 29–37.

Horton, J. and Kraftl, P. (2006) 'Not just growing up, but going on: Materials, spacings, bodies, situations', *Children's Geographies*, 4(3): 259–76.

Ingold, T. (2011) *The perception of the environment: Essays on livelihood, dwelling and skill*, Abindgon: Routledge.

Kullman, K. (2010) 'Transitional geographies: Making mobile children', *Social and Cultural Geography*, 11(8): 829–46.

Kyttä, M. (2003) *Children in outdoor contexts: Affordances and independent mobility in the assessment of environmental child friendliness*, PhD dissertation, Helsinki: Helsinki University of Techncology.

Law, J. (2004) *After method: Mess in social science research*, Abingdon: Routledge.

Law, J. and Urry, J. (2004) 'Enacting the social', *Economy and Society*, 33(3), 390–410.

Lester, S. and Maudsley, M. (2007) *Play, naturally: A review of children's natural play*, London: National Children's Bureau.

Ling, R. (2007) 'Children, youth and mobile communication', *Journal of Children and Media*, 1(1): 60–7.

Livingstone, S. (2002) *Young people and new media: Childhood and the changing media environment*, London: Sage.

Livingstone, S., Haddon, L., Vincent, J., Mascheroni, G. and Ólafsson, K. (2014) *Net children go mobile: The UK report*, London: London School of Economics and Political Science.

MacLure, M. (2010) 'The offence of theory', *Journal of Education Policy*, 25(2): 277–86.

Madge, C. and O'Connor, H. (2005) 'Mothers in the making? Exploring liminality in cyber/space', *Transactions of the Institute of British Geographers*, 30(1): 83–97.

Mascheroni, G. and Ólafsson, K. (2014) *Net children go mobile: risks and opportunities* (2nd edn), Milano: Educatt.

Massey, D. (2005) *For space*, London: Sage.

Mayall, B. (ed) (1994) *Children's childhoods: Observed and experienced*, Washington, DC: Routledge Falmer.

Ofcom, 2011, *UK children's media literacy*, http://stakeholders.ofcom.org.uk/market-data-research/media-literacy/archive/medlitpub/medlitpubrss/ukchildrensml11/.

Pain, R., Grundy, S., Gill, S., Towner, E., Sparks, G. and Hughes, K. (2005) '"So long as I take my mobile": Mobile phones, urban life and geographies of young people's safety', *International Journal of Urban and Regional Research*, 29(4): 814–30.

PPSG (Playwork Principles Scrutiny Group) (2005) *The Playwork Principles*, Cardiff: Play Wales.

Sandercock, G.R.H., Ogunleye, A. and Voss, C. (2012) 'Screen time and physical activity in youth: Thief of time or lifestyle choice?', *Journal of Physical Activity and Health*, 9(7): 977–84.

Stewart, K. (2007) *Ordinary affects*, Durham, NC: Duke University Press.

Sturrock, G. and Else, P. (1998) *The playground as therapeutic space: Playwork as healing (The Colorado Paper)*, Sheffield: Ludemos Press.

Waterman, C. (2010) 'Moving the deckchairs on the good ship "Childhood"', *Education Journal*, 122: 12–13.

Whatmore, S. (2002) *Hybrid geographies: Natures, cultures, spaces*, Thousand Oaks, CA: Sage.

Wood, C., Meachem, S., Bowyer, S., Jackson, E., Tarczynski-Bowles, M.L. and Plester, B. (2011) 'A longitudinal study of children's text messaging and literacy development', *British Journal of Psychology*, 102(3): 431–42.

Woodyer, T. (2008) 'The body as research tool: Embodied practice and children's geographies', *Children's Geographies*, 6(4): 349–62.

Part Three:

Playfulness and wellbeing

Understandings of play for children with profound and multiple learning disabilities (PMLD)

Stephen Smith

One young person was taken to the trampoline in her wheelchair, the playworker said 'Do you want to go on the trampoline?' The young person did not respond and so the playworker started to put her in a hoist. The young person began to show physical signs of distress when the playworker started to hoist the young person from their wheelchair and onto the trampoline. Once she was out of the hoist and on the trampoline, the staff member was jumping up and down causing her to bounce up and down. This led to smiles, then laughter and the young person having a very enjoyable time. (Field notes)

Introduction

Playwork practice in the UK is underpinned by the Playwork Principles (PPSG, 2005), which make a number of assumptions about children and play. This study develops an argument showing how the idea of play as freely chosen and personally directed needs careful consideration and perhaps a broader understanding for playworkers working with children with profound and multiple learning disabilities (PMLD), as the opening vignette illustrates. Building on an earlier desk-based study (Smith, 2010), observations and semi-structured interviews were carried out in an afterschool club and holiday play scheme for children with PMLD in south east England. During the interviews, staff said that they felt that some of the playwork theory and ways of describing play in the Playwork Principles (PPSG, 2005) do not relate to their work with children with PMLD. For this reason, playworkers who are working with this group may look for other ways to help guide their practice.

The aim of the research was to explore staff understandings of and attitudes towards the play of children with PMLD and to question whether the Playwork Principles (PPSG, 2005) can effectively support those who work with this group. Drawing on observations, interviews and the literature on working with disabled children, a focus on communication, relationships and playfulness emerged, which has the potential to support playworkers working with children with PMLD.

The chapter opens with a description of the fieldwork methods before briefly introducing the playwork ethos and how this is articulated in the Playwork Principles (PPSG, 2005). It then explores perspectives on disability and particularly PMLD, opening up the exploration of how adults might support the play of children and young people with PMLD, where volition and communication are particular challenges. In the absence of language, other forms of communication come to the fore, meaning staff need to work at building an understanding of nonverbal signals and metacommunication (Bateson, 1972). In a context where mobility aids and personal care routines can dominate, it is suggested that the idea of playfulness in these routines as well as in play activities can both draw on metacommunication and use it to create playful relationships. Examples from the fieldwork are interwoven throughout to illustrate the arguments being made.

The research context and approach

The setting was a special school in south east England that also provided play and recreation activities in the form of afterschool clubs and holiday play schemes for children with PMLD. The research participants were all teachers and teaching assistants during school time and playworkers in the out of school service. The school has a policy of only using school staff to work in the out of school service, as it is felt that the children with PMLD need workers who know them very well and are able to meet care and medical needs. The out of school staff team are divided into two groups, those who work specifically with the children with PMLD and those who work with the other disabled children who attend. This meant that the research focused on a small team of five staff, and while this was a small number in terms of data collection, it was felt of great value to have participants with experience and specialist knowledge of children with PMLD.

The research project was approved by the University of Gloucestershire's Faculty Research Ethics Committee. Informed consent was obtained from the staff prior to starting the research. Issues of consent from the children and young people were discussed at length. Given that the children and young people were not the focus of the research, and also that the research aimed to observe (rather than alter) normal practice, it was agreed that their consent was not required. However, it was felt that consent should be sought from parents and/ or staff acting in loco parentis, and that sensitivity should be used in terms of the children's consent to be present at various points during the session. Confidentiality and data protection protocols were fully observed.

The approach to the research was inductive and from a social constructivist perspective, allowing emerging concepts to be shaped and generated through the experience of data collection (Creswell, 2007). Six observations were completed in the afterschool club and play scheme. Observations aimed to identify how staff initiate, recognise and respond to playfulness in children with PMLD, and to what degree the children were active agents. It was important that participants were observed as naturally and as unobtrusively as possible, so observations were recorded in written form, capturing as much detail as possible. Observations included both play activities and times when the children were not explicitly engaged in play activities, for example being put into hoists and preparing for personal care routines.

Semi-structured interviews were carried out on an individual basis. This provided the opportunity for each member of the team to discuss their work without pressure from their colleagues. Using open questions enabled the researcher to listen to the participants and formulate discussions to gain further insights into their work. Interviews built on the observations and aimed to identify: how staff members define their role in the setting, their understanding of the children's play, what informs their practice, their feelings about the work and their training.

The Playwork Principles

The Playwork Principles (PPSG, 2005) underpin all playwork qualifications in the UK and outline the professional and ethical framework for playwork practice. They should be taken as a whole, but for reasons of brevity, the focus here is on the second principle, which defines play as 'a process that is freely chosen, personally directed and intrinsically motivated. That is, children and young people determine and control the content and intent of their play, by following their own instincts, ideas and interests, in their own way for their own reasons.'

In appreciation of the complexities of play Brown (2008, p 123) provides a critique of this definition and suggests that we risk 'misleading ourselves, society and most importantly the children with whom we work, if we hold fast to this untenable definition'. He gives examples of how some children are coerced or directed in their play by others and that they still gain much benefit from it.

Smith (2010) suggests that the Principles may not apply to 'all' children (as the Principles explicitly state) and that this definition of play could be problematic for those who support children and young people with PMLD. The Playwork Principles describe the role of the playworker as being 'to support all children and young people in the creation of a space in which they can play'. In one sense, it may seem that children and young people with PMLD have very little control over the physical design of the space or little choice as to what resources to use. However, paying attention to building open and responsive playful relationships may be considered a helpful approach to co-creating a space where the children and young people can play.

Throughout the history of playwork theorising, there have been several attempts to understand and fully interpret what playwork might look like in practice (for example, Sturrock and Else, 2005; Brown, 2008; Hughes, 2012). Some of the staff team in the study were undertaking playwork qualifications and becoming recognised as playworkers, meaning that their role as playworkers was now guided by the Playwork Principles (PPSG, 2005). Conversations with the staff team highlighted tensions and contradictions around concepts such as 'freely chosen, personally directed play' and 'intervention'. For example, one interviewee said

> "But the [children with] PMLD I've got, we have to make sure that we are playing with them, we are providing activities, like you know doing stories with them, doing sensory stuff, because they don't have the ability so we try to support that and to get them to do it as well, you know, hand over hand things."

Interviewees raised concerns that the Playwork Principles do not fully relate to young people who need such high levels of support and interaction. Staff felt that the way that they were working went against the "whole theory of the whole play thing" and that play is rarely 'chosen' by the young people.

Profound and Multiple Learning Disabilities (PMLD)

At this point, it is worth giving some consideration to what is meant by PMLD. It is recognised that people with PMLD are some of the most marginalised, and have some of the highest support needs, remaining highly reliant on services (PMLD and Mencap, 2008). 'PMLD' is a label used in the United Kingdom to describe those who are affected by the most severe impairments of cognition and consciousness deriving from neuro-developmental disorders (Simmons, 2011). Ware (1996, cited in Carnaby, 2004, p 4) suggests that the severity of their learning difficulty indicates that those with PMLD are 'functioning at a development level of two years (in practice well under a year)'. This is reflected by Simmons (2011), who states that the abilities of children with PMLD are often compared to those of a neonate because they are at a pre-verbal stage of development.

Simmons (2011) lists several descriptors from the literature describing those with PMLD as 'pre' a range of capacities or abilities, highlighting the dominant understanding of them as failing to reach normative developmental milestones. For example, they are described as pre-verbal, pre-volitional and pre-intersubjective. He argues, however, that children with PMLD experience and engage with their surroundings in ways 'more complex than existing conceptual frameworks capture' (Simmons, 2011, p 1).

Described as pre-communicative, children with PMLD are viewed as not having the ability to comprehend the objective world and as lacking 'contingency awareness' (Simmons, 2011). In particular, much of the literature describes people with PMLD as having substantial difficulty in intentional communication. Strong relationships are required by communication partners to ensure that changes in communication ability and health as well as physiological and psychological changes are appreciated. During the observations a young person was asked if they liked the music that was playing, young person said no, the staff member played it anyway. They appeared to be teasing the young person who responded by smiling. Despite this dominant understanding of children and young people with PMLD in the literature, in this scenario, there appears to be a sophisticated level of playful communication operating at a non-literal level. As Watson (2014, p 1) states, the concept of playfulness offers the potential to change perceptions of children with PMLD from passive children who are 'done to' to children who are inherently playful, have personalities, strengths, likes and dislikes.

How do people recognise that someone with PMLD wants to play? There may be individuals who are unable to provide clear messages that they want to play with something or someone. One of the staff talked about how they found this position quite challenging and how a large part of their role with the young people was centred on communication. This was due to the communication not being very clear, making it hard to understand what kind of play the young people want to engage in. In particular, if there is no previous relationship to build on "you are just clueless as to what sort of thing they will enjoy. You just approach with a couple of things" (interview).

Three interrelated themes emerged from the interplay between the literature and the data from observations and interviews: communication beyond words, relationship and invitations and playfulness. These go some way towards navigating the contradictions expressed by the staff between their practice and the Playwork Principles.

Communication beyond words

Although much of the literature describes children and young people with PMLD as 'pre-communicative', this tends to refer to the use of language or other forms of intentional communication. The term metacommunication was used by Gregory Bateson (1972) to describe the ways we communicate about communication, the non-verbal messages we send alongside the words used, for example, the signals that communicate playful intent or that convey the message 'this is play'. It is these spaces that the staff members are operating in where communication requires a deeper understanding of the young person in context as well as the ability to offer and provide new experiences confidently.

It could also be that staff are following cues from the children and young people that are driven by a deeper knowledge, and that what may appear as adult-led may be more intuitive than realised. Although staff often talked about not knowing what children wanted, in observations, they did appear to pay careful attention to metacommunicative signals and responses to their own cues.

A closer look at Sturrock and Else's (1998) play cycle may provide a useful link between Bateson's ideas of metacommunication and building playful relationships. The model describes the process of play and has five elements: the metalude, the play cue, the play return, the play flow and, finally, annihilation. From the play cue and return to that cue, a play frame is established. This model can be applied to the scenario where the staff member appeared to be teasing a young person about the music playing.

Throughout this exchange, the staff member and the young person appeared to be engaged in a play cycle, with cues and returns establishing the frame, although the young person did not issue the initial play cue. Perhaps a particular feature of this and many other frames observed is that the young people were not playing 'with' anything but were often being played with, it was the staff that were playfully interacting with the young people, as these field notes show:

> The adult issues a play signal to the young person and closely observes facial expressions, body language or any other communication. Staff wait for a response, the young person responds, positively or negatively. If there is no response the adult issues another cue, the adult engages the young person in a communication frame and playfully interacts throughout. Throughout the exchange the metacommunication from the staff is positive.

These playful communication frames were evident across the observations and were mostly ended by the staff who changed the activity or moved onto the next routine such as feeding or personal care. It was then down to the staff to begin a new frame. While these exchanges may not precisely meet the definition of play as freely chosen and personally directed, it is clear that staff issued cues to test for returns that indicated that the young person wanted to engage in that play frame, and then worked to establish and maintain that frame.

One of the principles underpinning Sturrock and Else's (1998) play cycle is that there is a danger that the play may become adulterated, that is, 'contaminated' by adult desires or urges to instruct, or dominated by the playworkers' own 'un-played out material' (Sturrock and Else, 1998). When interviewed, the staff expressed concern about this. However, given recognition of the higher levels of support needed by children and young people with PMLD, although the potential for adulteration may be higher, it is accepted that the trigger needs to come from the supporting adult who also carries a responsibility of response and frame-holding. For example, one interviewee said, "I would say yes, if they are relaxed and I can see that there is nothing bothering them, I think I would assume that child would probably like to play", and another: "I mean as a playworker, I would encourage to see if they are responding to the play we are providing." This issue is further explored in the two following sections on relationships and playfulness.

Relationships and Invitations

Casey (2005) proposes that for adults to fully support disabled children and young people in their play, there may be a need to become very closely involved and to move into the 'spirit' of play with them. This allows the adult to support, facilitate and 'scaffold' play in ways that are rarely achievable from a distance. However, adults may be concerned that they will lose authority over children if they do this. In response, Casey (2005, p 60) poses three questions:

1. Why are we afraid of giving up control?
2. What do we think will happen?
3. If the child or children aren't in control of their play, is it still play?

Casey (2005) emphasises a connection between fully entering into the spirit of play during appropriate moments and demonstrating respect while showing what is valuable to them. The suggestion is that this is a catalyst for a deeper understanding of the child's experience that may alter relationships, possibly towards a more equal partnership and a holistic knowledge that enables adults to support a child's play fully. This leads to further reflections on 'intervention and non–intervention' as an element of playwork that affords children the maximum 'autonomy' in their play, while making sure that they are not exposed to serious risks of harm, or what has been referred to as 'low intervention, high response' (NPFA, 2000, p 7). It requires being highly alert to 'subtle invitations' to join in, as such requests can rarely be seen as unambiguous. There needs to be sensitivity to a range of cues, facial expressions, body language, sounds and interests. These 'subtle invitations', or cues (Sturrock and Else, 1998) or metacommunication (Bateson, 1972) convey messages about allowing permission to support participation and to recognise and value children's authentic experiences.

The challenge posed by Casey is of adults understanding and developing the ability to make subtle interpretations and judgements that have a foundation in 'empathy and knowledge' (Casey, 2005, p 61), as we can only draw on interpretations rather that a supposed 'true knowledge' as to what is occurring during play.

When staff were asked, 'how do the young people indicate that they want to play?', they described how it is mostly them who will approach the young people and how they often cannot rely on any play signals or play cues from the children, but issue cues and pay attention to metacommunicative responses. Staff rely more on trial and error and receiving affirmation through positive response rather than a definite or even subtle play signal. It could be argued that the trial and error and the interpretation of the response are ways of supporting play rather than controlling play and therefore is a type of positive intervention rather than adulteration, but, as with any adult involvement in play, the potential to adulterate remains. There are also added variables such as the young people may not like what is happening, or they might be tired, in pain or upset. If there was no response or the young person did not appear to enjoy it, the playworker would try something else. However, since it was mostly the playworker who issued a play signal and the young person who responded, staff felt that this was not freely chosen, personally directed or intrinsically motivated by the young person.

During the research, a conversation took place about the playworker's thoughts regarding the opening vignette on the trampoline, where it seemed that the playworker made a young person take part in an activity in which they had indicated that they did not want to take part. Their response was as follows:

> "It's like a different student, a mainstream student, they have more interest in things, they want to explore more, and be involved more, and so do the special needs, but the thing with the special needs is that some of the experience has not been fulfilled, so let's say, mainstream kids, let me use the example of the trampoline again, with mainstream kids, they can see the trampoline, they can feel that jump, they can feel it by watching it, they can feel it by watching me and make a connection by watching and can feel it by watching me jumping, this is the reaction I am getting of going high, and that kid, maybe because he jumps on the floor, that the way he connects it psychologically and may not realize it, but this is the feeling I get when I am jumping on the trampoline. Especially with my kids, because they have never jumped so they cannot understand the actual feeling when they are watching me jump and this experience, it's a very psychological thing...So sometimes you need some physical prompts to get on there and just take it slowly, because it's all about trying and seeing what works and what doesn't work and doing it their pace, most of the time it works." (Interview)

Playfulness

Given the complexities of supporting the play of children and young people with PMLD, it was decided that an essential feature of the research would be to observe the staff team's approach to their work in total. In particular, this meant observing sensitive times such as personal care and the use of equipment such as the hoist, as these formed a significant part of the staff team's role. It was seen as valuable to the research to observe the staff team's approach to these routines as they involve a great deal of contact and sensitivity as well as many potential opportunities for playful encounters and of their relationship building with the young people. During the observations, the staff team did appear to be highly focused on the young people, not just for physical and personal care and medication, but also to ensure that they were having fun. They made decisions confidently and worked within the parameters of choice and understanding and with what they have grown to know about the young people and the nuances of their communication. Corke (2012) highlights the importance of the interactive styles that practitioners adopt when communicating with those with PMLD, and suggests that playfulness can be a key element of good relationships.

Corke (2012) notes playfulness has been an area of scholarly interest since the 1930s. Dewey (1933) suggested playfulness rather than play was an essential component of education. He saw playfulness as an 'attitude of mind', whereas play is a 'passing outward manifestation of this attitude' (Dewey, 1933, cited in Corke, 2012, p 9). Lieberman (1977, cited in Corke, 2012, p 9) described playfulness as 'an intriguing phenomenon and qualitative ingredient in play that goes beyond the childhood years'. Playfulness is also highlighted by Sutton–Smith (1997, p 147), who states that play is often described in terms of its form or content, like playing games or sports, whereas being playful is more of a reference to a 'mood of frolicsomeness, light heartedness, and wit'.

As Corke (2012) notes, there are multiple ways of understanding playfulness, just as with play. Drawing on work by Maxwell et al (2005), she acknowledges two sides to playfulness, one that is seen as fun-loving and the other as frivolous. Exploring whether adults find it easy to be playful, she notes that while they can show aspects of being fun-loving, they are less likely to be frivolous and that adults may be more at ease being playful when it is associated with humour. Humour has a stronger link to cognition than playfulness or laughter, which is pertinent when working with those who are functioning at very low developmental levels. Those with PMLD may be unable to appreciate humour but may find great benefits from the effects of playfulness through the use of laughter.

In her study of playfulness in young children with PMLD, Watson (2014) acknowledges Sturrock and Else's (1998) play cycle and extends it into a playfulness cycle intended to aid understanding of the often very subtle cues given by children and young people with PMLD. She notes

> Although it is possible for playfulness in children with PMLD to be child-led, motivated by some inner drive, another child or a particularly engaging toy, this study has shown that it is likely that children with PMLD will also often need a 'trigger' from those around them, which is why the 'offer' of playfulness has been included in the cycle. (Watson, 2014, pp 2–3)

In addition, playfulness is more likely to arise if conditions are right, and this necessitates paying attention to whether the environment is right for that child, being willing to be playful, and attuning to the playful metacommunications of the child. The playfulness cycle supports staff to recognise and extend playfulness and comprises seven elements: 'permission' and preparation; attunement; 'offer' of playfulness (may be openness to playfulness, a playful activity or playful approach); recognition of signs in the child; co-regulation; playful response; reattunement; and back to 'permission' and preparation, with the cycle repeating (Watson, 2014, p 3).

Returning to the interrelated theme of communication beyond words, Watson (2014, pp 3–4) suggests a number of signs of playfulness in children with PMLD, emphasising that these will be individual to each child, but may include:

- physical – subtle changes in facial expression, stiffening, increased movement of body and eyes, finger flexing, relaxing, flapping, postural change;
- emotional – twinkling eyes, open-wide eye gaze, smiling, laughing, raised eyebrows, open mouth, tongue out, increased expressive vocalisation, happy sounds;
- social – moving nearer, reaching out, increased eye contact, leaning towards.

One observation showed how a staff member used hand clapping to gain the 'young person's attention and eye contact, the young person follows and claps while smiling, the staff follows this cue and claps some more and starts talking and laughing with the young person' (field notes). Throughout this vignette, both Sturrock and Else's (1998) play cycle and Watson's (2014) playfulness cycle can be observed, showing also how the first play cue is issued by staff. The cue was not issued because the young person appeared bored or distressed but because of a willingness to engage the young people in playful activities.

The response to the children throughout the observations was mostly playful, as this observation of lifting a young person into the hoist shows:

> The hoist was not working, staff making this fun, explaining to the young person and being light hearted about it, comforting the young person as there are some signs of concern shown by young person, staff making the situation fun, tickling the young person and saying that the young person is 'like an octopus', using fun language, staff get a different hoist and as the child is lowered are saying "down, down, down, down", until the young person is back in their wheelchair. (Observation)

Another observation captured staff saying to the child while being hoisted that, "they are going to be put onto the roof". All could have been more serious interactions and misinterpreted and like the subtle difference between being playful and domination or making fun of and just making fun. This was also captured in one of the interviews: "My general response, I would say, is really positive, and always, come out with some sort of play, if you are shaking hands or if you are trying to touch and feel, then I will be doing it in a playful manner" (Interview).

Concluding reflections

Brown's (2008) critique of the Playwork Principles does highlight how children can gain benefit from play that is not entirely freely chosen although the examples he gives are centred on children coercing or forcing other children to play rather than adults. The lack of free choice and intervention-heavy working practices could place huge guilt on playworkers, particularly when the staff at the setting feel that they are adulterating the play as described by Sturrock and Else (1998). It could be that it is the interpretation of the playwork literature that is causing difficulties for the playworkers, since there are ways of supporting play by using interventions that may be confused with adulteration (although any certainty in this regard would be difficult).

For some of the staff there were some comments with regard to the approach of letting the children explore without getting involved, showing patience and ensuring that the young people were freely choosing their play. However, mostly, the staff described how they were constantly relying on facial expressions, body language and deep understandings that required time and a deep knowledge of the person. Another key element that was missing was that none of the children with PMLD were playing with each other. This could reinforce the staff's feeling of isolation from the notion of freely chosen play (PPSG, 2005) and a minimal intervention approach that underpins the espoused playwork practice as described in the Playwork Principles.

For the staff team, the issue of choice gave rise to a range of feelings and comments. All of the interviewees were asked how the young people make choices in the play setting. One staff member found this to be a particularly 'tough one' to answer, saying

> "We provide the option of choice to be honest, let's say we've got five games, we will be providing those five games, so they may have only those five games, that we are actually choosing for them. So they will be choosing out of those five games…we are approaching with the game, some sensory lighting or the music, and if you see that it is not working, or if the child is not quite happy or they are not getting involved, then we may try something different. So it is more of that type of choice, rather than allowing them one hundred per cent choice of choosing the game, it is much more restricted and narrower than with a mainstream child."

While this could be viewed as being true in many adult-led services, it appears that the level of staff control of choice was even greater with children and young adults with PMLD, as the staff team were choosing everything that the young people experience, from where they are moved to, to what activities are chosen. Staff were constantly making decisions for the individuals and choices are typically narrowed down to two options. It was felt that this was largely down to difficulties in communication and that any more than two choices would be too confusing for the young people.

The story of the trampoline, recounted in the opening vignette, could be seen as an example of adult control over the young person's own choice. Clearly this was an experience that the young person would not have had if the playworker was following a narrow understanding of playwork theory, since it could be argued their actions were highly directive, and therefore going against the principle of freely chosen play (PPSG, 2005), or that the young person's cues and returns were being ignored (Sturrock and Else, 1998).

What all this demonstrates is the importance of forming deep relationships to enable the staff not only to facilitate choice making but also to introduce options and new experiences for the young people. It is these relationships that are also essential in all other areas of communication when working closely with young people with PMLD.

When critically reviewing staff understandings and attitudes to the play of children and young people with PMLD, it could be argued that the staff team observed were operating in a space that exists outside the espoused theories of play that are prescribed by the Playwork Principles (PPSG, 2005). Within the staff team there were feelings that the Playwork Principles were not applicable to their work with children and young people with PMLD. It could be that the playwork sector may need to listen to such feelings and address interpretations of the Principles and playwork theory that appear to exclude practices that are, to some degree, adult led.

Communication was a highly emotive subject for the staff and was linked closely to staff members' understanding of and response to the play cues and signals issued by the children and young people. Staff explained that the play was mostly initiated by them and felt that this was an area that was contradictory to the Playwork Principles. It could be that staff were responding to cues that were more subtle than they were aware of and that a deeper exploration into metacommunication (Bateson, 1972), play signals and the play cycle (Sturrock and Else, 1998) could suggest that the team are being responsive but at a deeper and more intuitive level. Using playfulness during care routines as well as specific 'play activities' is a way of building relationships and developing sensitivity towards metacommunication that can assist in understanding choice through responses to initial play cues from staff.

References

Bateson, G. (1972) *Steps to an ecology of mind*, Chicago, IL: University of Chicago Press.

Brown, F. (2008) 'The Playwork Principles: A critique', in F. Brown and C. Taylor (eds) *Foundations of playwork*, Maidenhead: Open University Press.

Carnaby, S. (2004) *People with profound and multiple learning disabilities: A review of research about their lives*, London: Mencap.

Casey, T. (2005) *Inclusive play, practical strategies for working with children aged 3 to 8*, London: Paul Chapman Publishing.

Corke, M. (2012) *Using playful practice to communicate with special children*, Abingdon: Routledge.

Creswell, J.W. (2007) *Qualitative inquiry and research design: Choosing among five approaches* (2nd edn), Thousand Oaks, CA: Sage.

Dewey, J. (1933) *How we think*, New York: Houghton Mifflin.

Hughes, B. (2012) *Evolutionary playwork and reflective analyticpractice* (2nd edn), Abingdon: Routledge.

Lieberman, J.N. (1977) *Playfulness: Its relationship to imagination and creativity*, London: Academic Press.

Mencap (2001) *No ordinary life: The support needs of families caring for children and adults with profound and multiple learning disabilities*, London: Mencap.

Maxwell, S., Reed, G., Saker, J. and Story, V. (2005) 'The two faces of playfulness: A new tool to select potentially successful sales reps', *Journal of Personal Selling and Sales Management*, 25(3): 215–29.

NPFA (National Playing Fields Association), Children's Play Council and Play Link (2000) *Best play: What play provision should do for children*, London: NPFA.

PMLD Network and Mencap (2008) *About profound and multiple learning disabilities*, www.pmldnetwork.org/PMLD%20Definition%20 factsheet%20-%20standard.pdf.

PPSG (Playwork Principles Scrutiny Group) (2005) *The Playwork Principles*, Cardiff: Play Wales.

Simmons, D. (2011) 'The "PMLD ambiguity": Articulating the lifeworlds of children with profound and multiple learning difficulties', paper presented at the Nordic Network on Disability Research (NNDR) 11th Annual Conference, Reykjavík, Iceland, 28 May.

Sturrock, G. and Else, P. (1998) *The playground as therapeutic space: Playwork as healing (The Colorado Paper)*, Sheffield: Ludemos Press.

Sturrock, G. and Else, P. (2005) *Therapeutic playwork reader I*, Sheffield: Ludemos.

Sutton-Smith, B. (1997) *The ambiguity of play*, Cambridge, MA: Harvard University Press.

Smith, S. (2010) *An exploration of disability and special educational needs in playwork*, Gloucester: University of Gloucestershire, unpublished.

Smith, S. and Willans, B. (2007) 'There's no place like a play space: An appreciation of disability and playwork', in W. Russell, B. Handscomb and J. Fitzpatrick (eds) *Playwork voices: In celebration of Bob Hughes and Gordon Sturrock*, London: The London Centre for Playwork Education and Training, pp 167–75.

Ware, J. (1996) *Creating responsive environments for people with profound learning and multiple disabilities*, London: David Fulton.

Watson, D. (2014) *'Go-getters' and 'clever little cookies': A summary of a multi-method study on playfulness and children with PMLD*, Bristol: University of Bristol.

TWELVE

Therapeutic playwork: exploring playworkers' perceptions of therapeutic playwork training and its usefulness in supporting children in afterschool clubs

Claire Hawkes

Introduction

This study developed from observations that playworkers in afterschool clubs in a county in the south of England were struggling to respond to what they saw as challenging behaviour. The purpose of the study was to extend playworkers' understanding of Sturrock and Else's (1998) model of therapeutic playwork and explore their perceptions of its usefulness in afterschool settings. They attended introductory training and then reflected on their practice.

Throughout their childhoods children deal with a range of issues, some more traumatic than others, for example, making and breaking friendships, parents returning to work, changing schools, moving house, hospitalisation, family reorganisation, bullying, separation and death. This is aside from the experiences of those labelled as 'vulnerable' (such as those in the care of the local authority, witnesses of domestic violence, those experiencing abuse or living with impairments or disorders). These issues, emotions and anxieties can manifest themselves in children's play (Axline, 1964; Sturrock and Else, 2005). Through freely chosen play (where the content and intent of play is driven by the child), children can explore themselves and the world around them. They may unconsciously or consciously play with and through issues which they are facing. Play is paradoxical; it is both real and unreal, seen as a safe place to express and explore reality and the imaginary, as events can be replayed, endings changed or games stopped. The signals (verbal and non-verbal) that send the message 'this is play' permit behaviour that may be unacceptable elsewhere; acts can be forgiven as 'only playing'. In addition, psychodynamic theories of play suggest that playing has a latent, symbolic content beyond conscious articulation, alongside its manifest content (Sturrock and Else, 2005).

Many children spend a significant proportion of their time in childcare settings such as afterschool clubs (Wallace et al, 2009). As a local authority Childcare Development Officer, my work involved supporting the playworkers who worked in these settings. During my visits to childcare settings, playworkers voiced concerns about supporting children who showed anxieties and challenging behaviour in their play. Typical behaviour included swearing, shouting, aggression, bullying and teasing. The playworkers expressed a need to understand these play expressions and take on a more supportive role.

This study explored, through training and reflection, the potential for afterschool clubs to be environments where children can play out any emotions and issues and playworkers can support this healing potential of play through what Sturrock and Else (2005) term 'therapeutic playwork'. This perspective does not suggest that playworkers provide play therapy sessions or diagnosis; rather it is exploring the playwork setting as a holistic environment that lends itself to supporting children curatively. The chapter sets the context for the study, in terms of policy and common sense understandings of childhood and play, and what a therapeutic approach may offer. It then describes methodology and methods used before discussing the reflections from the training offered to playworker working in afterschool childcare.

Understandings of childhood

Playwork does not operate in a vacuum (Russell, 2011); government policies and public attitudes regarding the purpose of childhood and play affect the playworker, since policy dictates the allocation of resources. Neither does policy operate in a vacuum: it is influenced by political, economic and social trends. The dominant understanding of childhood, the way childhood is valued, both in policy terms and in broad adult–child relations, generally falls into three (often parallel but contradictory) constructs: angel, devil and the developing child (James et al, 1998). All three constructs see children as fairly passive recipients of adult knowledge and pay little attention to children's agency. Childhood is seen as a rehearsal time to generate skills needed for adult life when they will contribute to society by being active in the employment market (Moss and Petrie, 2002). Children are seen as empty vessels, a blurred dualism of victims and threats, angels who need protecting or devils who need correcting (Moss and Petrie, 2002).

There has been a plethora of policies in England concerning children and families but rarely do they mention 'free-time' or play, as such there is 'no single coherent government message about how play is understood and constructed' (Powell and Wellard, 2008, p 9). With no agreed definition of the value of play, social policy mostly acknowledges it only for the instrumental value in aiding the journey to adulthood. (Note that these UK policies apply to children and families in England. There are different policies in Wales, Scotland and Northern Ireland.)

Policy advocates and endorsers have generated a powerful rhetoric that marginalises other perspectives; as such policy frameworks are grounded in theories of child development, fundamentally focusing on adult support for children to reach their full potential (Russell, 2011). Moss (2007) identifies how, within the developmental paradigm, policy has professionalised the role of the adult, legitimising intervention to ensure that a child is within the 'normal' trajectories on approved development scales. Powell and Wellard (2008) identify this as a 'utilitarian' perspective, seeing children's play only in terms of its contribution to learning, social development, obesity reduction or crime reduction (Lester and Russell, 2008). The assumption here is that play must always be good for children (Brown, 2003). As such play time becomes scrutinised by adults to ensure it is used 'appropriately', and any inappropriate content is curtailed (Guldberg, 2009). Unless linked to development, play is seen as merely silly and foolish (Sutton-Smith, 1997).

The rise in childcare

There has been a significant increase in out of school childcare in the UK as a result of successive government strategies. The launch of the National Childcare Strategy (DfEE, 1998), together with concerns over litigation and the child protection element of the Children Act 1989 led to more emphasis on play provision where children stayed until they were collected by parents (Smith, 2010).

Most afterschool childcare clubs operate on school sites or are connected to schools, and Ailwood (2003) suggests dominant discourses of play in educational settings exert a powerful 'pedagogical force'. Smith and Barker (2000) note that playworkers often imposed school guidelines and behaviour within the club environment. The regulations governing out of school play provision also influence practice. With their legal force within the Children Acts of 1989 and 2004 and Childcare Act 2006, regulations reinforce the developmental paradigm by imposing standards on staffing, adult–child ratios, procedures and child protection. At the time of the research the policy framework influencing UK out of school care provision was the Early Years Foundation Stage (DfE, 2012) which became mandatory for all early years providers (including out of school provision catering for children under 8 years of age) in 2008. Although there have been changes to regulations since, the developmentalist influence remains prevalent.

Understandings of playwork

Scholarly interest in play spans many disciplines including psychology, biology, anthropology, geography and neuroscience. This interest is largely due to play having a multitude of meanings (Sutton-Smith, 1997). This could be a strength or it could be argued that this elusiveness leads to its malleability.

The dominant discourse of childhood and play influences playwork as there is an emphasis on managing, protecting and controlling children, 'channelling them into forms considered developmentally healthy and productive' (Prout, 2005, p 33). There is, however, an alternative perspective where the instrumental value of play is acknowledged, but so too is the intrinsic value. Children need to play for the sake of playing (Hewes, 2006). As Russell (2011, p 7) highlights 'Emotion regulation, stress response systems, attachment systems…creativity and flexibility, openness to learning can all be linked to the sheer nonsense, vitality and enjoyment of playing'. Rather than the developmental paradigm positioning children as dependents (where adults pass on knowledge), this perspective sees children as experts in their play (Beunderman, 2010).

In 1992 the UK playwork sector developed a set of values and assumptions which were replaced in 2005 with the Playwork Principles, the 'professional and ethical framework for playwork…[describing] what is unique about play and playwork' (PPSG, 2005). A playworker working to the Playwork Principles creates flexible environments that enable freely chosen, personally directed play, taking a low-intervention approach. The playing child is the focal point, playworkers remove barriers and create conditions conducive to play (Brown, 2009). The instrumental value of play is understood but adult agendas are put aside as much as possible and the intrinsic value of play is given priority.

Sturrock (2003, p 92) suggests that there is a correlation between the loss of opportunities to play in the wider environment and the increase in 'erratic behaviour, hyperactive syndromes, violent outbursts, suicide and drug use'. He argues that these behaviours suggest a deprivation, a form of 'dis-ease' as a reaction to supressed play needs. Given this, it has been argued (for example Hughes, 2001; Brown, 2009) that playwork settings can act as compensatory play environments, offering important 'opportunities and experiences that have been lost from daily life' (Brown, 2009, p 1). These are places where children can play freely because the adults supporting them understand and advocate the importance of play.

For this research, understanding the working environment was critical. Playworkers in UK afterschool clubs have to work within the childcare context, with its developmental discourse and demands of regulation and inspection regimes. At the same time the Playwork Principles require playworkers to give precedence to the play process over adult agendas. This creates tensions for playworkers, and it is suggested that the approach discussed here may help navigate these tensions.

A therapeutic perspective

Sturrock and Else's (1998) model of therapeutic playwork is predicated on the assertion that play is healing. Influenced by depth psychology, in particular Carl Gustav Jung, they outline a new paradigm, a perspective where the play space has 'ameliorating' potential. If adult psychotherapy involves the 're-playing of neuroses formed in childhood' (Sturrock and Else, 1998, p 4) to understand or release neurosis, then the playwork setting could potentially offer a healing environment by supporting children to play through potential neuroses at the time of formation, thus remedying their development and life in the present, too. The symbolic (latent) elements of playing are important to the child at the time of playing; children are driven to express deeply symbolic material through play. From this perspective, the play space becomes a stage for various enactments which may have meaning for the individual child. The playworker trusts children to 'express' whatever they need through 'playing out' and appreciates the existence of latent meaning or symbolism in these play expressions (termed the 'deep ludic' – derived from *ludo* (Latin for 'I play')), understanding that 'the past informs the play in that expectations, desires, beliefs, abilities and choices of the child will inform the play actions' (Else, 2008, p 81). Adults may only see the manifest content (understood as skills rehearsal) and not appreciate latent elements. However, if adults appreciate this symbolic expression (playing out of material) and develop a heightened sense of self-reflection, they could support the playing child more curatively.

Therapeutic playwork, as described by Sturrock and Else (1998), considers free play with a psychoanalytic application (although not wholly in the traditional Freudian sense). This perspective they call 'ludocentric' (play centred), with the playing child being the primary focus since the attendant adult services the play. The focus of therapeutic playwork is not on diagnosing children but on an understanding and appreciation of observation, both of the playing child and the attendant adult. The healing potential is in the form of children's play expressions, images, thoughts and desires manifesting from the space around them using 'toys, clay, earth, other elements, other children (and sometimes adults), found and forged materials and "stuff"' (Sturrock, 2003, p 89).

Influencing therapeutic playwork is Freud's (1920) notion of uncovering repressed content; alongside Jung's (1969) more mythical understanding of manifest and latent material, conscious and unconscious contexts, the 'collective unconscious' and archetypes. Sturrock and Else (1998) take these concepts and also consider playing out material without any rational analysis. As with all creative processes, play can allow fantasy material where unconscious contents could surface into the conscious. Many of these symbols are common across cultures and time, echoing Jung's archetypes of the collective unconscious, a useful reference for appreciating the significance, if not precisely interpreting the content of play expressions. Sturrock (1996, p 18) advocates that an understanding of the latent symbolic expressions would help playworkers in their practice, aiding them in 'making judgements about the play intervention and content of the child's play'. He is not advocating that playworkers become clinical psychologists, instead he suggests that the 'guesses' of the symbolism will suffice and appreciates meaning will vary among playworkers. Polysemic guesses (multiple and uncertain meaning) are acceptable as playworkers work in a field of unknowing.

The sensitive adult

To support the playing out of symbolic material and not 'adulterate' the play space (put an adult agenda over the playing child's) adults need to be highly skilled and sensitive to reading the language of play. In their model of 'psycholudics' (the study of the mind and psyche at play), Sturrock and Else (1998) present a technical language for describing the play process. They argue that the play sector needs to create its own language where the essence of the work remains the same but the new vocabulary is aimed at a more 'transcendent means of working' (Sturrock and Else, 1998, p 5). They describe six elements of the play process, making up a full 'ludic cycle' critical to healthy development: metalude (the internalised formation preceding the cue); cue (the invitation to play, which comes in many forms and could be to another person, an object or the environment); return (the answer to the invitation to play); frame (the psychological and/or physical boundary to the play); flow (where the child is immersed in the play, this could last seconds or weeks); annihilation (play ends as the child no longer wishes to engage in play). Through understanding the ludic cycle, playworkers will be able to 'co-operate intelligently' (Sturrock and Else, 1998, p 8). The ability to interpret diverse cues and respond appropriately is seen as a fundamental skill. If play cues are repeatedly ignored or responses are inappropriate then the play cycle may break down causing a range of behaviours that Sturrock and Else (1998) term 'dysplay'.

Playworkers can create a 'holding' environment (a Winnicottian term, similar to the concept of containment) where the 'play frame is the holding limitation or boundary for the projected ludic material' (Sturrock and Else, 1998, p 11). This is a space which is initiated by the child and retains meaning for the child. Playworkers need to be reliably available to the child, aware of their part in the play process; providing a supportive enclosure in which children consider it safe to express symbolic material, 'play[ing] out love and hate, conflict and resolution, creativity and destruction as a prelude to growth' (Sturrock, 2003, p 95). Drawing on Winnicott's (1971) concept of 'potential space' and Ogden's (2001) 'analytic third', Sturrock (2003) talks of the 'ludic third', a space created between the playing child and the attendant playworker.

The effect of play on adults

The idealisation of childhood creates images of play as essentially good, but in reality play is not always nice (Sutton-Smith, 1997). Children can play with strong emotions or concepts such as power and identity, which can be upsetting or frightening for playworkers. Play can be nasty: 'taunts, pranks, initiations, bullying, racism, excluding, obscenities, toilet humour, rhymes and songs, and games of power and resistance against adults' (Russell, 2006, p 7). Conflict is a part of children's play (Corsaro, 2003). Adults' idealisation of play, alongside literal readings of manifest play expressions, can obscure appreciation of more symbolic meaning and lead to understanding such play expressions as challenging behaviour.

Playworkers should have an appreciation of how play expressions affect them and be conscious of their own unplayed-out material

(Sturrock, 2003). Influenced by the Jungian concept of 'inner psychic reality', Sturrock and Else (1998) advocate the playworker should be sensitive to the different ways adults may take over play with their natural power and authority, termed 'adulteration'.

Unavoidably, adults bring their personal history to the play space and in some cases this can include unresolved issues from their past which rise to the surface and manifest themselves, contaminating the child's play process. Play becomes polluted by the playworker's conscious and unconscious thoughts. Therapeutic playwork suggests that through developing an awareness of their own unplayed-out material, their 'triggers' and 'lures', playworkers can recognise this unplayed-out material and its potential to adulterate the child's play.

Common to all therapeutic relationships is the notion of transference, where feelings or attitudes are unconsciously transferred from a situation or person in the past on to another, usually the analyst (Gelso et al, 1991). The holding environment of the play space makes it highly likely that transference will occur. Playworkers may see children upset or elated from their school day and 'acting out'. Sometimes emotions are projected onto toys, the environment and other children, but also onto the playworkers. These play expressions, particularly if they are aggressive in nature, could be seen as challenging behaviour (Sturrock, 2003). In turn playworkers need to be mindful of counter-transference, the projection of their own feelings, emotions and unplayed-out material onto the child. Sturrock and Else (1998) highlight that there needs to be an opportunity for playworkers to reflect on and analyse their actions, emotions and feelings, limiting counter-transference. Other therapeutic practitioners are required to have supervision or a form of therapy themselves, in order for emotions to be played out, away from the direct relationship with a client. There are no systems for similar levels of support and supervision for playworkers in the UK.

Sturrock (2003) suggests that playworkers need to operate in a 'witness position' where they are fully present but mindful of their own preconceptions, prejudices and unplayed-out material. Brawgs Continuum (Sturrock et al, 2004) (Figure 12.1) offers a model for reflecting on responses to the playing child. Drawing on Battram's (1999) model of complexity it develops a dynamic continuum, playworkers move up and down the continuum, constantly counterbalancing their behaviour as they are pulled in one direction or the other.

Figure 12.1: Brawgs continuum

External	**Didactic**	**Ludocentric**	**Chaotic**
Internal	**Non-ludic**	**Paraludic**	**Ludic**

Source: Sturrock et al, 2004.

The upper layer considers the range of playwork behaviour from 'didactic' (very directive, typical of the development discourse) to 'chaotic' (almost negligent and out of control). Between these two extremes of order and chaos is 'ludocentric' (supportive of play), also known as the 'zone of complexity'. The lower layer considers the range of internal emotions that play provokes in playworkers, these range from 'non-ludic' (the desire to correct the behaviour), to 'ludic' (uncaring or overly absorbed in their own play due to unplayed-out material). Between these two extremes is the 'paraludic' (playing with the child but supporting play in the witness position).

The direction of playwork

Playworkers have a challenging balancing act of working both within the dominant progress rhetoric (Sutton–Smith, 1997) and to the more intrinsic principles of the sector. Psycholudics is an attempt to re-privilege the child at play, making the playing child the focus and acknowledging that the play process has a healing function. Although some aspects of therapeutic playwork, in particular the play cycle as a technical tool to understand the play process, are embedded within the Playwork Principles (PPSG, 2005) and within playwork qualifications, the symbolic/latent nature of play is less often acknowledged, leaving opportunity for the meaning to be lost or open to broader interpretation. This research sought to explore whether a more comprehensive understanding of this aspect of the model might help playworkers to be more prepared in their responses and desire to support children in afterschool clubs.

Methodology and methods

The epistemological position of this study was social constructivism, where knowledge of the playworker's world is constructed. Instead of testing a hypothesis, it built a picture by gathering data, looking for patterns, consistencies and meanings. At the same time, the intervention was intended to bring about real change for the playworkers; in this sense the methodology included aspects of action research, although time did not permit a fully iterative approach. The methodology was therefore a hybrid of participatory action research and ethnography.

The group of participants was self-selecting from out of school workers across the county, and was a representative mix. The research followed the guidelines for ethics and was approved by the Faculty Research Ethics Committee; in particular, voluntary informed consent was gained from all participants and data confidentiality and security processes were observed. These playworkers took part in two workshops (12 hours in total), which introduced therapeutic playwork concepts and techniques, encouraged reflection and reflexivity, and challenged playworkers to look both at themselves and their practice. The researcher took part in the therapeutic playwork training to enable the gathering of a 'thick description', a typical ethnographic characteristic (Creswell, 1994), allowing patterns of behaviour, common values and beliefs, and shared experiences among the playworkers to be revealed and further explored.

Semi-structured informal interviews were then used to generate further data on reflections and changes to practice. The workshops introduced a light touch application of therapeutic playwork concepts, highlighted the manifest/latent aspect of the model, the necessity of understanding the self in terms of unplayed-out material and the potential to adulterate. The workshops were led by Gordon Sturrock, one of the authors of the original Colorado Paper (Sturrock and Else, 1998); this allowed the participants to understand not only the paper and its original concept without bias from other perspectives, but also its author's own reflections and continued deepening commitment to the approach since publishing.

Reflections

Overall participants felt that they could understand playwork from a new perspective, one that had challenged them both personally and professionally. Some quotes are shown below (unacknowledged due to confidentiality) that demonstrate the participants' feelings and personal journeys from the study. The 'light touch' application of therapeutic playwork led to changes in practice that encouraged a more ludocentric application of playwork.

While reflecting on the workshops, some common elements arose in particular around enjoyment, language and change. Enjoyment came from the feeling that the training filled a gap in their knowledge. The intensely personal nature of the course may have also fulfilled a desire to work more collaboratively (some previously explained they felt isolated in their practice). Their experiences demonstrated that they were already providing an informal therapeutic role and there was a commonality that motivation came from wanting to enhance the play space.

There was a reluctance to use the 'technical language', suggesting that more needs to be done on raising awareness in the playwork sector to understand the play cycle in its entirety.

The participants said that the workshops generated a change in practice: "it's changed everything", in particular how they saw behaviour: "It reinforced to me that children respond to the emotions they feel and often they don't have the words to describe how they are feeling." Local authority development workers also noted how it altered their approach to advising playwork settings: "It completely changed how I look at an afterschool club and what they offer." This suggests that although brief, the topics covered in the workshops were enough to develop an interest in the paradigm and a 'light touch application' was supportive to playworkers. It encouraged participants to become more reflective practitioners.

Four prominent themes arose from these elements and from analysing the interview transcripts: reflection, play expressions, tensions in practice and paradigm shift.

Reflection (unplayed-out material leading to adulteration)

The reaction during and after the main exercise of the first workshop was intense, as it was a very personal exercise aimed at supporting them to think about their own unplayed-out material. This dominated both workshops and had an impact on practice. The experience generated some extreme emotions. All the participants commented on the value of self-exploration. Participants could see how they affect the child's play space and how their unplayed-out material may contaminate. This underpinning concept of therapeutic playwork made a difference to practice almost immediately. Within everyday practice there had been little emphasis on such self-reflection. Even those that considered themselves to be reflective had not challenged themselves in this way or had the confidence to challenge others.

Play expressions (playing out material – latent symbolism)

There was acceptance of the idea of latent symbolism:

> "Children will act out through play even though sometimes
> we don't realise they are doing it, so when you've got them
> maybe fighting out with some dolls or teddies it's quite
> reasonable to think that they actually might be acting out
> a scenario that they have witnessed or been part of."

Many said that they believed that they were informally providing therapeutic environments. The training gave participants confidence to talk to children and not shy away from subjects. One participant highlighted that in youth club environments the expectation is that "young people may divulge things to you that are particularly difficult" and that it is "harder for people who worked in the day with preschool children and nursery children to make that transition and maybe that's about them not wanting to investigate because it might actually mean that something will come up."

This might suggest exploring some of the material covered in youth sector training may be advantageous to playworkers.

A thorough understanding of the deep symbolism of play was absent in the reflections and interviews. Using the play cycle and self-reflection beyond mere technique and into the realms of depth psychology was briefly discussed and intrigued the group; however, the concept was overshadowed by individuals' self-reflection and unplayed-out material. Had there been more time this would have been more fully explored. This adds to the understanding that the course gave a 'light touch' version of therapeutic playwork.

Tensions in practice (the development rhetoric)

The reflections highlighted that the development rhetoric was dominant and did influence all the clubs. This might suggest that Smith and Barker's (2000) findings have not changed in the intervening years. Some clubs did impose the school rules, or developed coping strategies that permitted playful behaviour (shouting, running, climbing trees) after the school staff had left for the day. Those situated on school sites without a dedicated space felt that teachers were carrying out overt and covert surveillance. Tensions existed between utilitarian views and working to a form of practice that recognised the Playwork Principles. Some participants commented on feeling isolated in early years settings as playwork was valued less than the early years pedagogy. One participant had tried to raise the profile of playwork by requesting space on the day nursery's team agenda but their manager felt that this information was not considered a priority. This is disappointing as the participant felt strongly that the skills could transfer to early years and help bridge the feeling of a divide between the two sectors. This echoes Rennie's (2003) observations that playworkers manage a constant balancing act. Those that had premises a short walk off the school site considered this to be invaluable in separating the expectations and 'rules' between school and club.

The reflections also evidenced Palmer's (2003) understanding of practice being a mixture of theory, individuals' beliefs and external influences. Although practice was diverse (playwork theory was evident albeit with fuzzy edges) there was a shared respect for playwork with a belief that clubs were separate from the school day and offered an opportunity for children to play for the sake of playing. It is interesting that to some, the concept of free play was new (particularly those working in early years environments). The light touch version of therapeutic playwork supported a deeper understanding of theory, and this helped practitioners become confident in their ability to tip the balancing act more in favour of a ludocentric approach.

Paradigm shift (the desire to understand a different perspective)

The degree to which participants voiced a need for a 'paradigm shift' had not been anticipated. Playworkers felt more needed to be done to explore this perspective and transfer this knowledge to generate a change. All participants felt that they had "just scratched the surface" and wanted to know more. Initially the group's perception of their training needs focused on specific situations such as bereavement, bullying or divorce. However, in the second workshop the group voiced a need for more generic training in communication skills with children, reading children's expressions, body language and neuro-linguistic programming. This suggests that the first workshop changed their understanding of what skills they already had; being intuitive with their experience and emotions gave them confidence in supporting children in specific situations.

The group commented that they could not get more information of this kind from other avenues. Despite attending lots of training, including level 3 qualifications, the group felt that they had not encountered this approach or understanding before and felt it made a positive impact on their practice. Although the latent symbolism of play is not recognised within playwork qualifications, the play process, the importance of reflection and the concept of adulteration are included. The group felt strongly that therapeutic playwork theories should be included within qualifications: "We don't equip workers today in a way that maybe we should do."

As well as a personal thirst for more knowledge (on playwork, therapeutic playwork and psychological theories), there was a drive to champion this 'light touch' version of therapeutic playwork. The group all cited the tutor as "inspiring", "passionate" and "fascinating". What they particularly valued was the fact he was well read in a range of psychological and psycho-analytical theories. The group enjoyed and responded to this level of passion, as it generated a collective energy that inspired them. They wanted to recreate this. The group voiced disappointment at being 'fed up' with bodies that represented the playwork sector, feeling that the therapeutic playwork perspective fitted more with the reason why they had come into playwork and it was not given enough recognition or consideration. The group felt that more needed to be done across the UK to inspire and upskill the workforce with this knowledge. More locally, the group wanted to inspire playworkers by becoming 'play champions'. The consensus from these participants was that "everybody should do it [this training]".

Participants explained how the workshops supported their communication with all children; all the interviews (including the author) contained reflections on their own children and other contexts of working with children, for example, Special Educational Needs, early years, youth work and Children's Centres. It was felt that the skills of self-reflection, communication and the technical play process were not limited to playwork, a point argued in Sturrock et al (2004).

Conclusion

This study investigated the use of therapeutic playwork concepts with playworkers and, although small scale, has been able to draw conclusions which could potentially enhance the Childcare Development role and support settings to operate in more ludocentric and therapeutic ways. Sturrock and Else's (1998) therapeutic playwork model has been explored, together with perceptions of ability to provide therapeutic playwork spaces following light touch training.

The research confirms the literature's identification of a 'tension' between policy's instrumental value of play and the principles of the UK playwork sector, which focuses on the primacy of the playing child over adult agendas. The instrumental value of play is acknowledged but so, too, is its intrinsic value. Therapeutic playwork, predicated on the assertion that play is healing and offers a stage for enactments of symbolic expression, was welcomed by the research participants. This perspective validated feelings that some were already providing an informal therapeutic role but felt unprepared in supporting play expressions that were often understood as challenging behaviour. It was a new perspective for all the participants, overall the knowledge was valued and produced a desire to learn more.

The workshops challenged participants both personally and professionally. The self-reflection exercises demonstrated how adults' personal history, beliefs and unresolved issues can contaminate the play space. The play cycle is acknowledged within playwork qualifications, but often in a simplistic or technical manner that does not account for ideas of play's latent as well as manifest content. This 'new' information and new perspective was seen to be critical in changing practice.

The research demonstrated that clubs can provide a space for the expression of latent material. Participants perceived behaviour through a different paradigm, seeing that it could be the expression of transference, latent material or a breakdown in the play process (dysplay). Participants reported being more reflective practitioners (sensitive adults) able to read the play process and be more aware of adult-led agendas such as promoting prosocial behaviour. The group felt strongly that more needed to be done (both nationally and locally) to champion and advocate therapeutic playwork.

In addition to the core aims of this enquiry, the research highlighted that fact that the underpinning concepts of therapeutic playwork could be beneficial to those working in other disciplines. The research participants worked in a variety of settings, including afterschool clubs, children's centres, youth clubs and day nurseries. Therapeutic playwork was considered to be supportive to practitioners beyond the ages typically limited to playwork in out of school clubs (4–12 years).

References

Ailwood, J. (2003) 'Governing early childhood education through play', *Contemporary Issues in Early Childhood*, 4(3): 286–99.

Axline, V. (1964) *Play therapy*, Boston, MA: Houghton Mifflin.

Barker, J., Smith, F., Morrow, V., Weller, S., Hey, V. and Harwin, J. (2003) *The impact of out of school care: A qualitative study examining the views of children, families and playworkers*, DfES Research Report 446, London: DfES.

Battram, A. (1999) *Navigating complexity: The essential guide to complexity theory in business and management*, London: Industrial Society.

Beunderman, J. (2010) *People make play*, London: National Children's Bureau.

Brown, F. (2009) *What is playwork? Children's Play Information Service fact sheet No 14*, London: National Children's Bureau.

Corsaro, W. (2003) *'We're friends, right?': Inside kids' culture*, Washington, DC: Joseph Henry Press.

Creswell, J. (1994) *Research design: Qualitative and quantitative approaches*, London: Sage.

DfE (Department for Education) (2012) *Statutory framework for the Early Years Foundation Stage*, Runcorn: DfE.

DfEE (Department for Education and Employment) (1998) *Meeting the childcare challenge: A framework and consultation document*, London: The Stationery Office.

Else, P. (2008) 'Playing: the space between', in F. Brown, and C. Taylor (eds) *Foundations of playwork*, Maidenhead: Open University Press, pp 79–83.

Freud, S. (1920) *A general introduction to psychoanalysis*, New York: Horace Liveright.

Gelso, C.J., Hill, C.E. and Kivlighan, D.M. (1991) 'Transference, insight, and the counselor's intentions during a counseling hour', *Journal of Counseling and Development*, 69(5): 428–33.

Guldberg, H. (2009) *Reclaiming childhood: Freedom and play in an age of fear*, London: Routledge.

Hewes, J. (2006) *Let the children play: Nature's answer to early learning*, Edmonton, Canada: Canadian Council on Learning.

Hughes, B. (2001) *Evolutionary playwork and reflective analytic practice*, London: Routledge.

James, A., Jenks, C. and Prout, A. (1998) *Theorizing childhood*, Cambridge: Polity Press.

Jung, C.G. (1969) *On the nature of the psyche*, London: Ark Paperbacks.

Lester, S. and Russell, W. (2008) *Play for a change: Play, policy and practice – A review of contemporary perspectives*, London: National Children's Bureau.

Moss, P. (2007) 'Meetings across the paradigmatic divide', *Educational Philosophy and Theory*, 39(3): 229–45.

Moss, P. and Petrie, P. (2002) *From children's services to children's spaces*, London: Routledge.

Ogden, T. (2001) *Conversations at the frontier of dreaming*, London: Karnac Books.

Palmer, S. (2003) 'Playwork as reflective practice', in F. Brown (ed) *Playwork: Theory and practice*, Buckingham: Open University Press, pp 176–90.

PPSG (Playwork Principles Scrutiny Group) (2005) *Playwork Principles*, Cardiff: Play Wales.

Powell, S. and Wellard, I. (2008) *Policies and play: The impact of national policies on children's opportunities for play*, London: National Children's Bureau.

Prout, A. (2005) *The future of childhood*, London: Routledge.

Rennie, S. (2003) 'Making play work: The fundamental role of play in the development of social relationship skills', in F. Brown (ed) *Playwork: Theory and practice*, Buckingham: Open University Press, pp 18–31.

Russell, W. (2006) *Reframing playwork: Reframing challenging behaviour*, Nottingham: Nottingham City Council.

Russell, W. (2011) 'Pyramid playwork: Four triangular analyses of playwork as the production of space where children can play', *IPA World Conference*, July, Cardiff: Play Wales.

Smith, H.H. (2010) *Children's empowerment, play and informal learning in two after school provisions*, PhD thesis, London: Middlesex University.

Smith, F. and Barker, J. (2000) '"Out of school", in school: A social geography of out of school childcare', in S. Holloway and G. Valentine (eds) *Children's geographies: Playing, living, learning*, London: Routledge, pp 245–56.

Sturrock, G. (1996) 'A diet of worms', in G. Sturrock and P. Else (eds) *Therapeutic playwork reader one (1995–2000)*, Sheffield: Ludemos, pp 10–20.

Sturrock, G. (2003) 'Towards a psycholudic definition of playwork', in F. Brown (ed) *Playwork: Theory and practice*, Buckingham: Open University Press, pp 81–98.

Sturrock, G. and Else, P. (1998) *The playground as therapeutic space: Playwork as healing (The Colorado Paper)*, Sheffield: Ludemos.

Sturrock, G. and Else, P. (2005) *Therapeutic playwork reader one*, Sheffield: Ludemos.

Sturrock, G., Russell, W. and Else, P. (2004) *Towards ludogogy, parts I, II and III: The art of being and becoming through play.* Sheffield: Ludemos.

Sutton-Smith, B. (1997) *The ambiguity of play*, Cambridge, MA: Harvard University Press.

Wallace, E., Smith, K., Pye, J., Crouch, J., Ziff, A. and Burston, K. (2009) *Extended schools survey of schools, pupils and parents: A quantitative study of perceptions and usage of extended services in schools. Research Report DCSF-RR068.* London: Department for Children, Families and Schools and Ipsos MORI.

Winnicott, D.W. (1971) *Playing and reality*, Harmondsworth: Penguin.

THIRTEEN

Play, playwork and wellbeing

Nic Matthews, Hilary Smith, Denise Hill and Lindsey Kilgour

Introduction

Wellbeing and wellness are phrases that have increasingly found favour within public policy and the lexicon of health-related professional communities, particularly in the UK (ONS, 2011; Cabinet Office and DoE, 2013; DoH, 2014). Individuals and groups seeking to advocate action to address health and economic inequalities and social injustices also draw on the terms to bring attention to disparities in opportunities and life chances (Wilkinson and Pickett, 2009; Marmot, 2010). Despite the growing visibility of wellbeing it remains a contested term associated as much with objective measures of quality of life (in economic, educational and psychological terms) as with more subjective and colloquial notions of happiness. This versatility means it is hard to come to an agreed meaning (Ereaut and Whiting, 2008; OECD, 2009) and identify research strategies that capture its essence. Working definitions commonly identify links to a positive state of mind and body, feeling safe, a capacity to cope and an ability to build positive relationships (for example, Foresight Mental Capital and Wellbeing Project, 2008; Ben-Arieh et al, 2014). While such definitions reflect a range of influencing factors, it is suggested that wellbeing research is framed by 'binary language' (for example, characterised as objective versus subjective or state versus process) (Amerijckx and Humblet, 2014). As a consequence, the challenge for policy makers, advocates for social change, researchers and practitioners is to find a meaningful way to articulate what wellbeing is and how to understand it within the context of individuals' lives and for different demographic groups.

This chapter details a year-long project undertaken with the staff of a playwork charity in the south west of England (*Play Gloucestershire*) and the children[1] they worked with. The active engagement of children and playworkers (also referred to as play rangers in this chapter[2]) in the project allowed insight into what attending an open access play setting[3] might bring to a child's wellbeing. Facilitated by the play rangers, the children's experiences were elicited through visual and participatory methods. This ensured the work was child and play-centred, authentically documenting the activities and interactions that characterise the free play environment fostered by the professionals and volunteers operating across the sites involved. For the play rangers, the project was an opportunity to undertake some training on and understand more about wellbeing and how their practice might contribute to its enhancement. This is valuable in its own right but equally it is becoming critical for the sustaining of play services that professionals in the sector understand how their work may link with, or support, the work of other professional groups engaging with young people. The latter can be beneficial when seeking funding and can encourage playworkers to advocate for the value of play among other professional communities (for example, those linked to health and social work). The importance of collating evidence on the wider impact of play initiatives, and the need to increase the opportunities for play, were set out by Gill (2014). The challenges to the sector and the potential value of the health agenda to playwork provision are discussed later in the chapter as this framed the context to the project and the approach adopted.

Childhood wellbeing research: concepts and contexts

The characterisation of wellbeing research as 'binary' is indicative of the fact that many studies focus on particular facets of wellbeing. In drawing together the literature on children's wellbeing Amerijckx and Humblet (2014) rightly argue that the concept is multi-dimensional and operating at multiple levels, yet studies tend to be located on 'five structural theoretical axes' (p 409): subjective versus objective; individual versus community; state versus process; material versus spiritual; and positive versus negative. Furthermore, the studies also seem to focus on 'the salience of one pole of the axis' (p 411). This was more likely to be the negative, objective, material 'end' at the expense of the more subjective and positive dimensions. This characterisation reflects the breadth of domains, from the individual to the societal level, which can inform a child's wellbeing and also some of the disparities in the quality of life experienced by children. A recent Report Card from UNICEF *Children of the recession* is indicative of the uneven ways in which national economies have dealt with and come through the 2008 recession. It highlights the economic and social challenges for governments but also the potential to address child poverty and wellbeing through social policies (UNICEF, 2014). It is against such a socio-political background that providers of UK play services seek to sustain activities that engage children and contribute to their quality of life.

The mix of variables linked to wellbeing can make it harder for those wanting to understand and promote it to articulate what it is and how they might influence it. The most well-rehearsed dimensions within the research literature focus on the quality of relationships, environments and 'the self and freedoms' (Dex and Hollingworth, 2012, p 15). UNICEF, for example, monitors six dimensions of wellbeing: family and peer relationships, material wellbeing, health and safety, educational wellbeing, behaviour and risk. Further research has explored life satisfaction on the basis of individual differences such as: age and gender (Knies, 2012), ethnicity (Valois et al, 2003), and socio-economic status (Marmot, 2010). There is also work that focuses on how wellbeing is influenced by different settings including: schools (Fryenberg et al, 2009), neighbourhoods and home life (Tisdale and Pitt-Catsuphes, 2012) and outdoor environments (Thompson Coon et al, 2011). What is striking is that while the value of play has been examined, the contribution of play to wellbeing is a less well-developed field of enquiry (see Play England, 2008; Dell Clark, 2013; Abdullah et al, 2014).

Childhood wellbeing research: approaches and agendas

The current understanding of the concept is underpinned by cross-sectional work from well-established national (UK) and international organisations such as UNICEF, The Children's Society, the New Economics Foundation and the Office of National Statistics. This is increasingly being complemented by a body of research that seeks to describe a holistic picture of childhood wellbeing.

The wellbeing of children has been monitored internationally by the Health Behaviour in School-aged Children (HBSC) research group since 1983. The school-based, self-completion survey work, undertaken on a four-year cycle across 44 countries, offers insight into the social determinants of children's general health and wellbeing (for example, HBSC, 2009; Currie et al, 2012). UNICEF has also contributed to the quantitative research literature through its *Report Cards* (for example, UNICEF, 2007; 2014) and the qualitative literature through commissioning work such as that completed by Ipsos Mori Social Research Institute and Nairns (2011). This project, with young people in the UK, Spain and Sweden, involved two phases: non-participant ethnographic work with 24 families; and in-school discussion groups and in-depth interviews. The work considered explicitly the relationship between materialism, inequality and wellbeing reflecting the current research interest on how economic conditions, austerity, social policy and consumer culture inform quality of life.

Other international projects (for example *Young Lives* which focuses on international development and child poverty) have utilised creative methodologies and longitudinal work to complement cross-sectional studies and has argued that children's accounts of their experiences are crucial to understanding agency in wellbeing (Crivello et al, 2009; Morrow and Crivello, 2015). In the UK the New Economics Foundation and The Children's Society have completed a mixed methods study on childhood wellbeing (Abdullah et al, 2014). Together, these projects respond to a call for research to look holistically at wellbeing and for that work to feed into policy and inform practice.

The importance of continuing to monitor wellbeing at a national and international level is highlighted by the most recent *The good childhood report* (The Children's Society, 2015) which suggests that in the UK young people's overall life satisfaction has 'stalled'. The latest *Children's worlds* survey suggests that children's self-reported wellbeing was largely positive but that they were more satisfied with family and friendships than school life and their local area (Rees and Main, 2015). The latter is an important consideration for playworkers, particularly those seeking to promote children's use of space in their neighbourhood through free, open-access provision.

Play as a way to wellbeing: taking an assets approach to wellness

It was observed earlier that despite research spanning five theoretical axes more needs to be done to bring those axes together and offer a holistic view of wellbeing. This is a challenge for researchers and practitioners seeking to understand the domains which influence wellbeing. The team for the current project drew on frameworks used in assets-based health strategies as one way of doing this. This approach to health promotion has three guiding principles: to use the language of assets (resources already at someone's disposal) rather than deficits (needs to be met); to focus on the determinants of health not poor health; and to recognise the value of psycho-social factors to positive health outcomes. It is a holistic approach which looks at how factors at the population, community and individual level have an impact on health and wellbeing. Examples might include environmental conditions, social networks and adopted health behaviours, respectively (Morgan and Ziglio, 2007).

This layering was important for the project. While the work was about exploring what an open access, free play service might contribute to attendees' wellbeing through the children's own words and participation, it was also about locating playwork in a wider wellbeing context as a community asset with the capacity to link to wider health and social care agendas. To date the research literature has focused on asset-based initiatives in public health, community development and in education but there is potential to also use it in play contexts. For the project team, the approach offered a clear articulation of the mix of experiences, competencies, relationships and settings that can contribute to wellbeing. This offered the *Play Gloucestershire* team a health-related framework which shared their interest in promoting resilience, self-efficacy and connectedness among young people.

The project utilised the 40 development assets identified by the *Search Institute* grouped under eight categories: positive identity, social competencies, constructive use of time (for example, participation in the arts and sports), support, positive values, empowerment, boundaries and expectations and commitment to learning (within an educational context) (Scales, 1999; Search Institute, 2006). These have specifically been assessed through quantitative means in schools since 1990 but it was felt that there was scope to use the assets framework in different settings through qualitative approaches (also see Matthews et al, 2015). Other frameworks have been used by, for example, The Children's Society in its *Ways to wellbeing* report (Abdullah et al, 2014). This mixed-method study followed up work undertaken by the New Economic Foundation which assessed the evidence regarding those activities that contribute to wellbeing among adults, identifying *Five ways to wellbeing* (Thompson and Aked, 2011). Abdullah et al (2014) looked for the five themes among children. Common ground was shared in four: connecting, being active, learning and giving. There was also some support for the fifth theme 'taking notice' (mindfulness) but in addition 'playing, creativity and imagination' was seen as worthy of being a category in its own right for children.

Within these frameworks the themes are set out differently but there are commonalities in that they focus on what is accessible to young people (the resources/assets at their disposal), the significance of people and relationships and the activities that are available. In combination these build a picture of wellbeing that is drawn from young people having the opportunity to: participate in divergent activities that foster creativity and competence; develop meaningful connections with peers and adults who provide social support; and live in neighbourhoods that afford them security and a chance to take risks. The focus on wellbeing as a process, promoting positive values, community and the 'spiritual' attends to the earlier assertion that wellbeing research tends to focus on negative axes.

Playworkers and children at play: partners in research

The Playwork Principles (PPSG, 2005) define what is unique about playwork, articulating a particular approach to working with children and young people at play. In doing so, wellbeing is mentioned explicitly. Principle 1 refers to 'the healthy development and wellbeing of individuals and communities' and Principle 8 encourages playworkers to adopt a style of practice that balances 'risk with the developmental benefit and wellbeing of children'. Furthermore, the Playwork Principles make reference to reflective practice and playworkers acting as 'advocates for play when engaging with adult led agendas'.

The latter was important to the project. Part of the context to the work was recognition of the current climate in which playwork operates. A changing economic environment, in particular, has tested the sector (McKendrick et al, 2014). First, providers of community play services are operating under increasing financial pressures and this affects their ability to sustain services. Second, funding comes from outside the play sector, this results in playworkers looking to social services, health and other agencies for resources and collaborations. These partnerships require playworkers to engage with other policy agendas and understand how their practice can support and fit with those from other professional communities (Play England, 2008). A collection of papers in the first issue of the *Journal of Playwork Practice* argues specifically that, despite the challenges playworkers face, the potential to collaborate and bring playwork to a wider audience is an opportunity not to be missed. In that volume Smith (2014) particularly highlights the 'reflective practitioner researcher' role. Playworkers are well placed to produce practice-based research in partnership with researchers and, what is more important, in collaboration with the young people with whom they engage.

Research that puts the voice of young people 'front and centre' requires professionals to enhance their understanding of research possibilities and also appreciate how their tacit knowledge can contribute to the evidence base on playwork. It is also important that the methods used encourage the young participants to be active agents in the research process. Such naturalistic enquiry alongside cross-sectional work will ensure children are visible within research into their wellbeing (Dex and Hollingworth, 2012).

Playwork and participatory research: co-producing knowledge

Article 12 of the United Nations Convention on the Rights of the Child (1989) sets out the right of children to express their own opinion on matters that pertain to them. This reinforces the need for practitioners and researchers to engage young people actively in research and evaluation activities. This has led to a growing interest in participatory research techniques and creative methodologies that put children's voices at the centre of enquiries into childhood. Despite the interest and value in working *with* children there is demand to see more work that identifies children as the co-researchers or co-creators of knowledge. France et al (2002) referred to children as 'competent reporters' of their own lives. Leitch (2008) argues subsequently for the use of creative methods to capture children's experiences, with the children also acting as co-interpreters. For playworkers there is potential to support the call for more child-centred research by using participatory techniques within their practice. This can help to build the evidence-base for what playwork brings to children and local communities.

Central to participatory research is the focus on empowerment and emancipation; a desire to soften the hierarchical relationship between the researcher and the researched (Schäfer, 2012). It is valuable for exploring playwork within open access play settings as the approach means that young people are already in an environment/space where they are familiar and comfortable (O'Kane, 2008). Playwork also draws on storytelling, drawing, photography and other child-led activities that are less dependent on literacy and dialogue. Furthermore, playworkers are skilled at developing ongoing and meaningful relationships with the children with whom they engage. They are, therefore, well-placed to be co-researchers as they are integral to the play experience and accomplished at working with children. This can facilitate inclusive research that reflects the child's perspective offering a 'portal' into their experiences using their skills and capacities (Carter and Ford, 2013). However, the challenge of using participatory approaches to elicit research materials from children is to ensure the robustness of the data.

The more creative the means of data collection, the more concerns can be raised about the analysis, interpretation and representation of the materials, particularly in terms of the retention of the child's perspective. That caveat aside, the growing body of research literature that incorporates participatory and visual techniques recognises that such approaches bring something different to adults' understanding of children's lives. The primacy of language as the 'privileged medium for the creation and communication of knowledge' (Bagnoli, 2009, p 547) remains but this can and should be complemented by methods that allow children an alternative avenue for self-expression.

Designing and delivering the Art of Wellbeing project

This small-scale participatory research project involved researchers from the University of Gloucestershire and the team at *Play Gloucestershire*. Ethical clearance was given by the researchers' Faculty Research Ethics Panel. Approval covered the data collection procedures, the information leaflets given to children and parents and the voluntary informed consent forms that the children signed. The project had two objectives: to pilot a training programme for playworkers in community settings which would promote awareness of issues associated with childhood wellbeing and child-centred research techniques; and to use participatory methods to identify and examine critically how open access play provision might contribute to children's wellbeing. Building a picture of how children engage with open access play services and how this might support wellbeing is a challenge as such provision is by its very nature informal. However, this also makes it a suitable setting for blending visual and oral data. It is also necessary to acknowledge the environment encouraged a 'fluid' engagement with the discussions, as is appropriate in research that seeks to address issues of hierarchy (Schäfer, 2012) and encourage participation on the children's terms.

There were two concurrent phases of work. First, the research team delivered a one-day training event that included sessions on wellbeing and on creative methodologies. Follow-up support was then offered at the sites used for play sessions. A series of three semi-structured discussions were held with the play rangers pre- and post- training at intervals reflecting key phases in the project. The culmination of the play rangers' engagement with the research team was a professional development event for playworkers at which a member of *Play Gloucestershire* gave a presentation about their experiences. Part of that presentation was based on the second element of the work. Using 578 drawings, 61 photos (taken by play rangers, session volunteers and children) and associated discussions as narratives (Veale, 2005; Kostenius and Öhrling, 2008), the play rangers facilitated conversations with the children attending their play sessions about their experience of being involved in outdoor play sessions. Subsequent analysis involved thematic analysis of interview transcripts (Morse and Richards, 2007) and content analysis of visual materials (Rose, 2001). This chapter focuses predominately on the photo elicitation.

The project involved children from three different types of environment across the county, identified by the play rangers: a group living and playing in a high density, inner city urban setting; a group living and playing in a suburban market town; and a group living and playing in a rural town setting. These reflected sites where *Play Gloucestershire* had well established provision and a history of working with the children. Due to the nature of the play provision being offered, all settings were located in areas with a level of deprivation and identified need.

The play rangers were asked to identify up to 30 photographs from each site that represented everyday play at the site, a variety of play types such as creative play, deep play, socio-dramatic play (Hughes, 2002) and key events. They were asked to identify pictures that were taken over a period of time rather than pictures from just one day. As part of the photo selection process, play rangers were asked to ensure that permissions were in place for all children in the photographs. The selected photographs were put into albums and transferred on to an iPad.

Following this selection process, on arrival at the sites, children were invited to be part of the research project that the play rangers were undertaking with the university team. The play rangers explained that they wanted to find out what the children thought about play, play rangers and wellbeing and that together they would be looking through a collection of photos from their site and chatting about them. If the children wanted to take part then they read through and signed the voluntary informed consent form for that site. Groups of around ten children at a time signed the voluntary informed consent form to be involved and agreed to be recorded. The voice recorder on the iPad was then set to record and the children took control of the iPad and started to scroll through the photos one by one.

The method was tested out at the rural site prior to October half term. As with all sessions, fine weather could not be guaranteed and for this initial session the weather was particularly wet and windy. The children were described as having 'very high spirits' and were excited about the iPad. The debrief session with the play rangers after this initial session flagged a number of issues worthy of consideration prior to further data collection sessions at other sites:

1. working outdoors and the weather: too wet (rain drops on the screen and general water proofing needed), too windy (background noise), too sunny (too much glare on the screen);
2. the initial novelty factor of having an iPad on site: give the children time to become familiar with it and to get past any initial excitement of using one;
3. on site distractions: if there is something more exciting happening on site or very large numbers of children then it is likely that play rangers will be needed elsewhere.

It was advised that in any of the above situations, it would be best to delay the data collection. However, key days and dates were identified when each of the play rangers would undertake the data collection with the children at their site.

A picture of wellbeing: assets at the children's disposal

The research literature suggests that wellbeing is derived from young people having: access to creative and divergent activities; the opportunity to foster meaningful relationships with peers and adults; and an environment that afford them a sense of safety without precluding opportunities for risk tasking. In seeking to build the picture of what this looks like in open access play settings the project team undertook a thematic analysis of the discussions held between the play rangers and the children attending the play sessions. A total of 136 minutes of audio, from nine sessions, across the three sites were transcribed into 110 pages of transcript. These pages were matched to the photographs being discussed before being coded against the 40 separate developmental assets for middle childhood (ages 8 to 12) (Search Institute, 2006). The analysis showed that all four categories of external assets; *support, empowerment, boundaries and expectations* and *constructive use of time* and three categories of internal assets; *positive values, social competencies* and *positive identity* were represented. Notably, the one category not represented was *commitment to learning*, however this is linked explicitly to school rather than being something that can be related directly to the outdoor play environment.

A recurrent theme was the role, importance, relationship to, and significance of, the play rangers. A third of the photographs discussed with the children included play rangers in them. In the majority of the photographs, the play rangers were not the focus of the image yet within the narrative discussion of them the children identified the play ranger and commented positively about them and their significance in their lives. This was gauged not only through the transcription of the discussion but also through the paralanguage in the audio recordings. Children spoke excitedly and animatedly about the play rangers (Figure 13.1):

"Cathy, Cathy!"
"You didn't use to call her Cathy."
"Jessie J, Jessie J."
"J J Jessie J."
"Jessie J, Jessie J, Jessie J, Jessie J."
"She looks so cool there."

Figure 13.1: "Jessie J!"

Source: Play Gloucestershire

And they spoke fondly of those that they missed:

> "I could just take her out of the photo, right now."
> "Ahh."
> "We miss Cathy."

The children's enthusiasm when talking about the play rangers aligns to the categories of *support: other adult relationships* and *boundaries and expectations: adult role models* which affirm the valuable role of non-family adults in the lives of young people. This aligns to contemporary wellbeing research findings which emphasise the importance of the quality of relationships, inclusive of the role of significant adults in children's lives (Dex and Hollingworth, 2012; Tisdale and Pitt-Catsuphes, 2012; Abdullah et al, 2014). Such support helps to create a climate where young people can feel safe and thrive.

This environment provides the foundations for a second theme, that of children as active agents in the design and implementation of activities. This included children commenting on creative play activities:

> "We were really bored, so me, L and other people decided to make a telly."

> "L took the telly home, didn't he, and then his sister sent him back for the remote control like it was a proper telly. She said 'I can't change channels without a remote control', it was brilliant, I absolutely loved it. So he came back and said 'We've got to make a remote control', and so we did."

There were also examples of young volunteers highlighting where they had led activities (see Figure 13.2):

> "Oh that's when we did the parachute wasn't it?"
> "Oh yeah and we all went inside."
> "And we asked them 'What do you love about outdoor play?' and everyone said [what they loved]."

As part of this latter example, the play ranger responded: "Yeah, it was an amazing moment for me when you were all under the parachute... and everybody did it...it was really brilliant."

Figure 13.2: Parachute

Source: Play Gloucestershire

Such observations illustrate how this play environment encourages *Empowerment*; a perception of being appreciated and valued. The ideas of the children are respected and facilitated by the play rangers, they are involved in decision making on the site and they have the chance to help others as young volunteers. Such an environment empowers individuals and offers opportunities for positive shared experiences with peers ("'we've got to make a remote control' and so we did"). While *support* and *empowerment* are externally derived assets such vignettes also show how creative, freely undertaken play promotes *positive values*; helping others and being responsible for generating their own 'amazing moments'.

A third theme focused on the range of activities in which the children were involved. This was by far the most prominent area covered in the discussions, probably due to the nature of the focus of the research and the selection of photographs. Two thirds of the photographs showed activities such as football, face painting, cooking, den building while one third focused on general play such as hanging out around the swings or smiling for the camera. Children described the activities in which they had been involved.

[talking about the game of bottle top bingo they had made]

"There's me, there's J, there's K."
"We were playing bingo."
"Yeah, we were playing bingo and B, not B, J won."
"You can remember who won?"
"Yeah, J won."

"Face painting!"
"What are they actually doing?"
"Face painting!" [several]
"Or arm painting!!'
"And do you know the weirdest thing, happening over there, same kids, painting their arms again!"

This range of activities supports the *Ways to wellbeing* theme 'playing, creativity and imagination' (Abdullah et al, 2014) as a valuable means of enhancing wellbeing among young people.

The themes of food, healthy eating and cooking recurred throughout the discussions and contribute to *Positive Values* (individual responsibility) and a healthy lifestyle. A sixth of the photos depicted food in one way or another: children eating fruit, riding the smoothie bike, making soup and cooking on the fire (Figure 13.3). This is perhaps unsurprising as preparing, cooking and eating food around the fire is a focal activity at the play sessions. However, what was more surprising was the consistently enthusiastic and positive way in which the children spoke about the activity. The children commented:

"He's eating!"
"I'm eating!"
"Melon. He's eating water melon."
"Yeah melon, watermelon."
"Favourite fruit?"
"Apples."
"Grapes, I don't like melon."
"Grapes are the best and strawberries."
"Pineapple, pineapple!!" [several]

On another occasion they commented:

> "That's when we made M's red soup for the first time."
> "We made like this soup and it has all red ingredients in it like tomatoes and peppers and all that."
> "Only red stuff."
> "So did everyone eat it?"
> "Yeah" [several]
> "I did, I loved it…I loved it."

Figure 13.3: Red soup

Source: Play Gloucestershire

Asset-based models seek to 'rebalance' public health strategies, promoting the importance of health literacy; the ability to make informed choices about health-related matters. Health literate individuals have the skills to achieve and sustain good health (Peerson and Saunders, 2009). Such literacy starts with young people having access to age-appropriate health messages (Marmot, 2010). This can be realised through play settings via participatory activities such as cooking around a fire pit. Health literacy is a personal health 'asset', through which individuals can take responsibility for their actions. Engaging in the preparation and eating of food with significant adults and peers can encourage healthy behaviours. It is recognised that opportunities to experience the positive effects of 'protective factors' (access to support systems that encourage positive values) increases the likelihood of longer-term wellbeing (Fenton et al, 2010).

The final theme to emerge was that of confidence and self-esteem that strongly links to the category of *Positive Identity*. While reviewing the photos, particularly those that depicted activities rather than general play, children identified the activities they had planned and led:

> "Oh I remember that was in half terms when me and M ran it."
> "Yeah." [several]
> "And me and M done the water balloon fight, that game."
> "That was fun."
> "And drip dunk."
> "That was good. You organised that very well."
> "I know!"

They also discussed the ones they aimed to organise in the future:

> "Guys, shall we do another Christmas party?"
> "YES!"
> "Me and you should run it again."
> "And me."

This level of confidence illustrates their perceived sense of personal power and self-esteem while touching on key *Social Competencies* around planning and decision making within the context of the play setting.

Future wellbeing research: a place for child-centred participation research

The project was participatory in nature utilising opportunities for reflection on practice and professional development for the play rangers involved. For the young people engaging in the free play facilitated by the play rangers there were opportunities to share memories and experiences through their own words, images and pictures. While these are valuable, and helpful in terms of providing insights into what benefits come from outdoor play services, an extension of such work is to move toward more explicit participatory action research (PAR) (see Chapter Nine, this volume: Fitzpatrick and Handscomb). PAR leads to changes in the power relationships between the researchers, the researched and the audience of the work. The associated methods (inclusive of longitudinal, creative and visual techniques) encourage the creation of 'slow knowledge', that is knowledge not easily extracted through traditional methods such as cross-sectional survey work (Clark, 2010). Such work is advocated by researchers who recognise how the research process can be used to bring about social change. However, a challenge to building the body of work grounded in participatory methods is the extent to which the approach can be accommodated within playwork practice under current funding regimes.

This chapter has already contextualised UK playwork as operating within a changing financial climate. The calls for child-centred, participatory methods may well be tempered by the requirements of funding bodies which may want an 'upfront' articulation of the research design and dissemination activities prior to confirming funding. Franks (2011) suggests this can limit the extent to which research can be truly child-centred; rather 'pockets of participation' (p 15) within programmes of research may be a way forward. Given the importance of child wellbeing to the agendas of funders in health and social work, playworkers will continue to find partners in these sectors. These collaborations may 'prescribe from above' established research protocols but that should not discount a place for more creative methodologies. An adult researcher, or playworker, cannot presume to know how a child is experiencing their childhood, however, encouraging the use of practitioners as co-researchers and young people as active agents in research and co-constructors of knowledge is crucial for understanding what outdoor play services can contribute to childhood wellbeing.

Notes

[1] Play Gloucestershire primarily work with children aged 5 to 15. Children participating in the research project were self-selected and included some young volunteers

[2] In the UK, the term 'play rangers' is used to describe those who work in a number of public parks and open spaces rather than at a dedicated site

[3] 'Open access' is a term used in the UK to differentiate play sessions or settings where children are free to come and go and those that are contracted childcare, where children are looked after until collected by a caregiver.

References

Abdullah, S., Main, G., Pople, L. and Rees, G. (2014) *Ways to wellbeing: Exploring the links between children's activities and their subjective wellbeing*, The Children's Society, www.childrenssociety.org.uk/sites/default/files/Ways%20to%20well-being%20report%20FINAL.pdf.

Amerijckx, G. and Humblet, P.C. (2014) 'Child well-being: What does it mean?', *Children and Society*, 28(5): 404–15.

Bagnoli, A. (2009) 'Beyond the standard interview: The use of graphic elicitation and arts-based methods', *Qualitative Research*, 9(5): 547–70.

Ben-Arieh, A., Casas, F., Frønes, I. and Korbin, J.E. (2014) *Handbook of child well-being: Theories, methods and policies in global perspective*, Volume 1, Dordrecht: Springer.

Cabinet Office and DoE (2013) *Increasing opportunities for young people and helping them achieve their potential*, London: DoE.

Carter, B. and Ford, K. (2013) 'Researching children's health experiences: The place for participatory, child-centered, arts-based approaches', *Research in Nursing and Health*, 36(1): 95–107.

Clark, A. (2010) 'Young children as protagonists and the role of participatory, visual methods in engaging multiple perspectives', *American Journal of Community Psychology*, 46(1–2): 115–23.

Currie, C., Zanotti, C., Morgan, A., Currie, D., de Looze, M., Roberts, C., Samdal, O., Smith, O.R.F., and Barnekow, V. (eds) (2012) *Social determinants of health and well-being among young people: Health behaviour in school aged children (HBSC) study: International report from the 2009/10 survey*, Copenhagen: WHO Regional Office for Europe.

Crivello, G., Camfield, L. and Woodhead, M. (2009) 'How can children tell us about their wellbeing? Exploring the potential of participatory research approaches within young lives', *Social Indicators Research*, 90(1): 51–72.

Dell Clark, C. (2013) 'The state of play', *International Journal of Play Special Issue*, 2(3): 161–2.

Dex, S. and Hollingworth, K. (2012) Children's and young people's voices on their wellbeing, *CWRC Working Paper* No 14, www.cwrc. ac.uk/resources/documents/FINAL_Dex__September_2012__ Report_on_childrens_voices_on_wellbeing_Working_Paper_ No_14.pdf.

DoH (2014) *Care Act 2014*, Norwich: The Stationery Office, www. legislation.gov.uk/ukpga/2014/23/pdfs/ukpga_20140023_en.pdf.

Ereaut, G. and Whiting, R. (2008) *What do we mean by 'wellbeing'? And why might it matter*, http://dera.ioe.ac.uk/8572/1/dcsf-rw073%20 v2.pdf.

Fenton, C., Brooks, F., Spencer, N. and Morgan, A. (2010) 'Sustaining a positive body image in adolescence: An assets-based analysis', *Health and Social Care in the Community*, 18(2): 189–98.

Foresight Mental Capital and Wellbeing Project (2008) *Final project report*, London: The Government Office for Science.

France, A., Bendelow, G. and Williams, S. (2002) 'A "risky" business: Researching the health beliefs of children and young people', in A. Lewis and G. Lindsay (eds) *Researching children's perspectives*, Buckingham: Open University Press, pp 150–62.

Franks, M. (2011) 'Pockets of participation: Revisiting child-centred participation research', *Children and Society*, 25(1): 15–25.

Fryenberg, E., Care, E., Freeman, E. and Chan, E. (2009) 'Interrelationships between coping, school connectedness and wellbeing', *Australian Journal of Education*, 53(3): 261–76.

Gill, T. (2014) *The play return: A review of the wider impact of play initiatives*, Children's Play Policy Forum, https://timrgill.files.wordpress.com/2014/08/evidence-review-colour-low-res.pdf.

HBSC (2009) *Young people's health in Great Britain and Ireland: Findings from the health behaviour in school-aged children study 2006*, Edinburgh: HBSC International Coordinating Centre.

Hughes, B. (2002) *A playworker's taxonomy of play types* (2nd edn), London: Playlink.

Ipsos Mori Social Research Institute and Nairns, A. (2011) *Child wellbeing in the UK, Spain and Sweden: The role of inequality and materialism. A qualitative study*, www.unicef.org.uk/Documents/Publications/IPSOS_UNICEF_ChildWellBeingreport.pdf.

Knies, G. (2012) Life satisfaction and material well-being of children in the UK, *ISER Working Paper Series* No. 2012–15, www.econstor.eu/handle/10419/65927.

Kostenius, C. and Öhrling, K. (2008) '"Friendship is like an extra parachute": Reflections on the way school children share their lived experiences of well-being through drawings', *Reflective Practice*, 9(1): 23–35.

Leitch, R. (2008) 'Creatively researching children's narratives through images and drawing', in P. Thomson (ed) *Doing visual research with children and young people*, London: Routledge, pp 37–58.

McKendrick, J., Horton, J., Kraftl, P. and Else, P. (2014) 'Conclusion: Playwork and its geographies in financially challenging times', *Journal of Playwork Practice*, 1(1): 96–9.

Marmot, M. (2010) *Fair society, healthy lives: The Marmot Review*, London: The Marmot Review.

Matthews, N., Kilgour, L., Christian, P., Mori, K. and Hill, D.M. (2015) 'Understanding, evidencing, and promoting adolescent well-being: An emerging agenda for schools', *Youth and Society*, 47(5): 659–83.

Morgan, A. and Ziglio, E. (2007) 'Revitalising the evidence base for public health: An assets model', *Promotion and Education*, 14, Supplement 2: 17–22.

Morrow, V. and Crivello, G. (2015) 'What is the value of qualitative longitudinal research with children and young people for international development', *International Journal of Social Research Methodology*, 18(3): 267–80.

Morse, J.M. and Richards, L. (2007) *Read me first: For a user's guide to qualitative methods* (2nd edn), London: Sage.

OECD (Organisation for Economic Co-operation and Development) (2009) *Doing better for children*, Paris: OECD, www.oecd.org/els/social/childwellbeing.

O'Kane, C. (2008) 'The development of participatory techniques: Facilitating children's views about decisions which affect them', in P. Christensen and A. James (eds) *Research with children: Perspectives and practices* (2nd edn), London: Routledge, pp 125–55.

ONS (Office for National Statistics) (2011) *Initial investigation into subjective well-being from the opinion survey*, www.ons.gov.uk/ons/dcp171776_244488.pdf.

Peerson, A. and Saunders, M. (2009) 'Health literacy revisited: What do we mean and why does it matter?', *Health Promotion International*, 24(3): 285–96.

Play England (2008) *Play and health: Making the link*, http://playengland.org.uk/media/120486/play-and-health-policy-brief-03.pdf.

PPSG (Playwork Principles Scrutiny Group) (2005) *Playwork Principles*, Cardiff: Play Wales.

Rees, G. and Main, G. (eds) (2015) *Children's views on their lives and well-being in 15 countries: An initial report on the Children's Worlds survey, 2013–14*, York, UK: Children's Worlds Project (ISCWeB).

Rose, G. (2001) *Visual methodologies: An introduction to the interpretation of visual materials*, London: Sage.

Scales, P.C. (1999) 'Reducing risks and building development assets: Essential actions for promoting adolescent health', *Journal of School Health*, 69(3): 113–19.

Schäfer, N. (2012) 'Finding ways to do research on, with and for children and young people', *Geography*, 97(3): 147–54.

Search Institute (2006) *40 Developmental assets for middle childhood (ages 8–12)*, Minneapolis, MN: Search Institute.

Smith, H. (2014) 'Prospects for participatory research on wellbeing with playwork practitioners and children at play', *Journal of Playwork Practice*, 1(1): 90–5.

The Children's Society (2015) *The good childhood report 2015*, London: The Children's Society.

Thompson Coon, J., Boddy, K., Stein, K., Whear, R., Barton, J. and Depledge, M.H. (2011) 'Does participating in physical activity in outdoor natural environments have a greater effect on physical and mental wellbeing than physical activity indoors? A systematic review', *Environmental Science and Technology*, 45(5): 1761–72.

Tisdale, S. and Pitt-Catsuphes, M. (2012) 'Linking social environments with the wellbeing of adolescents in dual-earner and single working parent families', *Youth and Society*, 44(1): 118–40.

Thompson, S. and Aked, J. (2011) *Five ways to wellbeing: New applications, new ways of thinking*, London: New Economics Foundation.

UNICEF (2007) 'Child Poverty in perspective: An overview of child well-being in rich countries', *Innocenti Report Card 7*, Florence: UNICEF Innocenti Research Centre.

UNICEF (2014) 'Children of the recession: The impact of the economic crisis on child well-being in rich countries', *Innocenti Report Card 12*, Florence: UNICEF Office of Research.

Valois, R.F., Zullig, K.J., Huebner, E.S. and Drane, J.W. (2003) 'Dieting behaviors, weight perceptions, and life satisfaction among public high school adolescents', *Eating Disorders*, 11(4): 271–88.

Veale, A. (2005) 'Creative methodologies in participatory research with children', in S. Greene and D. Hogan (eds) *Researching children's experience: Approaches and methods*, London: Sage, pp 253–72.

Wilkinson, R.G. and Pickett, K. (2009) *The spirit level: Why more equal societies almost always do better*, London: Allen Lane.

Closing thoughts

FOURTEEN

What do we want research in children's play to do?

Wendy Russell, Stuart Lester and Hilary Smith

Introduction

It is traditional for a concluding chapter to *reflect* on the content of
the book and offer comment on meaning and future direction. What
is offered here is an alternative optical metaphor, that of *diffraction*.
Reflection implies seeking a singular, accurate mirror image of the
studies presented here, reducing their multiplicity to more of the
same. In this way it establishes a fixed direction for future (re)search
in pursuit of a goal of enlightenment about children's play and adults'
role in supporting it. In physics, diffraction occurs when waves hit a
barrier or a slit resulting in a different movement and patterning. It
is a relational phenomenon (or perhaps a phenomenon of relating); a
diffractive analysis in research and other forms of knowledge production
requires paying attention to patterns of interference. As Haraway (1992,
p 301) says: 'Diffraction does not produce "the same" displaced, as
reflection and refraction do. Diffraction is a mapping of interference…A
diffraction pattern does not map where differences appear, but rather
maps where the effects of difference appear.'

Extending this, Barad (2007, p 25) suggests diffraction is 'an apt
metaphor for describing the methodological approach…of reading
insights through one another in attending to and responding to the
details and specificities of relations of difference and how they matter.'

Multiple readings extend thinking rather than repeating sameness; it
is an approach that is generative rather than reductive, leading to more
questions but also discerning patterns and potentials.

In putting such an approach to work here, this final chapter draws
on concepts from new materialist, posthuman, Deleuzian and post-
qualitative approaches to offer an account of the practice-based studies
in this book and what these might mean for research in children's
play. These approaches have emerged from transdisciplinary work
across fields as diverse as philosophy, life and physical sciences, and

anthropology (for example, Barad, 2007; Braidotti, 2013). They disturb traditional research methodologies (for example, MacLure, 2010; 2013; Lather, 2013; 2015), and have been applied in a variety of contexts including early years education and childhood studies (for example, Lenz-Taguchi, 2014; Taylor and Blaise, 2014) and young teen sexualities (for example, Renold and Ringrose, 2011), but less so to middle childhood play scholarship, although examples are emerging, including Kane (2015), Lester (2013; 2016) and Russell (2016).

The chapter reads these approaches through each other and through theorisations of the social, political and economic landscapes of childhoods, children's play and research in children's play in order to pay attention to the patternings of relations of difference. It also weaves in participants' contributions to a workshop at a Professional Development Event (PDE) hosted by the 'Professional Studies in Children's Play' postgraduate programme team at the University of Gloucestershire in January 2016. This is an annual event where graduating students present their research to current students, alumni and others in the sector. It was just such an event in 2013 that Professor Berry Mayall attended and gave us the encouragement to publish this collection of studies. The discussion at the 2016 PDE event explored the question 'what do we want research [in children's play] to do?' Responses to this provocation highlighted a number of contradictory hopes for research that were embedded in the professional context of adults working to support children's play. They are used here to provide a loose structure to the chapter, beginning with a consideration of epistemology: what/how we can 'know' about children's play and what different epistemologies *perform*. It then moves on to explore how the process of knowledge production plays out in practice and policy domains, in terms of what the dominant policy and research paradigms might do and what they might exclude. From this, the discussion broadens out into a consideration of the expressed desire for research and other forms of knowledge production not only to understand but to change the world in myriad small ways. Finally, the chapter ends with some further provocations to challenge dearly held assumptions regarding the ethics of the pursuit of knowledge, particularly about children's play.

Insights offered are partial, tentative and unfinished; like the studies themselves they are messy, situated, contingent and incomplete. They are not to be taken as final judgements; what matters is the process of attending to relations of difference, to small specificities as a way of disturbing habitual modes of understanding in order to bring in some of what has traditionally been excluded and to see what more might be said and done.

What is to be known?

This collection, while loosely themed, does not cohere around a single point of organisation other than a general interest in studies of children's play, which in itself remains intangible and elusive. Although many of the authors in this book were new to academic research and its associated conventions, they are not novice practitioners, far from it, and they bring a wealth of diverse practice knowledge. For some, their initial desire when approaching their research projects was to prove the worth of their work; thesis supervisors will be familiar with the process of scaling down ambition both in terms of the size of the projects students want to do and in their claims. These studies are small-scale; within current dominant research paradigms, that often implies that they are less significant than large-scale projects that seek to show 'what works'. As this chapter discusses, there is a growing number of researchers interested in developing approaches and methodologies that can work with what becomes occluded in such large-scale studies: the details of each situated experience and the differences that become homogenised in headline 'findings'. As such, these studies are concerned with the singular rather than the universal. They pay attention to the messiness, uncertainty and unpredictability of practice, and some of the chapters here certainly do that. In contrast to the still-dominant European-American research tradition, attention is given to micro-processes rather than products. It is practice fieldwork, that is, ways of being affected by what is happening in an open and generous manner (ethical practice). While many chapters apply what may be traditional methods, the approaches are not determined by these: they are experimental (in the sense of trying out something new to see what happens), partial and concerned with practice techniques and materials in order to add to what is known rather than reduce singular events to more of the same. The chapters are produced by being involved in the world, not objective by-standers; as such they are not trying to prove pre-established ideas but to generate or animate new ideas and practices. They are modest attempts that arrive at *'particular conclusions in particular locations for particular studies'* (Law, 2004, p155, emphasis in the original).

One of the aims of the book is to question the assumption that research sits outside of practice and is therefore subject to different rules. The chapters are representative of practice-based research – that is, they show implicitly and explicitly the dilemmas of practice. Practice in children's play is always a process of (re)searching, an obstinate curiosity; one is always working with the not yet known, never to be fully captured in words or known once and for all. Practitioners' ways of knowing include their sensations, memories, intuitions, insights, perceptions, movements and imaginations, as is shown particularly in the chapters employing more-than-representational methodologies (for example, Williams, Chapter Four; Coppard, Chapter Five; Fitzpatrick and Handscomb, Chapter Nine; Dickerson, Chapter Six).

The focus on practice-based research in children's play in the UK and the USA implies an adult practitioners' gaze. While this is not a singular, universal gaze (and indeed some chapters in this collection have made efforts to move beyond 'gaze' to an embodied engagement), it is important to pay attention to the material and discursive effects of dominant understandings of the nature and value of childhood and children's play, together with the desires and multiple knowledges brought by practitioners to the research arena. Such desires were apparent in the flip chart notes of roundtable discussions held at the PDE workshop on the question 'what do we want research to do?', which showed a range of contradictory feelings and responses. Several used metaphors of light to express a desire for clarity of understanding about play, for example:

1. Shine some light on play and playwork.
2. Clarify what play is.

This, together with other statements such as 'prove the importance of play, playwork, play environments', illustrates expectations of research to be able to discover fixed, boundaried, absolute and universal truths and to represent these accurately in language. Others were perhaps more nuanced in their language, using terms such as 'explore, raise questions'. Some, as a part of the 'carousel' process of visiting the flip notes of other groups, added challenges to the expressed desires for certainty. One flip chart sheet had, 'answer questions', to which had been added, 'Whose questions? Generate more questions or change the questions.' Similarly, one comment of 'solve problems' had the additional comment, 'Create problems'. Yet another: 'Show results, prove things, disprove things' to which had been added, 'Can research do this?'

The opening chapter of this book briefly considers this last question in terms of raising a challenge to posivitism in the social sciences, and this is picked up again here. Building on the Enlightenment principles of reason, science, progress and liberty, positivism in the social sciences applied the 'scientific method' from natural sciences, with the assumptions that knowledge could only be derived from empirical study, that there were deterministic and universal laws of human behaviour that can be objectively measured by rigorous methods and instruments, and that social science should be used to solve social problems (Demers, 2011). Although it has been argued that such a simplistic view hails more from philosophy of science than the actual practice of scientific research, positivism has persisted (Lather, 2005; Demers, 2011), albeit in a more measured form (often termed post-positivism or critical realism) that acknowledges complexity and observer fallibility but seeks to overcome these by the use of multiple and triangulating methods. In this way, objectivity refers not to individual researchers but to the amalgamated methods; fundamentally, there is still a belief in an objectively existing truth that, although attempts to discover it may be flawed, should still remain the ultimate goal of research.

Two interrelated questions emerge here: first, why is it that positivism has persisted so doggedly in the face of sustained criticism, and second, what does such an epistemology do? Perhaps it has persisted because there is a desire for certainty, as reflected in the hopes expressed at the workshop for research to finally decide what it is that play is. It is far more comforting to think a phenomenon can be known than that it cannot. On a more cynical level, Demers (2011) suggests that government agencies and big business fund positivist research that serves their interest, whereas they are less likely to fund humanist or posthumanist research that is critical of the economic and political status quo, an idea that is revisited later in this chapter.

In addressing the second question, a belief in final proofs and truths relies on a clear delineation of the subject of research: what *exactly* is play? Definitions are useful, and certainly the *process* of trying to agree a definition – something that play scholarship has yet to achieve – is illuminating and enjoyable, in terms of what it says about both substance and perspective. However, defining does more than clarify the phenomenon itself. In order to define, boundaries have to be set, so there needs to be a distinction between 'play' and 'not-play', a distinction that can apply always and only to the play/not-play duality. Play becomes a thing that is 'outside of history and structure, decontextualized but measurable' (Lather, 2005, p 5), separated from the daily flows, messiness and rhythms of children's lives (Lester, 2013). For example, the stories of being a child during the second world war told by the interviewees in the chapter by Willans (Chapter Three) show how play was interwoven into everyday movements and routines, such as their meanderings on the journey home from school, playing marbles on the way, or having to hide behind trees to avoid enemy aircraft. In Coppard (Chapter Five, p 85) one of the observers muses on the 'vague land between playing and not playing'.

Boundary-making practices do more than create a play/not-play duality. They also *perform* by excluding other ways of knowing about play. The more precise a definition, the more exclusive it is likely to be. Propositional knowledge progresses incrementally, building on initially tentative propositions until they become basic premises that a community of scholars accepts as given. They are abstractions with their own internal logic. One example of this is the particular understanding of the relation between play and children's development that sees the purpose of play as a mechanism for learning skills needed in adulthood. Despite critiques of the foundational studies making such claims (for example, Smith, 1988; 2010; Sutton-Smith, 1997; 2003), this basic premise is so firmly entrenched that it will take more than a few academics to dislodge its hold on policy, professional, commercial and child rearing practice. It is evident in the discussions on professionals' understandings of the value of play in Dickerson (Chapter Six), Kinney (Chapter Seven) and Hawkes (Chapter Twelve).

Such continual and self-referential 'upgrading', based on original premises that have become accepted truths, continues to exclude ways of appreciating play that no longer fit the basic premises. Foucault's (1972, p 207) words on trying to define science itself as a thing independent of context (that is, to separate it from its discursive formations and subsequent effects – its 'doings') can apply also to attempts to pin down both definitions of play and its relation to learning and development: 'all the density of the disconnections, the dispersion of the ruptures, the shifts in their effects, the play of the interdependence are reduced to the monotonous act of an endlessly repeated foundation.'

Perhaps these 'endlessly repeated foundations' occlude what first enchanted practitioners and scholars about children's play. In becoming worthy of scientific study of this ilk, play risks losing its playfulness, its joy, its pure nonsense and its entanglement with everything else that produces everyday life.

The effects of narrow perspectives are not only felt in an isolated realm of knowledge; they matter in terms of adults' relationships with children. As Barad (2007, p 185) states:

> Practices of knowing and being are not isolable; they are mutually implicated. We don't obtain knowledge by standing outside the world; we know because we are *of* the world...The separation of epistemology from ontology is

a reverberation of a metaphysics that assumes an inherent difference between human and nonhuman, subject and object, mind and body, matter and discourse…what we need is something like an *ethico-onto-epistem-ology* – an appreciation of the intertwining of ethics, knowing and being.

Traditional epistemological foundations and their accompanying classifications, resemblances and oppositions are concerned with a need to verify; these are disrupted by drawing attention to the ways in which something different comes to matter thereby re-configuring and constituting new forms of engagement and relatedness. It is a quest for 'more life…a particular form of boosting aliveness, one that opens us to our being in the midst of life through a thoroughly ontological involvement' (Thrift, 2008, p 14).

One further comment remains on the situated knowledges informing definitions of play and the intertwining of knowing, doing and ethics that can be made in relation to the specific definition of play employed by the UK playwork sector. Although not all of the chapters in the book are about playwork, many make reference to the Playwork Principles (PPSG, 2005), the professional and ethical framework for playwork practice (see the Appendix for the full statement). These Principles give the following definition of play as: 'a process that is freely chosen, personally directed and intrinsically motivated. That is, children and young people determine and control the content and intent of their play, by following their own instincts, ideas and interests, in their own way for their own reasons.'

This definition was formulated to apply to the particular social and political landscape in which playwork operates: as such, it is a clear example of how 'knowledge' is situated. Understood as a code of conduct for the sector, the intention of the Playwork Principles is to fulfil a number of functions including protecting service users, giving credence and professional status, giving guidance to practitioners, and helping to create and maintain professional identity (Banks, 2004). Within this context, the definition of play becomes a formal statement of service ideal that can be useful in terms of resisting expectations from other adults to control or direct children's play towards particular adult-determined outcomes. Nevertheless, it also creates tensions, as discussed in Jackson (Chapter Eight), Smith (Chapter Eleven) and Hawkes (Chapter Twelve).

This definition is situated in the dominant disciplinary perspective of the era and landscape where it was formulated, that of twentieth-century minority world psychology and its attendant assumptions of the individual child as 'autonomous subject exercising rational agency over both human and non-human others from which they are ontologically discrete' (Russell, 2016, p 197). What is of interest here is to consider what such a definition might exclude. What happens if the human subject is decentred, no longer seen as apart from nature but an entangled part of it? This requires a radical dissolution of the nature/culture binary, the foundational assumption within humanistic, constructivist epistemologies of the separateness of the given (nature) and the constructed (culture).

Disturbing the nature/culture boundary implies a reconfiguring of other comfortable dualities, and in particular that of subject/object (to which might also be added human/non-human; adult/child; play/not-play, mind/body). Furthermore, fixity becomes unseated: phenomena are no longer singular and unitary but nomadic, always becoming (Braidotti, 2013). Barad (2007) coined the term *intra-action* as a substitute for *interaction* 'in order to stress that the actors in a performative relationship should not be seen as distinct entities, acting upon each other from "outside", but as entangled agencies which establish each other as well as being created themselves' (Keevers, 2009, p 20). As Russell (2016, p 198) notes,

> At the risk of over-simplifying her [Barad's] work, what this does is radically reconfigure understandings of the ways in which space and time are produced...'Play-spaces'...do not pre-exist independently of their production, but emerge through the intra-actions of bodies, affects, histories, material and symbolic objects and so on. Space becomes relational, dynamic and always in the making.

Many of the chapters in the book specifically consider children's lives spatially, particularly – but not only – those in Part Two, and the two oral history projects (Harris, Chapter Two; Willans, Chapter Three). Several experiment with ideas from posthumanism, new materialism and performative, more-than-representational approaches that offer different ways of knowing, being and acting. 'Thinking differently shifts focus from what is happening inside individual minds to what is produced within and in-between bodies and materials that constitute the spaces of encounter' (Lester, 2013, p 137). From this perspective, research into children's play focuses 'less on fixed boundaries between play and not-play, this play and that play, good play and bad play, and more on the dynamic flows and forces of those entanglements and the possibility of becoming-different' (Russell, 2016, p 198). It is not a question of what play might mean but how does it work, not with the expectation of a definitive answer but simply being more attentive to the particular and singular set of circumstances from which playful moments emerge.

Such a perspective highlights the entanglements of epistemology, ontology and ethics, something that was apparent from the PDE workshop. Since participants were all practitioners, there was a clear desire for research to make a difference for their practice as well as for children's play itself. In particular, there were several references to influencing policy, a topic to which the chapter now turns.

Influencing policy

In response to the question, 'what do we want research to do?' many participants, in flip chart comments and discussion, expressed a strong desire to influence the policy process, both in terms of policies directly concerning children and families and broader policies that affect children's everyday lives (for example, town and spatial planning, highways and welfare policies). The relationship between policy and practice is felt sharply in the current political landscape of austerity and the biggest cuts in UK public spending since the beginnings of the welfare state (Slay, 2012), with children's play services being especially vulnerable to local government cuts (McKendrick et al, 2015). Comments included 'help us articulate and advocate what we do', 'inform and influence policy and policy makers', and 'provide evidence'. These three statements offer slightly different positions in the research, practice and policy tension triangle (Lester and Russell, 2008), from finding ways to 'represent' what play practitioners do (and, by implication why it matters), to influencing policy processes (which is more than merely 'proving' value), to the contested concept of evidence itself. In both the USA and the UK, the turn towards evidence-based policy has meant a shift away from critical research that challenges the inequitable status quo towards a resurgence of positivism in qualitative research (Lather, 2015; Edwards et al, 2016). Evidence is required to show which interventions are most effective – and cost-effective – in addressing identified social problems. Such positivism employs what St Pierre (2015, p 76) terms '1980s methodology' and its attendant concepts of reliability, replicability, validity, triangulation, data coding, audit trails, inter-rater reliability and so on, with the 'gold standard' being the randomised controlled trial and its assumptions of 'causation and final truth'. While such tools can be useful, they 'only answer certain kinds of questions' (Bristow et al, 2015, p 128), implying other forms of 'evidence' can also 'count'. As Edwards et al (2016, p 1) point out:

> this assumption that every problem in society has an evidence-based solution is part of a modernising, new managerialist approach to governance in which social values and moral issues are reduced to technical rationality, cut adrift from political debate involving interests and power, while social justice, material conditions and social inequalities are obscured from view.

Nevertheless, no matter how rigorous, reliable and replicable the methods used, it is not only evidence that influences policy. The significant body of work on policy networks and advocacy coalitions highlights how the policy process is rarely driven by rational choice and is much more likely to be incremental (building on slight shifts from what has gone before) and open to influences from other interest groups (Hudson and Lowe, 2006). As Voce's (2015) story of the English Play Strategy and Lester and Russell's (2013) account of the Welsh Play Sufficiency Duty illustrate, what influences agenda setting and the other messy, iterative and interdependent processes in policy development and implementation depends on myriad and often unpredictable events, connections, disconnections, relationships, ideologies, interests, influence and power resources (in the form of political and legal authority, information or finance) as well as 'evidence'. Play advocates can have different roles to play in terms of promoting different forms of value for their practice: as Kinney describes in Chapter Seven, policymakers may focus on instrumental value of play services, but a case can be made also for intrinsic and institutional value (Holden, 2006). Play advocates need to find ways of articulating all three (see Matthews et al, Chapter Thirteen for an example). The argument made here is that more-than-representational and diffractive methodologies can help enliven the drab accounting of linear and technical 'what works' evidence and can also open up the cracks to expose what these methods exclude.

Some models for impact evaluation, albeit those at the lower levels of standards of evidence (Bristow et al, 2015), emphasise the need to identify the theory behind the interventions. Known as theory-driven approaches to evaluation, these include Theory of Change (Fulbright-Anderson et al, 1998) and Realist Evaluation (Pawson, 2006). Although both these approaches would fit in the 'post-positivist' camp, they do perhaps allow for more critical approaches that can make visible basic assumptions and what they exclude.

This brings the discussion back to questions of theory and its place in practice-based research in children's play. The next section considers the theoretical assumptions embedded in much social policy concerning children and young people that may speak to instrumental value, and the final section explores what theory can offer for articulating value differently and what this might mean for research.

Policy processes as material discursive practice

The theories embedded in policies concerning children and families are often discussed within policy literature as paradigms (Moss, 2007) or narratives (McBeth et al, 2014). Both approaches bring slightly different emphases to exploring the assumptions inherent in the ways policy understands the nature and value of childhood, and, implicitly or explicitly, the material effects of these assumptions, but employ different methods for analysing these. Despite challenges raised by the social studies of childhood that emerged in the second half of the twentieth century (Prout, 2005), the overwhelming paradigm/narrative in policies relating to children and families remains future focused, seeing childhood as an apprenticeship for an autonomous, producing and consuming adulthood (Moss, 2007), with education policies aiming to build future industry leaders and social services and youth justice policies aiming to limit the burden of the poor on the state (Katz, 2011; Edwards et al, 2016). These are deficit models that fix childhood as separate from adulthood. Both are encapsulated in this foreword to the Open Public Services White Paper (HM Government, 2011, p 4):

> The failure to educate every child to the maximum of their abilities is not just a moral failure to accord every person equal worth, it is a piece of economic myopia which leaves us all poorer. For in a world rendered so much more competitive by globalisation, we can no longer afford to leave talents neglected. Every pair of idle hands, every mind left uncultivated, is a burden on all society as well as a weight on our conscience.

Such language exemplifies 'the conflation of fiscal rationality and morality' as a 'hallmark of neoliberal governmentalities' (Janzen and Jeffrey, 2013, p 122). It can be understood as what Ryan (2014) terms 'biosocial power' – a particular configuration of Foucault's (2008) concept of 'biopolitics' as applied to children and childhood – acting on the minds and bodies of children in order to produce the self-governing citizen. Ryan locates the children's playground as a site of biosocial power, as a 'technology of conduct...to both constitute and govern the liberal democratic subject' (Ryan, 2014, p 87). Such a technology navigates the tensions between positioning childhood as a site of freedom and constraint, particularly in terms of those children identified as social problems in need of state intervention. In tracing the history of the public playground in the USA, Ryan draws parallels with contemporary political narratives that have resurrected the 'moral underclass discourse' (MUD) (Levitas, 2004). Many (but not all) of the chapters in this book discuss play provision in areas of deprivation; although there is little class analysis presented, this is perhaps an element of difference that is elided through homogenising grand narratives of childhood play.

A powerful example of the entanglements of policy narratives, developments in science and technology, professional practice, global capitalism and neoliberalism can be seen in the dramatic increases in the use of psychopharmaceuticals as a form of governance of difference among children and young people (Janzen and Jeffrey, 2013). Another example can be seen in the use of neuroscientific evidence as a political strategy for 'framing and taming' policies on early intervention (Edwards et al, 2016). In the UK, early intervention policies (for example, Allen, 2011) cite evidence from neuroscience to show the effects of environment on brain development from conception and through the early years. The argument has been forcibly and emotively made 'that focusing on babies' brain development is the only way to prevent a multiplicity of social problems from unemployment, lack of social mobility and educational under-achievement, to crime, violence and anti-social behaviour' (Macvarish, 2013, p 1). There are critiques of the research itself, including how neuroscience is still contested and not 'policy ready' (Edwards et al, 2016), how it has been overgeneralised and oversimplified in policy and professional discourse (Bruer, 2011), and how claims that plasticity and sensitive periods being limited to the early years are contestable (Rose and Abi-Rached, 2013). However, what is of interest here is what such material discursive practices *do*.

In their critique of this biologising of parenthood, Edwards et al (2016, p 2) state: 'pseudoscientific "brain science" discourse is co-opted to bolster policy claims about optimal childrearing. This discourse frames poor mothers as the sole architects of social disadvantage, and its taming strategies of early years intervention are entrenching gendered and classed understandings and social inequalities.'

These two examples illustrate the power of ideologically led policies that select evidence strategically; what this means for research in children's play is that practitioners and advocates need to pay attention both to what scientific evidence might exclude and to other ways of knowing, being and doing. In reality, play advocates have to navigate this policy landscape. The desire for research to prove that play practitioners can help meet policy agendas is understandable. Ethically, the argument here is that the field also needs to seek different ways of articulating why children's play – and adult attention to supporting the conditions for play to emerge – matters.

Changing the world through re-enchantment

This chapter has highlighted some of the contemporary challenges faced by practitioners/(re)searchers in co-creating opportunities for children's play. It is set against a backdrop of increasing individualisation and commodification of all aspects of life (Garrett, 2009) where life itself has become the main capital of neoliberalism (Braidotti, 2013). The ways in which bodies and desires are subjugated to economic imperatives and political ideologies is a dominant cliché of global capitalism. However, the disenchantment and totality that such regimes may present are not given and prefigured; there is always an excess, something always escapes. Indeed, playing contains micro-revolutionary possibilities for re-working oppressive power structures, generating feelings of 'being connected to an affirmative way to existence' (Bennett, 2001, p 156). The multiple entanglement of subject and objects that come about through movement, encounters, affects and so on, and that produce moments of playing, also constitute the emergence of practice wisdom. What is known and the 'knowers' of this knowledge co-emerge and shape each other through doing (speaking/acting/thinking), and by doing they continue to collectively co-create practice (Keevers et al, 2012).

Alongside the expressed desire for proofs and truths and the challenges to these, the flip chart notes from the PDE event also articulated a desire to 'challenge the status quo' and 'to disrupt and disturb common understandings', and for bigger aims to:

- make society better;
- change the world and the way we feel about the world – more just and fair;
- continue to be enchanted with the world.

Some hope might be drawn from the chapters in this book, many of which raise a challenge to dominant paradigms and begin to explore alternative approaches to research that can offer an ethical and political stance and that can help to re-enchant the study of children's play and adults' relationship with it. There is a place for theory here; as MacLure (2010, p 277) says, 'we need theory to block the reproduction of the bleeding obvious, and thereby, hopefully, open new possibilities for thinking and doing.' This is not the theory that tucks a stable world into pre-established boxes to be ticked for the audit culture, it is the theory that 'defamiliarises, complicates, obstructs, perverts, proliferates' (p 5), in sum, that offends. It offends because it moves away from the individual psychological subject or sociological agent that we thought we could not think without towards decentring the human and attending to the entanglements of the nonhuman, of matter, movement, affect. It dissolves binaries such as nature/culture, adult/child, subject/object, theory/practice, discourse/matter; it is never complete, it is messy, fluid, nomadic. This is not only a question of theory as epistemology, it is an ethico–onto–epistemology that can move away from neat but exclusionary segmentations and categorisations to take account of the messy fluidity and heterogeneity of just getting on with life, to produce more just and equitable accounts.

It is hard, this theory, because it is so very different. It is difficult to step out of traditional ways of doing theory, of the language that locks ideas into the things it is trying to leave behind: certainty, interpretation, progress, fixity. Novelty is uncomfortable, as is uncertainty. It requires altering habits (of qualitative research, common sense understandings and language) and developing sensibilities appropriate to a methodological decentring of the human subject and disturbing of the status quo of worn out binaries and human exceptionalism.

As we introduced in the opening chapter, MacLure (2010) suggests one way of addressing this is through Massumi's (2002) 'exemplary practice'. This is not a matter of applying theory to examples, which Massumi says would change what is being explored through the application of the concepts. Massumi's examples are not generalisations or particularities, they are singularities. Although they are singular, they can stand for other instances. What matters are the details, and these details can be sites for connections, disruptions, digression and diversion, producing difference rather than more of the same. It is generative rather than restrictive, drawing in what has gone before and reading this diffractively through new insights. Examples can emerge from 'the wearying mass of ethnographic data' (MacLure, 2010, p 282) as a kind of glow, something that catches the attention in an affective, visceral manner. While all this may seem a far cry from the solid and certain evidence required of policy makers, there is a space for enlivening 'evidence' through the telling of small moments of enchantment, stories, nonsense conversations.

Such approaches are beginning to be seen in collaborative work. One is the European COST-funded project on 'New Materialism: networking European scholarship on "how matter comes to matter"' (http://newmaterialism.eu). It can also be seen in the work of the Common Worlds Childhoods Research Collective (http:// commonworlds.net), 'an interdisciplinary network of researchers concerned with children's relations with the more-than-human world' in order to trouble the normalising effects of anthropocentrism – or perhaps the anthroponormativity – of traditional childhood studies (Taylor and Blaise, 2014). As Lenz-Taguchi (2014, p 87), says:

> the research produced is political in its emphasis on creating and inventing new forms of possible realities in the analysis. In this way the world might, as Haraway (2008) suggests, become a 'more liveable place', where children have increased power to act, to play and learn together with performative agents that can also be other than merely human agents.

As a final provocation, intended to disturb what is held most dear, a couple of comments from the flip charts at the PDE event can provide some cautionary – and playful – troubling of the play field's 'endlessly repeated foundations' (Foucault, 1972, p 207) and 'reproduction of the bleeding obvious' (MacLure, 2010, p 277). Perhaps we should 'stop trying to overthink everything', and ask the question 'is play on too much of a pedestal?'

References

Allen, G. (2011) *Early intervention: Smart investment, massive savings*, London: Cabinet Office.

Banks, S. (2004) *Ethics, accountability and the social professions*, Basingstoke: Palgrave Macmillan.

Barad, K. (2007) *Meeting the universe halfway: Quantum physics and the entanglement of matter and meaning*, Durham, NC: Duke University Press.

Bennett, J. (2001) *The enchantment of modern life: Attachments, crossings and ethics*, Princeton, NJ: Princeton University Press.

Braidotti, R. (2013) *The posthuman*, Cambridge: Polity Press.

Bristow, D., Carter, L. and Martin, S. (2015) 'Using evidence to improve policy and practice: the UK What Works Centres', *Contemporary Social Science*, 10(2): 126–37.

Bruer, J.T. (2011) *Revisiting 'The myth of the first three years'*, Kent: Centre for Parenting Culture Studies, Kent University.

Coleman, R. and Ringrose, J. (eds) (2014) *Deleuze and research methodologies*, Edinburgh: Edinburgh University Press.

Demers, D. (2011) *The ivory tower of Babel: Why the social sciences are failing to live up to their promises*, New York: Algora.

Edwards, R., Gillies, V. and Horsley N. (2016) 'Early intervention and evidence-based policy and practice: framing and taming', *Social Policy and Society*, 15(1): 1–10.

Foucault, M. (1972) *The archaeology of knowledge*, London: Routledge.

Foucault, M. (2008) *The birth of biopolitics*, New York: Picador.

Fulbright-Anderson, K., Kubisch, A. and Connell, J. (eds) (1998) *New approaches to evaluating community initiatives, vol. 2: Theory, measurement, and analysis*, Washington, DC: Aspen Institute.

Garrett, P.M. (2009) *Transforming children's services: Social work, neoliberalism and the 'modern' world*, Maidenhead: Open University Press.

Haraway, D.J. (1992) 'The promises of monsters: A regenerative politics for inappropriate/d others', in L. Grossberg, C. Nelson and P.A. Treichler (eds) *Cultural studies*, New York: Routledge, pp 295–337.

Haraway, D.J. (2008) *When species meet*, Minneapolis, MN: University of Minneapolis Press.

HM Government (2011) *Open public services white paper*, Norwich: The Stationery Office.

Holden, J. (2006) *Cultural value and the crisis of legitimacy*, London: Demos.

Hudson, J. and Lowe, S. (2006) *Understanding the policy process: Analysing policy welfare and practice*, Bristol: Policy Press.

Janzen, C. and Jeffery, D. (2013) 'Prescribing practice: Pharmaceuticals, children, and the governance of difference', *Journal of Progressive Human Services*, 24(2): 117–39.

Kane, E. (2015) *Playing practices in school-aged childcare: An action research project in Sweden and England*, Stockholm: Stockholm University.

Katz, C. (2011) 'Accumulation, excess, childhood: Toward a countertopography of risk and waste', *Documents d'Anàlisis Geogràfica*, 57(1): 47–60.

Keevers, L. (2009) *Practising social justice: Community organisations, what matters and what counts*, PhD thesis, University of Sydney.

Keevers, L., Treleaven, L., Sykes, C. and Darcy, M. (2012) 'Made to measure: Taming practices with results-based accountability', *Organization Studies*, 33(1): 97–120.

Lather, P. (2005) 'Scientism and scientificity in the rage for accountability: A feminist deconstruction', paper presented at the First International Congress of Qualitative Inquiry, Champaign, IL, 5–7 May.

Lather, P. (2013) 'Methodology-21: what do we do in the afterward?, *International Journal of Qualitative Studies in Education*, 26(6): 634–45.

Lather, P. (2015) 'The work of thought and the politics of research: (Post) qualitative research', in N.K. Denzin and M.D. Giardina (eds) *Qualitative inquiry and the politics of research*, Walnut Creek, CA: Left Coast Press, pp 97–117.

Law, J. (2004) *After method: Mess in social science research*, Abingdon: Routledge.

Lenz-Taguchi, H. (2014) 'New materialisms and play', in L. Brooker, M. Blaise and S. Blaise (eds) *The Sage handbook of play and learning in early childhood*, London: Sage.

Lester, S. (2013) 'Playing in a Deleuzian playground', in E. Ryall, W. Russell and M. MacLean (eds) *The philosophy of play*, London: Routledge, pp. 130–40.

Lester, S. (2016) *Bringing play to life and life to play: Different lines of enquiry*, PhD dissertation, Gloucester: University of Gloucestershire.

Lester, S. and Russell, W. (2008) *Play for a change – play, policy and practice: A review of contemporary perspectives*, London: National Children's Bureau.

Lester, S. and Russell, W. (2013) *Leopard skin wellies, a top hat and a vacuum cleaner hose: An analysis of Wales' Play Sufficiency Assessment duty*, Cardiff: Play Wales.

Levitas, R. (2004) 'Let's hear it for Humpty: Social exclusion, the third way and cultural capital', *Cultural Trends*, 13(2): 41–56.

McBeth, M.K., Jones, M.D. and Shanahan, E.A. (2014) 'The narrative policy framework', in P.A. Sabatier and C.M. Weible (eds) *Theories of the policy process* (3rd edn), Boulder, CO: Westview Pres, pp 225–66.

McKendrick, J.H., Kraftl, P., Mills, S., Gregorius, S. and Sykes, G. (2015) 'Complex geographies of play provision dis/investment across the UK', *International Journal of Play*, 4(3): 228–35.

MacLure, M. (2010) 'The offence of theory', *Journal of Education Policy*, 25(2): 275–83.

MacLure, M. (2013) 'The wonder of data', *Cultural studies – Critical methodologies*, 13(4): 277–86.

Macvarish, J. (2013) 'Biologising parenting: Neuroscience discourse and parenting culture', paper presented at *The Family in crisis? Neoliberalism and the politicisation of parenting and the family*, University of East London, 28 June.

Massumi, B. (2002) *Parables for the virtual: Movement, affect, sensation*, Durham, NC: Duke University Press.

Moss, P. (2007) 'Meetings across the paradigmatic divide', *Educational Philosophy and Theory*, 39(3): 229–45.

Pawson, R. (2006) *Evidence-based policy: A realist perspective*, London: Sage.

PPSG (Playwork Principles Scrutiny Group) (2005) *The Playwork Principles*, Cardiff: Play Wales.

Prout, A. (2005) *The future of childhood*, Abingdon: Routledge.

Renold, E. and Ringrose, J. (2011) 'Schizoid subjectivities? Re-theorizing teen girls' sexual cultures in an era of "sexualisation"', *Journal of Sociology*, 47(4): 389–409.

Rose, N. and Abi-Rached, J. (2013) *Neuro: The new brain sciences and the management of the mind*, Princeton, NJ: Princeton University Press.

Russell, W. (2016) 'Entangled in the midst of it: A diffractive expression of an ethics for playwork', in M. MacLean, W. Russell and E. Ryall (eds) *Philosophical Perspectives on Play*, London: Routledge, pp 191–204.

Ryan, K. (2014) 'Governing the freedom to choose: biosocial power and the playground as a "school of conduct"', in F. Martínez and K. Slabina (eds) *Playgrounds and battlefields: Critical perspectives of social engagement*, Tallinn: Tallinn University Press, pp 85–108.

Slay, J. (2012) '2020: What welfare state?' *The NEF Blog*, 22 October, 2012. www.neweconomics.org/blog/entry/2020-what-welfare-state

Smith, P.K. (1988) 'Children's play and its role in early development: A re-evaluation of the "play ethos"', in A.D. Pellegrini (ed) *Psychological bases for early education*, Chichester: Wiley, pp 207–26.

Smith, P.K. (2010) *Children and play*, New York: J. Wiley.

St Pierre, E.A. (2015) 'Practices for the "new" in the new empiricisms, the new materialisms, and post-qualitative inquiry', in N.K. Denzin and M.D. Giardina (eds) *Qualitative inquiry and the politics of research*, Walnut Creek, CA: Left Coast Press, pp 75–96.

Sutton-Smith, B. (1997) *The ambiguity of play*, Cambridge, MA: Harvard University Press.

Sutton-Smith, B (2003) 'Play as a parody of emotional vulnerability', in J.L. Roopnarine (ed) *Play and educational theory and practice*, Play and Culture Studies Vol. 5. Westport, CT: Praeger pp 3–17.

Taylor, A. and Blaise, M. (2014) 'Queer worlding childhood', *Discourse: Studies in the Cultural Politics of Education*, 35(3): 377–92.

Thrift, N. (2008) *Non-representational theory: Space, politics, affect*, Abingdon: Routledge.

Voce, A. (2015) *Policy for play: Responding to children's forgotten right*, Bristol: Policy Press.

APPENDIX

The Playwork Principles

An Introduction

The Playwork Principles establish a professional and ethical framework for playwork. They are endorsed by the national training organisation for playwork – SkillsActive – by the Welsh Assembly Government and by Play Wales.

Where the Principles refer to children and young people, they mean all children and young people.

Playwork Principles

These Principles establish the professional and ethical framework for playwork and as such must be regarded as a whole. They describe what is unique about play and playwork, and provide the playwork perspective for working with children and young people. They are based on the recognition that children and young people's capacity for positive development will be enhanced if given access to the broadest range of environments and play opportunities.

1. All children and young people need to play. The impulse to play is innate. Play is a biological, psychological and social necessity, and is fundamental to the healthy development and wellbeing of individuals and communities.
2. Play is a process that is freely chosen, personally directed and intrinsically motivated. That is, children and young people determine and control the content and intent of their play, by following their own instincts, ideas and interests, in their own way for their own reasons.
3. The prime focus and essence of playwork is to support and facilitate the play process and this should inform the development of play policy, strategy, training and education.
4. For playworkers, the play process takes precedence and playworkers act as advocates for play when engaging with adult-led agendas.
5. The role of the playworker is to support all children and young people in the creation of a space in which they can play.

6. The playworker's response to children and young people playing is based on a sound up to date knowledge of the play process, and reflective practice.
7. Playworkers recognise their own impact on the play space and also the impact of children and young people's play on the playworker.
8. Playworkers choose an intervention style that enables children and young people to extend their play. All playworker intervention must balance risk with the developmental benefit and wellbeing of children.

The Playwork Principles are held in trust for the UK playwork profession by the Scrutiny Group that acted as an honest broker overseeing the consultations through which they were developed.

Index